Venerable Master Hsing Yun

A historical meeting between two religions—the Master greeted by His Holiness, Pope John Paul II at Vatican City.

Taking a look at the world's largest copy of the *Koran* inside the Roman Mosque in Italy, 1997.

Hsing Yun extends a warm welcome to the Dalai Lama, 1989.

The abbot of the Dhammakaya Foundation in Thailand escorts Hsing Yun for a tour of the grounds, 1994.

Ordains the first-ever Buddhist monastics
in Africa, 1994.

Venerable Master Hsing Yun leading disciples in walking meditation.

Venerable Master Hsing Yun

A group photo with delegates of the World Fellowship of Buddhists
Conference at Nan Tien Temple, Australia.

Leading the opening ceremony of the International Outstanding Buddhist
Women Conference at Fo Guang Shan, Taiwan.

A family portrait with his mother and siblings.

Buddha's Light Publishing exhibits books in languages other than Chinese at the Taipei International Book Exhibition held at Taipei World Trade Center (February 1, 2002).

A noted calligraphist, 1993 (Courtesy of Chen Chih-min).

Presiding over the International Triple Platform Full Ordination Ceremony in Bodhgaya, India, (February 15, 1998).

The Master leading a sea of B.L.I.A. members in the campaign for universal compassion and loving-kindness toward all, in Taipei.

The Master leading the welcoming ceremony to receive the Buddha's Tooth Relic, originating from Tibet, in a joint Sutric and Tantric Dharma Service held in Taiwan.

Master of Chinese Painting Chang Ta-Chien [Zhang Daqian] visited Fo Guang Shan and presented his work"One flower, one world; one leaf, one Buddha"as a gift to Venerable Master, (March 14, 1978).

Nobel Prize for Literature Laureate Alexander Solzhenitsyn at Fo Guang Shan, (October 21, 1982)

University of Berkeley Professor Dr. Lewis Lancaster receiving the *Fo Guang Tripitaka—Chan Canon* from Venerable Master on behalf of twenty-seven universities in the United States.

USA.

A magnificent view of Hsi Lai Temple, U.S.A.

國際佛光會世界總會成立暨第一屆
INAUGURATION OF BUDDHA'S LIGHT INTERNATIONAL ASSOCIATION &

Former United States Vice President Al Gore, the first deputy of head of state to visit Hsi Lai Temple, (April 29, 1996).

Inaugural ceremony of B.L.I.A. World Headquarters at Hsi Lai Temple, U.S.A., (April 16, 1992).

Conducting a chanting service for victims at New York's World Trade Center site after the September 11 attack, 2001.

Visiting Griffith University in Queensland, Australia, and meeting with the Chancellor the Honorable John Macrossan (2nd right), Vice-Chancellor Prof. Roy Webb (left), and Uri Themal, Executive Director of Multicultural Affairs Queensland, to discuss the establishment of the World Religious Institute, (November 29, 1999).

Fo Guang Shan Buddhist Hymn Choir performance.

Fo Guang Shan
Hall of the Gold
Buddhas, 2001.

The twelve links of dependent origination are like rosary beads that have been threaded together.

Eyebrows! They may seem useless, but are actually extremely useful.

A straightforward mind means the essence of Chan expressed with one finger.

Ask yourself if you have a clear conscience.

Joining palms harmonizes the ten dharma worlds within one heart.

Your pinky maybe the smallest, but it is the closest to the Buddha when you join palms.

Patience is the greatest strength.

Doesn't the whole universe belong to us!

Someone once asked a question, "What does Fo Guang Shan look like?" Some compared it to the five fingers of a hand or the petals of an orchid; others suggested a traditional monastery or a modern temple. In my opinion, all the respondents were both right and wrong. When I founded Fo Guang Shan, I did not have a set plan. I merely built when the causes and conditions were right. That is why Fo Guang Shan is made up of buildings of different kinds and encompasses a wide variety of activities.

Seeing the pagoda means seeing the Buddha. The Seven Pagodas of Fo Guang Shan.

A corner of Fo Guang Shan.

Fo Guang Shan Main Shrine.

The Main Shrine by night.

The Great Welcoming Buddha at night.

Fo Guang Shan Dragon Pavilion.

The Biography of
Venerable Master Hsing Yun

Handing Down the Light

Original Chinese Text by Fu Chi-ying
Translated by Amy Lui-Ma

BUDDHA'S LIGHT PUBLISHING
HACIENDA HEIGHTS, CALIFORNIA
U.S.A.

© 2004 Buddha's Light Publishing

Chinese edition © 1995 Fu Chi-ying and Venerable Master Hsing Yun

Published by Buddha's Light Publishing
3456 S. Glenmark Drive
Hacienda Heights, CA 91745
Phone: 626-923-5144; 626-961-9697   Fax: 626-923-5145
E-mail: itc@blia.org   Website: www.blpusa.com

Library of Congress Cataloging-in-Publication Data

Fu, Zhiying.
    [Chuan deng. English]
    Handing down the light : the biography of Venerable Master Hsing Yun /
Fu Chi-ying; translated by Amy Lui-Ma.-- Rev. ed.
        p. cm.
Includes bibliographical references and index.
    ISBN 1-932293-00-0 (alk. paper)
    ISBN 1-932293-09-4 (alk. hardcover)
    1. Xingyun, da shi—Juvenile literature. 2. Priests,
Buddhist—China—Biography—Juvenile literature. I. Title: Biography of
Venerable Master Hsing Yun. II. Title.
BQ962.S7487F813 2003
294.3'92'092—dc22
                                2003023662

Cover design by Chun-Er Cheng
Book design by Ching Tay
Printed in Taiwan.

CONTENTS

Words from Venerable Master Hsing Yun   *i*
Author's Note   *iii*
Acknowledgments   *vi*
Preface   *vii*

Part One
Many, Many Returns in Buddha Karma

1. To the Delight of All Buddhas   7
2. Promise on Mount Qixia   *19*
3. Facing Turbulent Times   *32*

Part Two
Crossing the Sea, Light in Hand

4. The Tangshan Monk Sets Sail   *45*
5. Ilan, the Cradle   *53*
6. Master of Innovation   *62*

Part Three
Nurturing and Cultivating the Seed of Buddhism

7. Heading South   *87*
8. Epoch of Buddha's Light   *97*
9. An Outstanding Disciple of Buddhism   *107*
10. Traditional Monastery, Modern Vision   *123*
11. Dharma Realization within the World   *136*
12. Good Affinities around the World   *150*

Part Four
Spreading the Dharma to Liberate All Beings

13. The Passing and Receiving of the Baton   *175*
14. Like Clouds and Water   *184*
15. Affection for the Isle, Heart for the Mainland   *195*

Part Five
Buddha's Light Held High

16. The Dharma Coming West   *217*
17. Buddha's Light International Association   *231*
18. Holding Space in an Embrace   *243*

Part Six
Returning on the Wings of His Vows

19. Heart of a Child   *265*
20. Devoted to the Buddhist Path   *283*
21. No Regrets Whatsoever   *292*

Endnotes   *304*

Glossary   *316*

Appendix Chronology of Venerable Master Hsing Yun   *324*

Words from Venerable Master Hsing Yun

Having marched through life for close to seventy years, I am but an ordinary monk who deems "preaching the Dharma a daily duty and benefiting all living beings a lifetime career." Whatever transpires in the outer conditions, I have always felt profoundly blessed to be in the favor of the Buddhas from the ten directions and with the affinity of all living beings. With them watching over and caring for me, I have been able to carry out the sacred mission that pertains to a monastic little by little. During these past few years, friends have taken such an interest in my life that they have been quite insistent on writing about it. Some of the results are exalting, others critical; some well-intentioned, others without much intention. All of them I invariably choose to regard as references for my practice and mirrors for my doings.

For some time now I have enjoyed the congeniality of those at Commonwealth Publishing Company, a refreshing group of idealists, enthusiasts, and professionals under publisher Kao Hsi-chun. When the group came up with the notion of publishing my biography, I was only too glad to comply.

Commonwealth's chief editor, Fu Chi-ying, was selected to author the text. After working closely with her over the next two years, I was left with no doubt that the task had fallen on the right shoulders. A receptive yet independent thinker, the skilled journalist persisted in taking her subject back in time without appearing to cross-examine me. I have nothing but positive things to say about the thoroughness of her research and investigation. The first draft alone struck me as being incredibly complete in its portrayal of my disposition, thinking, and spirituality. The essentials were all there in one articulate flow. I was won over instantly, which was not much of a surprise; that the senior disciples of Fo Guang Shan were was a surprise.

Too insignificant are one person's footprints along the river of no return that is history. I am willing to disclose the details of my life, work, faith, experience, thoughts, and feelings because, in so doing, Buddhists may be able to draw inspiration for their own cultivation. But most of all, I hope this offering of the records of my inner growth and outer journey will prompt everyone to rise in unison to extinguish the fire of worldly strife, to light in its place the light within each of us, and to create the joyful, harmonious pure land on earth.

Once again, my thanks to friends at Commonwealth and to Chi-ying for this book. Let me pray that the compassionate light of the Triple Gem be around you, dear readers, that health in body and mind, and propitiousness be yours!

Hsing Yun
Taipei Vihara
December 1994

Author's Note

From reporter, copy editor, and producer, to chief editor, I am lucky to have a career that allows me to work with something I love—words. Since finishing school over ten years ago, I have been counting my blessings daily. Yet, never had I thought of penning a book.

How strange are the causes and conditions taught in Buddhism! How wondrous they are!

I first had a personal interview with Venerable Master Hsing Yun six years ago for *Global View Monthly*. Two years later, a proposed biographical series by the Commonwealth Publishing Company featuring contemporary figures triggered unanimous efforts to solicit the book rights for the biography of the Master. As events snowballed, the first-ever chance to author a book fell into my lap. It was not until the Master had agreed and I had begun writing that I heard about how, for years, this project was the most sought-after among those who are far superior to me in scholarship and writing. But, green as I may have been, it seemed that I was the one with the right causes and conditions.

Over the course of the next 600 or so workdays, the Master tolerated and commiserated with the worldly, unknowing creature that I am. To the inquisitive and at times unrelenting journalist that I was trained to be, the Master accommodated to the fullest and showered with moving and inspirational quotes.

In no time he had freed me from the nagging thoughts of certain restrictions, which a biographical project on a living subject might otherwise entail. He showed me trust; he gave me room. I, too, soon found myself in touch with the openness and pureness beneath that towering countenance.

Below, I have shortlisted some of the primary source materials from which I drew information for this book:

- Nineteen personal interviews, each lasting two to three hours, that resulted in thirty-two, ninety-minute cassettes
- Interviews with thirty-eight relatives, teachers, disciples, devotees, friends, Buddhist scholars, Buddhist and non-Buddhist personalities, and members of the media
- Source texts: nineteen of the Master's titles; the complete lectures in four volumes; the complete diary, letters, notes, newspaper and journal clippings of his activities in Taiwan (since 1968), Hong Kong, Germany, and the United States; *Universal Gate* magazine; *Buddha's Light Newsletter*; *Awakening the World*; and major religious references such as *Biographies of the Eminent Masters, The Buddhist Religion and Buddhist Monasteries in Taiwan, The Chan School and Dao School,* the *Fo Guang Encyclopedia*, and others.

To further capture Master Hsing Yun's spirituality and life, I visited Fo Guang Shan in Kaohsiung, and other branch temples and related organizations numerous times; I traveled to his hometown of Jiangdu in Jiangsu Province, Qixia Temple in Nanjing where he was tonsured, Hong Kong, Germany, and the United States. I *hung* around as best I could for his lectures and classes, travels and visits, meetings and conferences, or when he entertained guests and devotees and reunited with loved ones. On one such tour last summer, he finally had something to say about my shadowing of him: "You sure are getting the *hang* of this!" he laughed.

The illustriousness of the venerable and his phenomenal feats have already been affirmed. This is not a book about an unreachable legend. I am merely trying to recreate an honest, intact record of this philosopher of life, his words and actions, his thinking and spirit—just as he is. My touch, I want to be light; my expression, I hope to be open. May readers not only find it a story of success but also benefit from the enormity of his wisdom and the intensity of his energy for life.

Although the protagonist is a Buddhist monastic, I have intended that the religious aspect be somewhat diluted; and, indeed, this is a book for everyone, not just Buddhists. Hoping to interest and inspire, and to ensure readability throughout, I have adopted an approach in its general presentation that may be more readily acceptable to the public. May readers, too, be led to reflect on their Buddha Nature and, ultimately, find the clear, pristine source of the river of life.

This text is entitled *Handing Down the Light* to represent the Dharma as a light which, when passed into the hands of Master Hsing Yun, shines across the five continents. Furthermore, the light—also representing his aspirations and deeds—shall continue to transmit messages of compassion, joy, generosity, appreciation, affinity, humility, and gratitude through the defilements within and without our minds.

The project has, for the past two years, kept me away from home and my loved ones more often than I would have liked. Gratitude is especially due to my parents, whose love and concern for their daughter and granddaughter seem boundless. Most of all, I must thank my loving husband, without whose support this task would never have been completed.

Lastly, may I offer this book for the benefit of all sentient beings.

Fu Chi-ying

Acknowledgments

Due to an increasing interest in Buddhism, and in the inspiring life of Venerable Master Hsing Yun in particular, English-speaking readers worldwide eagerly awaited publication of the English edition of *Handing Down the Light*. Following the release of the Chinese edition in 1995, which has sold over a 100,000 copies around the world, the first English edition was released in 1996. A second edition was published in the year 2000 after English-speaking disciples of Venerable Master Hsing Yun suggested ways in which the text could be improved.

We received a lot of help from many people and we want to thank them for their efforts in making the publication of this book possible. We especially appreciate Venerable Tzu Jung, the Chief Executive of Fo Guang Shan International Translation Center (F.G.S.I.T.C.), Venerable Yi Chao, and Venerable Hui Zai for their support and leadership; and Amy Lui-Ma for her translation. We want to thank Pey-Rong Lee, Mu-Tzen Hsu, Robin Stevens, Ching Tay, and Kevin Hsyeh for their efforts in bringing forth the third edition. Brenda Bolinger, Lucie Gonzalez-Kitchen, Mason Fries, Scott Herby, Laura Neustaedter, Madelon Wheeler-Gibb, and Corey Bell worked tirelessly on the second edition. Finally, we would like to acknowledge Jeanne Tsai, Fred Webb, and Edward Little for the first edition. We hope that each new edition will both benefit and inspire the reader.

Fo Guang Shan
International Translation Center
Hsi Lai Temple
Los Angeles, 2004

Preface

"Let your heartbeat resonate with that of all people! Let your blood flow in oneness with all beings!"

What exactly are we reading? A politician's election promise? A bestseller's blurb? A rave review of some rock star's pop-culture appeal? A physician's formula for healing?

This impassioned cry is actually Venerable Master Hsing Yun's socially conscious vision for spreading the Dharma.

In the warming presence of its universal, harmonizing energy, and its commitment to give confidence, joy, service, and hope to others, Humanistic Buddhism has opened hearts and transformed lives across the globe.

*   *   *

A lifelong search of mine has been to discover a religion that truly resonates with me. As a result, I have the utmost admiration for those whose personal spiritual paths have become clear to them. I am eager for the day when I, too, will feel confident about having found the right spiritual practice.

Over the last few years, I have been honored to spend time in Master Hsing Yun's company. However each time we met, I hesitated to ask him about Buddhist philosophy, encouraging him to speak instead about social trends, human ethics, educational systems, the media, politics between Taiwan and China, and much more. Hsing Yun always elaborated on these topics within the domain of "Humanistic Buddhism" and "Living Buddhism,"[1] the forms of Buddhism he advocates. His eloquent instruction and profound knowledge caused me to consider how students might have benefited from his teachings had he served as a professor. I learned an incredible amount during each of our lively exchanges.

I first came to admire the Master through his column in *Global View Monthly* and his personal reflections in *Universal Gate* magazine. While I saluted his philosophy and beliefs, I knew very little about his journey to promote Buddhism.

I yearned to learn more about:

- How he manages to make complex doctrines easy and understandable with such wisdom and compassion.
- How he makes these seemingly complex doctrines concrete and practical.
- What underlies his competence in running the multidimensional organization of Fo Guang Shan.
- The noble and innate qualities that enabled him to pass on the abbotship and complete Fo Guang Shan's succession at age fifty-eight, thereby creating a more expansive space for Buddhism.
- How he–with the strength of his vows, his causes and conditions, and his virtuous deeds–has been able to bring Buddhism to the corners of the world.

At long last, the story of Master's influence on the world will be told.

* * *

In depicting a character of such profound depth and dimension as Master Hsing Yun, Fu Chi-ying has undoubtedly succeeded.

Using a clear structure, fluid language, delightful photographs, and information from personal interviews, the author enables those who are both familiar and unfamiliar with the Master to experience his role in the creation of Fo Guang Shan and in the dynamic growth of Humanistic Buddhism.

The greatness of Master Hsing Yun, as presented in this biography, is threefold. He is:

- A religious reformer of remarkable resolve and cultivation
- A master innovator with the compassion and wisdom to spread the Buddha's teachings, and
- A caring educator who makes religion practical and accessible.

His will to reform stems from his determination; his will to innovate, from his creativity; and his will to educate, from his compassion. With each of these qualities, Hsing Yun is a Buddhist master from whom the world benefits, and a social educator whose influence reaches far and wide.

*　　*　　*

I have always believed that concepts are capable of redirecting the course of history; now I believe even more that religion is capable of redirecting the course of life. What is recorded in this book about the Master, are the philosophies and actions that have transformed many lives.

"Humanistic Buddhism" and "Living Buddhism," which the Master has spent a lifetime teaching, have not only changed the lives of countless Chinese people but will inarguably alter Chinese and world history in remarkable ways. Of course, his profound teachings have had the most impact on the dynamic and ever-changing island of Taiwan. The expansion of Buddhism in Taiwan has indeed been a miracle, surmounting even the tremendous growth of its economy.

The author eloquently describes Hsing Yun's journey to endear Buddhism to the hearts of people all over the world:

Each step he takes leaves behind trails of lotuses,
The wind rustling beneath his robe sweeps clean the
path to the Pure Land.

With a heart full of devotion and compassion, the monk from Yangzhou transcended the limits of time and distance to gracefully create a world of infinite Buddha's light.

As the Buddha's Light International Association (B.L.I.A.) rapidly expands worldwide, Master Hsing Yun will have many more miles of path to tread and more lessons of the Dharma to teach.

Kao Hsi-chun
Taipei
December 1994

---

[1] Living Buddhism: It emphasizes how to apply Buddhism in daily life.

Part One

MANY, MANY RETURNS IN BUDDHA KARMA

Hsing Yun at twenty-five.

His birthplace in Jiangdu. (Courtesy of Fu Chi-ying)

Qixia Temple, where Hsing Yun was tonsured.
(Courtesy of Fu Chi-ying)

Venerable Master Zhikai (1911-1979), born in Haian, Jiangsu, founded the Qixia Vinaya College. Hsing Yun was his only disciple, whom Master Zhikai educated with strict discipline.

Venerable Master Zhikai (second from left) and teachers at Qixia.

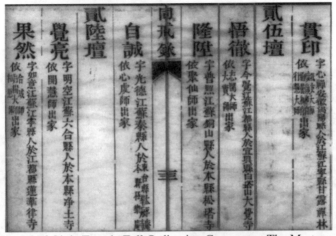

A record of Qixia Temple Full Ordination Ceremony. The Master was the leader of group 25, 1941.

In Nanjing, listening to his mother, 1994.

With his mother, Madam Lee Liu Yu-ying at Hsi Lai Temple
Preparatory Center, 1979.

Chapter 1

To the Delight of All Buddhas

*I*n March, Jiangnan[1] is a lush, green region alive with flitting orioles, floating butterflies, and budding peach and plum trees. Yangzhou is nestled in this fertile land, a mere three hours from Nanjing, the hub of ancient Chinese culture.

Yangzhou is a famous, historical city of political, social, and religious significance. One of nine provinces of the Xia Dynasty [c 2205–1766 B.C.E.], Yangzhou was the site where cultural and economic forces converged with the opening of the Grand Canal during the reign of Emperor Yang of the Sui Dynasty [589–618 C.E.]. Situated at the estuary of the Yangtze River, Yangzhou has been a favorite sojourn for the literati throughout the ages. Emperor Qianlong of the Qing Dynasty [1644–1911 C.E.] was known to have traveled through Jiangnan six times while he was ruler. Tang [618–907 C.E.] poet Li Bo [701–762 C.E.], in bidding his peer Meng Haoran [689–740 C.E.] farewell, once wrote:

> *Heading west, my old friend departs*
> *from Huanghe Lou.*
> *Among the mist and blossoms of the third moon,*
> *he sails for Yangzhou.*
> *Into the azure distance recedes the image of*
> *that lonely sail,*

> *Leaving behind the sight of the Yangtze*
> *flowing toward the sky above.*

Few other verses convey so simply the boundless beauty of Yangzhou. Once tranquil and pristine, Yangzhou is now quickly emerging as a dynamic metropolis in a country experiencing great change and reform.

Blessed Hometown of Jiangdu

Accessible by a forty-minute drive from Yangzhou is the county of Jiangdu, which in its pure simplicity and serenity has never been a tourist hot spot or a strategic transport location. But there is a distinct wonder about Jiangdu, for it is where one of the world's most illustrious religious leaders was raised.

There, in a gray-brick courtyard west of Xiannu Temple was the homestead of Venerable Master Hsing Yun, founder of Fo Guang Shan (Buddha's Light Mountain).

On the twenty-second day of the seventh moon on the lunar calendar in 1927, an infant's cry rang out from the home of the Li family who ran a humble incense business. This child was their second son, with an elder brother and sister who preceded his arrival. The birth of the boy, then named Guoshen, was anything but ordinary.

The matriarch of the family Mrs. Li[2] [née Liu Yuying], now a spirited and healthy elderly woman, still recalls every vivid detail:

> While I was in labor with your master, I dreamt of a little golden figure. He was rummaging through the odds and ends by my bed with quiet determination.
>
> "What are you looking for?" I asked.
>
> "He's looking for stalks of grain," said a white-haired old

man also present in the dream.

"My bed is stuffed with hay. How can there be any stalks of grain?"

At that moment, the little golden figure performed a miracle, and pulled a stalk of grain out from under the bed.

The old man then told me, "This *Dao*[3] shall be fruitful."

The prophetic dream was the first of several unusual occurrences. The chubby newborn was rosy-cheeked on one side and quite pale on the other. A pair of fine reddish lines colored the space between his nose and upper lip. Neighbors were soon gossiping about the "little monster who was born into the home of Li Chengbao."[4] To prevent the curious stares of the villagers, his mother loosely tied him with a sturdy piece of string and kept him indoors most of the time until, inexplicably, these unusual birthmarks vanished by the age of two or three.

Plum of the Li Family[5]

Hsing Yun has no recollection of these mythical tales. But each time his mother spoke at great lengths about the past, he would smile and listen contentedly as a son should. When others passed on these remarkable stories, his countenance was neutral, showing neither pride nor objection to his noteworthy birth.

After nearly fifty years, the Li home in Jiangdu was renovated. The revived two-story single-family home with a spacious courtyard now houses the youngest brother, Guomin, and his family. A stroll across Limin Bridge, near Xiannu Temple, brings into view the Grand Canal, which now suffers from devastating pollution and stagnation. Early on, Mrs. Li recognized the unique strength and courage of her son:

In those days, daily necessities had to be purchased on the

opposite bank of the canal. With the nation engulfed in war, nobody wanted to risk his life ferrying others back and forth for a mere pittance! However, your master who was only ten at the time, would strip to his waist, tie his shirt around his forehead, and plunge right in. The rushing current of the canal may have daunted many, but he would always bring home the necessities. Everybody thought this second son of ours was special; of all the plums in the Li family, this would be the one to watch.

Grandma, the Most Beloved

All the praise given to him for childhood gallantries mean little to Hsing Yun in comparison to the fond memories he has of his maternal grandmother, Madam Liu [née Wang]. Though illiterate, she could chant the *Diamond Sutra* by heart. She had also been a vegetarian for over half a century.

Many years later in a Buddhist seminar, Master Hsing Yun fondly recalled the religious influence his grandmother had on him as a child:

My grandmother became a vegetarian at the age of eighteen. Rising daily at dawn for her morning prayers, she would chant Buddhist scriptures like the *Amitabha Sutra* or the *Diamond Sutra* despite her illiteracy. My sister and I were raised under her wing, and the two of us would try to outlast one another as strict vegetarians. I was three or four then and completely unaware of the Buddhist teachings underlying vegetarianism. I was merely trying to please Grandma.

My childhood was spent in her company. Every day, sometime between midnight and daybreak, she would get up to meditate, cross her legs, rest her shoulders, assume the full lotus position, and control her breathing. In the process, her tummy would roar like rushing rivers and swelling seas. A sleepyhead roused from slumber, I would ask, "Grandma, why is your tummy crying so!"

"This is called mastership, mastership from practice," was her reply.

The devout practice of Hsing Yun's grandmother gave this inquisitive child and his older sister ample opportunity to accompany her to nearby temples where they paid homage and prayed to the Buddha. Occasionally, she would return home with the altar offerings, such as fruit or rice, which the children gladly consumed. An eager child trying to emulate his beloved grandmother, Hsing Yun experienced his first connections with the Buddha.

On occasion, monastics were received in their household. His grandmother was naturally the influence behind these visits. In an era of war and turmoil, the monastics impressed Hsing Yun tremendously with the gracefulness of their robes, the dignity of their demeanor, and the respect they received from villagers. He began to think, "How nice it is to be a monk!"

Hsing Yun held his grandmother up as the consummate role model because of her noble character. She was industrious, frugal, and kind. While he was away during his monastic training, he missed her most dearly. When he turned twenty, he returned home to see her. Sewing peacefully under a tree, she began to relate to him what she would expect for her own funeral, when the event took place. She had hoped that these arrangements would be left in the hands of this grandchild, who was now a monk.

Two years later, the Communist Regime took over the country. That was the last time the two of them were together. When his grandmother passed away, Hsing Yun was already in Taiwan and had no way of tending to her funeral as promised. He had been extremely close to his grandmother and his remorse was heart-

felt. In loving gesture to her, he made a regular practice of financially supporting his three uncles back at home, hoping to return–
if only in the slightest manner–what he had received from his grandmother.

Buddha Nature in the Tot

Though they were unable to offer him bedazzling riches or a
glorious ancestry, Hsing Yun's parents did bestow upon him the
gift of great character. He took after his father in moderation and
integrity, and his mother in gallantry and fairness. His grandmother's compassion added to the wealth of qualities from which he
was to benefit for life.

From a very early age, Hsing Yun has shared an exceptionally close and harmonious relationship with his older sister, Suhua. These affectionate siblings recently reunited after more than
forty years of separation. Reflecting on their childhood together,
Suhua brimmed over with the same tenderness, "He was so different from the rest of us." She could not remember her kid brother
ever fighting with anyone. In fact, a three-year-old Hsing Yun
would drag the family candy-jar to the courtyard, where its entire
contents would be given to friends in the neighborhood. There
were those who considered this generous act foolish, and teased
the son of the Li family for knowing little else but how to give
everything away to others.

Looking back over their childhood, Suhua realizes that her
younger brother had displayed characteristics of Buddha Nature
from a very early age. She surmises that his willingness to become a monk probably stemmed from causes and conditions of
many past lives.

In another instance, the five-year-old Hsing Yun spotted a
group of small chicks huddling together in the rain. He carried
them back home, one by one, and placed them before the wood-

burning furnace to help them dry off. One chick dashed into the fire in panic. When the child snatched it back, he found its lower beak had been burnt quite badly. To help the chick eat, he dug a tiny hollow in the earth, put in some rice, and let it feed from there. The chick was tenderly nursed back to health and eventually grew into a thriving and mature hen.

Suhua shared yet another episode vivid in her memory. On a deep wintry night, during a family gathering for fireside stories, an elder began a narrative about human suffering. The main character was a white-bearded, impoverished, ailing, and hunger-stricken old man living in the mountains. Before the storyteller could finish, her little brother had disappeared, only to be found underneath the table, weeping with sorrow for the poor old man! Even when others tried to comfort the boy, telling him that it was only a tale, he would not come away and he rejected dinner altogether because he wanted to give his portion to the suffering old man in the story. His anguish was not appeased until he was allowed to visit his maternal grandfather that evening, to whom he kindly offered his dinner.

Last year, after learning about her brother's homecoming, Suhua, along with her daughter and two sons, journeyed all the way from Liuzhou, Guangxi to Nanjing by way of a forty-eight-hour train ride.

In the courtyard of the brand-new home, which her brother had built for their mother's retirement, a serene Suhua looked every bit as lovely and genteel as she must have been in her youth. Recent travels have taken her to both Hsi Lai Temple in the United States and Fo Guang Shan in Taiwan. Although Suhua recognizes the influential and admired leader that Hsing Yun is today, deep down, she will always see him as her chubby, dimpled kid brother.

Mother, Mentor of Wisdom

The abundance of homes where "the wind swept the floor and the moon lit the house" demonstrated the confining poverty of the northern Jiangsu Province where the Li family resided. Manual labor was the primary means of livelihood, and schooling was only for the privileged few who could afford it. Hsing Yun's parents, though somewhat better off than others, were unable to send him to a private school. With a passion and eagerness for learning already in evidence, seven-year-old Hsing Yun found his first mentor in his illiterate mother.

The young Mrs. Li was frequently ill and often bedridden. Her loving second son would read to her from the *Qizi Duan*,[6] then popular in Yangzhou. She knew the work by heart and would correct his mistakes as he read, helping him build a larger vocabulary, encouraging his enthusiasm for reading, and reinforcing in him the principles of loyalty, filial piety, integrity, and moral virtue. Though many years have passed, he still remembers the names of all one hundred and eight characters, and their respective characteristics in the classic *The Water Margin* [*Shuihu Zhuan*].[7]

Family resources eventually permitted private schooling during the next two or three years. Unfortunately, this luxury was interrupted by local bandits and the occupation by Japanese troops. Little did he know that the passages from Confucian texts absorbed during this brief period would be the only formal education he would have during his entire life.

Strictly speaking, Hsing Yun has never spent a single day in a regular school nor has he earned a diploma, a multitude of which he has handed out over the years. He never formally attended college, but he has founded Hsi Lai and Fo Guang Universities and has been awarded an honorary doctorate. His disciples, among the most highly educated in the history of Chinese Buddhism, have degrees from Harvard, University of California Berkeley, and many other institutions of higher learning. Countless intellectuals have taken refuge with him. To them, his lack of a degree or diploma is irrelevant; to them, he is a true teacher and master.

His triumph over the expected illiteracy of northern Jiangsu residents illustrates a teaching he still propagates today: limitations are merely perceptions, and potential may be realized even in spite of the worst obstacles.

A Half-Century of Separation

Upon entering the monastery, Hsing Yun became a monk who transcended the three realms of desire, form, and formlessness. The vast compassion of his true nature has since been offered to all living beings. Still, the innate attachment to his mother was hard to let go of. When communication with his family was impossible and he had no way of knowing whether his mother was dead or alive, he would not celebrate a single birthday. In the Buddhist culture, one's birthday is an occasion to appreciate and honor one's mother for the suffering she experienced in giving birth. Hsing Yun was deeply saddened that he could not express his respect and love to his mother on this special day and chose instead to pay homage to the Buddha. Each year he would rise early, go before the Buddha, quietly light incense, and chant in solitude. He dedicated this practice to the health and well-being of his mother.

In 1986, Venerable Tzu Chuang, then Abbess of Hsi Lai Temple in Los Angeles, finally located Mrs. Li, who was indeed alive and well. To honor his mother on his sixtieth birthday, Hsing Yun held a grand Dharma function to show his gratitude and to celebrate not only his own birthday but also the birthdays of others who were of the same age. Invitations were extended to a thousand lay and sangha community members also in their sixties. At this special gathering, the Buddhist spirit of honoring one's parents was manifested through treating all parents as one's own, and a sense of sisterhood and brotherhood was forged among those of the same generation.

As family visitations from overseas resumed in China, his mother was able to join him on various trips to Japan, the United States, and Taiwan. At long last, mother and son were able to spend the Lunar New Year together at Hsi Lai Temple—their first in fifty years and the first since he entered monkhood. The family reunion was truly an intimate and touching one for both of them.

As much as he had missed his mother all those years, she too had suffered. She was condemned to hard labor, eking out a meager living. The family was ostracized for having a son who resided out of the country. Hsing Yun was harshly judged for having supposedly compromised his loyalty to the nation. His mother was not even allowed to keep a single photograph of him. When circumstances worsened, she was repeatedly detained and interrogated, and pressured with a devastating choice: "Leniency if you confess the whereabouts of your son, and punishment if you don't."

Thankfully, this painful and frightening era has now passed. Despite his lengthy and distant travels to spread the Dharma for the benefit of all sentient beings, Hsing Yun is dedicated to being a dutiful son. He continued to care for his mother from afar, arranging for visits and daily games of mahjong with her neighbors.

In the spring of 1994, Hsing Yun left Kaohsiung to return home. With a birthday cake, peach-shaped buns, longevity noodles, and flowers in hand, as well as disciples and devotees in tow, he went to celebrate his mother's big day. "How I've cried for you! My eyes are failing!" the mother was overheard whispering as she held her son's hand in her own. The gentle master proceeded to sit quietly with his mother, helping her enjoy her birthday cake.

Her Gift to All Living Beings

Mrs. Li, at ninety-four,[8] was a walking historical text. Having braved storms of epic proportions—the fall of the Qing Dynasty, the Xinhai Revolution,[9] the rise of modern China, the strife of warlords, the Sino-Japanese War,[10] the civil war between the Nationalists and Communists,[11] the Cultural Revolution,[12] and the recent reconnection between Taiwan and the Mainland—her words and actions are always full of instructive wisdom. Once, while walking about the grounds of Hsi Lai Temple with her son in the moist, cool morning air, they arrived at the slope to the left of the main entrance. Turning the key to a side door, Hsing Yun announced, "This door opens to a shortcut leading up to the temple."

"Main door or side door?" asked his mother. "In this world of ours, the best people take the main door, the mediocre wait for another, and the worst make no effort at all. There's no shortcut!" With a colorful, and at times turbulent foundation of experience, Mrs. Li embodied strength and perseverance.

Mrs. Li felt that her life's most momentous decision was to offer her son to Buddhism by permitting him to take tonsure. Her family members seem to have been blessed with exceptional longevity: she and her three brothers combined lived over 350 years; her four children, over 280 years; both generations, over 600 years.

On a visit to Fo Guang Shan during a conference for devotees, Master Hsing Yun asked his mother if she would like to say a few words. Contrary to her son's concern over her possible stage fright, she stood at the podium before an audience of twenty thousand and spoke with confidence: "Fo Guang Shan *is* the Pure Land; heaven *is* among us. May the Master guide you; may you attain the Way at Fo Guang Shan. You're all so kind. This old granny has little to offer you; I can only give you the gift of my son."

Afterwards, when they were alone together, Hsing Yun jokingly asked his mother, "How could you give me away so easily?

Don't you want me anymore?"

"So many need you. How can I keep you all to myself? You're not mine; you belong to everyone," she replied.

It is certainly true that from the instant a tearful Mrs. Li agreed to allow her beloved son to leave home and become a monk, he has been a great offering to all sentient beings.

Chapter 2

Promise on
Mount Qixia

*T*he bloodiest chapter in contemporary Chinese history opened on July 7, 1937 with the eruption of Japanese gunfire on Marco Polo Bridge in Hebei. Thereafter, Japanese militarists proceeded to wreak havoc on millions of innocent lives across the land.

On towards Destiny via the Unknown

It was under these dire circumstances that Hsing Yun's father left home on business. Hsing Yun would never see his father again, and the family never received news of his whereabouts. Financial ruin would plague the family for the next few years. Hoping to locate him herself, Mrs. Li decided to take twelve-year-old Hsing Yun with her to look for her husband in Nanjing. The year was nearing its end, and the northern winter was harsh and unrelenting. As the delicate young woman and her little boy, who had never in his life crossed the county gate of Jiangdu, began their journey, they had no idea where it would lead.

Their extraordinary quest led to the child's destiny. Perhaps, this was the fruition of many lives of connection with the Buddha.

Hsing Yun recounts what happened:

Midway to Nanjing, we bumped into the newly formed peace corps practicing their drills. As I was gazing intently at the scene, I was approached by a monk who was one of the receptionists at the temple on Mount Qixia (Cloud Dwelling Mountain). Probably thinking I looked cute with my round cheeks and big ears, he casually asked whether I would be willing to become a monk. Out of instinct, I quickly replied, "I'm willing!" Before long a message came from the abbot, Venerable Master Zhikai, "I've heard that you would like to leave home to become a monk. I will be your master!"

But how could his mother let him go? In her attempt to find her husband, she was about to lose her son. How was she going to face those at home? Still, young Hsing Yun insisted that he had given his word and would keep his promise. With a mixture of both sadness and understanding, she tearfully accepted his choice.

All alone, his mother headed home, while Hsing Yun stayed at Qixia Temple. His father was still missing, and villagers speculated that he was probably one of 300,000 innocents who perished in the Rape of Nanjing [1937 C.E.].[13] Although Hsing Yun did not remember much about his father, on his first homecoming he had the ancestral shrine renovated, the memorial tablets of both his maternal grandmother and father put in a place of honor, and requested that family members light incense and pray regularly.

Qixia was both a mountain and temple of historic renown. Under Master Zhikai, Hsing Yun received the Dharma-lineage name Wuche (Thorough Realization), and the Dharma name Jinjue (Instantaneous Awakening), and became a disciple of the forty-eighth generation of the Linji School of Chan Buddhism. He was the youngest student at Qixia Vinaya College. Because Qixia Temple was open to all monastics regardless of their tradition, they came from various destinations around China. Although Hsing Yun was tonsured at Qixia Temple, it was not his ancestral monastery. This was because in accordance with the monasterial regulations of the time, Dajue (Great Awakening) Temple of Yixing, where his master was tonsured, became Hsing Yun's ancestral monastery instead.

So Many Monks in Northern Jiangsu

As one considers the circumstances of Hsing Yun's decision to become a monastic, one may ponder over the phenomenal number of Buddhist monastics in contemporary China who originated from the northern Jiangsu Province. Well-known monastics from this area include Venerable Masters Zhiguang, Taicang, Nanting, Dongchu, Yanpei, Zhuyun, and others. It seems that there may be something special about this region.

The harsh environment is one unique and influential feature. The lowlands of northern Jiangsu is where the hopelessly silted Huai River is redirected by way of the constricted Grand Canal, which floods every year between summer and fall when the Huai swells. Moreover, because the land is formed by the continual rise of the sea level, the soil simply contains too much salt to be suitable for agriculture. Residents, lamenting over life's impermanence and toil, are often compelled to turn to spiritual practice for strength.

In addition, driven by the region's poverty, there was a shift of the rural population to urban cities like Shanghai. Professional pursuits were mainly limited to manual labor. Full of respect and admiration, the struggling villagers learned about peace and patience from the serene demeanor and tranquil lifestyle of the monastics.

The region was pervaded by the belief that an entire family lineage benefited from the vows and practice of one person committed to the monastic life. When monkhood for fathers and brothers improved the quality of life for those at home, those who had joined the monastic order frequently returned to lead sons and nephews onto the same path.

The Supreme Monastery of the Six Dynasties

Historic temples abound in the Zhenjiang, Jinshan, Jiaoshan, and Yixing counties of Jiangsu. One of them is Qixia Temple, built during the Six Dynasties Period [208–588 C.E.]. There in the shade of the luxuriantly forested Mount Qixia, where ancient and regal maples spread like evening clouds, the gathering literati used to stand and gaze at their surroundings, awestruck by its beauty.

Passing through the mountain gate, the steps leading to the temple are lined with old trees and new blossoms. A halfmoon-shaped lake shimmers in the sun. A twenty-five cent admission is collected in the garden, and then again at the temple to support their maintenance.

In the cool April air stands the majestic Vairocana[14] Shrine. On the lawn surrounding the five-story Relic[15] Stupa, young Hsing Yun spent many pleasant hours after class. Parts of the hexagonal stupa have since become time worn and have crumbled away. Inside the 1,500-year-old stone cave of a thousand Buddhas, figures of the bodhisattvas and arhats still maintain full lotus position, but unfortunately without their heads–evidence of violence against them by the ignorant Red Guards. The government's reconstructive efforts have only minimally helped salvage much of the beauty that once graced the stupa.

Its cloud-dwelling remoteness is probably what kept Qixia Temple from total ruin during the siege of the Cultural Revolution. The main shrine and its right and left shrines are still intact. But the waft of incense is thin and the presence of devotees rare. At times, an old monk, frail and alone, emerges. The novice monks, in groups of three or five, appear subdued and downcast. Though structurally sound, the temple has lost much of its vitality and vibrance.

Even the Buddha statue, which has undergone a half-century

of desolation, is unanimated. Gazing at those many splendored maples and long, resplendent walls, one cannot help but wonder about the two-thousand dawns and dusks Hsing Yun spent there.

Poor as a Temple Mouse

Naturally, in the scantiness of wartime livelihoods, there was a shortage of devotee visits and donations to the temples. Even though the laypeople were aware of the great virtue and merit of making offerings, most were simply too poor to do so. In those early days at Qixia Temple, Hsing Yun was as poor as a temple mouse.

He had to keep each letter he wrote to his mother for a year because he simply could not spare money for postage. A torn robe, he would mend with paper; a worn sole, he would fix with some cardboard; a lost sock, he would replace with a reject from another pair. He cannot recall ever having worn two socks of the same shade due to the meagerness of his possessions. He still vividly remembers the single bucket of water shared by all for morning cleansing. The act was restricted to the so-called *two times and a half*—first, soaking the towel; second, wiping the face and soaking it again; and for the remaining half, the final wringing of the towel. The facecloth used for washing often remained dirty. After the ritual, the cleansing water always turned to mud. Still, it was carried off and used to flush the latrine.

Food was also in extremely short supply. There was literally too little gruel for too many monks. Hsing Yun remembers that Qixia Temple once housed a sangha of over 400 monastics from all over China. Rice, often mixed with other grains, was served twice a month; otherwise the daily gruel, more a watery broth than anything else, was served with either beancurd dregs or salted turnips. The leftovers of the dregs, when sun-dried again, were contaminated by the droppings of birds that came to feast on them, and the turnips were often infested with maggots. The vegetable soup, lacking in ingredients and oil, was probably clean enough to do laundry in. Sometimes, with little snails and earthworms lining its bottom and bugs floating at the top, the soup started to reek during the chanting preceding the meal. All Hsing Yun could do was close his eyes, hold his breath, and gulp it down.

Our human condition renders us prone to sickness and pain. One time, Hsing Yun came down with a case of skin ulcers so horrendous that each time he removed his garb his ailing skin was painfully torn. Despite his pain and the danger he was in, he was unable to see a doctor due to the scarcity of resources.

In another instance, he contracted malaria. Monasterial discipline disallowed sick leave, and he was compelled to go about the daily routine like the others despite bouts of chills and fever. A half-month had elapsed before his master, who headed the Buddhist college, was informed of his condition and sent someone over with half a bowl of salted vegetables. Hsing Yun ate them in tears, moved with gratitude for this gift.

To anyone living in the affluent modern world, a half-bowl of salted vegetables might seem trivial, but to the stricken Hsing Yun, it was comparable to the most delicious of delicacies. The kind gesture awakened in him, the determination to spread the Buddhist faith in reciprocation for his master's graciousness, and it reinforced his view that no one should ever go hungry. Today, the kitchens in all the branch temples are ready around the clock to provide food for all those who come to the gate.

Nonsentient vs. Sentient, Unreasonable vs. Reasonable

There is no end to the suffering of the body; nor do the trials of the spirit get any easier.

The new kid at Qixia Temple often attended lectures for seven or eight hours at a time, palms joined together and knees pressed into the gravel until his arms were so numb that they no longer felt like his own and the gravel had sunk into his little knees. He was only twelve.

When he received the complete precepts of monkhood at fifteen, he began to realize the depth of their meaning. He vowed to accept the sentient with the nonsentient, and the reasonable with the unreasonable.

"I remember answering in the negative when the preceptor asked if I had ever killed. The next instant a bundle of willow twigs came down on my head. 'Not even mosquitoes and ants?' I quickly changed my answer to the affirmative. But the willows came down once again because, regardless of the victim, killing is a misdeed. Then the preceptor asked, 'Did your master send you?' 'I've come on my own,' I replied and was whacked a third time. 'So your master didn't send you? Since you decided to come on your own, you deserve a beating,' the preceptor said. 'Yes, the master sent me,' I humbly corrected myself once more. 'What if you weren't sent? Would you have come just the same?' And I was struck a fourth time."

The willow twigs banished arrogance and obstinacy; the beatings transformed one's attachment to ego, to the absence of it. As Hsing Yun's religious sentiments and integrity took shape, a personality evolved that "is content with every encounter, lives according to circumstances, is carefree in mind, and does everything with willingness and joy."

To the keenly inquisitive youth, that was just the beginning of his training. It became more difficult in the next fifty-three days. Each time he raised his head, wondering where sounds of the mountain or streams were coming from, the leading master in the preceptorial hall would catch him and the bamboo cane would strike: "What are you listening to? Close your ears! Young as you are, what sound can you claim as yours?" At that, Hsing Yun would hasten to gather mind and spirit and block out the sounds of the leaves that rustled like waves and the rain that beat on the eaves. But again a master's cane would find him, "Open your ears and listen! What sound is not yours?" At other times, he would be hit for peeping at the liturgical ceremonies taking place in the preceptorial shrine: "Your eyes are wandering! What is there that is yours?" Then, on exiting the hall, he would become aware of the grass that swayed with the breeze and the geese that soared with the clouds and, in panic, would shut his eyes to them. "Open your eyes to see! What is there that isn't yours?" He was struck once more.

This form of training, one of inclusion and acceptance of any and all circumstances, laid the groundwork for his practice and teaching, and nurtured a personality that is equally at peace with having and not having, hunger and satiation, day and night, more and less, advancing and retreating, largeness and smallness.

Master Zhikai, Disciplinarian and Reprimander

Venerable Master Zhikai treated his disciple with austerity, founded on deep love. During the Lunar New Year, all of the monastics would take time off to go home. Not Hsing Yun. He yearned to be reunited with his family but could not leave unless the master gave consent, and the master did not. Over the span of ten years, in fact, he had given his disciple only two sets of clothing. During the occasional tutorial, he treated Hsing Yun the way a traditional master treats a disciple, disciplining and reprimanding to strengthen and ennoble his will.

On one occasion, Hsing Yun was chided in class by another teacher. Master Zhikai, hearing of the news and thinking that his student might have been wronged, sent for the young monk. After the master had asked about the circumstances, he raised a teacup to his student and said, "You thought that by telling me about your money woes, I'd give you some money! Let me be frank. Even if I gave you the money I saved for tea, you wouldn't be able to spend it all. Yet, I'm not going to give it to you. You may not understand this concept now, but someday you'll appreciate my intentions."

As he grew in years and in wisdom, he came to appreciate the reasons and the profundity of those intentions.

The reason for denying him a visit home was because he needed to mature in and deepen his spiritual practice. Although he possessed a good nature, it was feared that exposure to outside elements might be distracting, and that he might regress and lose the desire for the Truth. Rigorous training was designed to teach him how to prevail with mental fortitude. Mastering this skill entailed the endurance of pain and poverty. In the end, he learned to let go of material life, and ceased to ask for more or to desire different circumstances.

After four decades, Hsing Yun returned to Qixia Temple to sweep the burial stone of his master for the first time. He, who rarely sheds a tear, prostrated before the memorial tablet of Master Zhikai, spoke of his own struggles to fulfill his master's wishes, prayed, and wept.

Media producer Zhou Zhimin who was touring with him records what she had witnessed:

The procession to his ancestral monastery was overwhelming. The sound of the bell and drum resounded as a solemn and important pronouncement. The Master's gait was weighty and his eyes were brimming with tears. Speechless and with great reverence, he prostrated before the Buddha time after time. When he was finally invited to speak, he broke down in tears before he could even begin. Ten minutes passed, and the abbot posed the request once more. The Master began again, "I was tonsured at Qixia Temple. Forty-six years, I have been away and today I am home to visit my ancestral monastery. How beautiful this place has been kept! With their lives, the venerables must have guarded this place, and with their hearts tended the grounds! How you all must have been there for him when Master Zhikai suffered, consoled him when he would have rather died! I can't possibly begin to thank you! ...I thought that I could be strong, but now that I am here at my ancestral monastery, I know not what to feel anymore..." With that, he wept again.

Master Zhikai died defending the Buddhist faith in the turmoil of the Cultural Revolution. He was buried in his hometown of Haian, Jiangsu. For many years now, Hsing Yun has financially supported his master's family. And during every homecoming, he chants sutras and prays in gratitude at his master's graveside.

Hsing Yun's family felt the heartache of his extended absence. His mother tried to visit him as often as she could. To be near him, his brothers Guohua and Guomin lived and worked at the temple for a few years. Terribly worried about her brother's badly worn shoes, his sister Suhua learned the special skill of making monastic footwear from a nun who lived miles away. Unsure of his exact size, she made two pairs—one larger and the other smaller—that she asked someone else to deliver. It was years later before Suhua would realize Hsing Yun had given them away to a couple of young novices much poorer than himself, and he continued to make do with the worn pair that he had.

The Young and Valiant Monastic

The six years on Mount Qixia laid the foundation for Hsing Yun's lifelong commitment to Buddhism. By the time he had been admitted to Jiaoshan Buddhist College, Zhenjiang in 1945, he had matured into an astute and compassionate young monk.

Jiaoshan Buddhist College, among the most reputable institutions of higher learning, was home to an outstanding faculty and student population. Its chancellor, Venerable Master Xuefan, is now the abbot of Qixia Temple. While he was there, Hsing Yun studied *The Compendium of Abhidharma* [*Abhidharmakosa*] under Master Yuanzhan and early Buddhism under Master Zhifeng. Master Mingshan, the vigilant eighty-year-old abbot of Jiaoshan and Baohua Temples, coached him on the doctrine of Yogacara for half a year and remembers the young man in his late adolescence as "very focused on his studies, very reticent then, but quite eloquent now." They have taken the time to get together periodically over these past few years and, whenever credited for having been the renowned mentor to a distinguished student, Master Mingshan smiles and says, "Hsing Yun has done much to revitalize Buddhism. Truly, he is my master now!"

Shiming, a classmate from Jiaoshan, takes pride in Hsing Yun's success and recounts the days they shared:

> You were so supportive of my two feature columns, *New Voice* and *Kalavinka*,[16] in the local Zhenjiang newspaper. Each time I asked for a piece of your writing, you would always gesture "no" first. This was to tell me that you would have it, when you motioned to me that you wouldn't. Then you would lower your head in silence, and the conversation and laughter of our mountain stroll would subside. I knew you were organizing your thoughts and beginning to compose a masterpiece. Then at study hall that evening, you would place in my hands the completed work.
>
> I later became a reporter for Nanjing's *Buddhism Monthly*. Once I was packing for another trip when you slipped a bundle of cash into my pocket, saying, "Your interviews are

very important. Make sure you feed yourself!" I smiled, and accepted your gift. When we met again on my return, I lifted my garb and jokingly asked you, "Can you tell I used your money wisely?" You were pleased with my ample belly and laughed heartily.

Books, and Their Causes and Conditions

In the 1930s, China witnessed an increased immersion of Western culture into its own. Without newspapers available in the typically reclusive orthodox Buddhist monastery where Hsing Yun lived, discontent began to stir amongst the young minds in the sangha, who were eager to keep abreast of the times. Fortunately, an evacuated country school left behind a library. The older monastics were indifferent, but Hsing Yun spent hours in this newly found retreat, away from the monotony of monasterial life. Without hesitation, he flung himself into the sea of Chinese classics and, to this day, admits to savoring historical texts and biographies the most. He was first introduced to contemporary Western thought though his studies of Western works. This opened a window within his heart to the world beyond the monastery and beyond China.

Today, Fo Guang Shan provides over twenty libraries for its international department, the lay community, students, and children. These facilities can be traced back to the circumstances that first bonded Hsing Yun to a library five decades prior.

Even though Hsing Yun did not receive much formal education, once he discovered the joy of reading books, he never stopped studying on his own. Every cent he had was invested in new titles; he would rather miss a meal than a book. Since then, a delightful volume is often the gift of choice between the Master and his disciples.

With his avid reading, Hsing Yun sharpens his comprehension and clarity, and seeks to draw his own conclusions. He adds commentaries and annotations, makes generous notes, jots down unforgettable lines, and always indicates the sources. When necessary, a perusal of his personal notes is equivalent to reading the book once again. This practice enables him to tutor the most intellectually gifted scholars among his disciples and has helped him become a best-selling author and articulate public speaker.

By the time he had left Jiaoshan Buddhist College in 1947, Hsing Yun had studied in the monastery for nearly ten years. The journey from Qixia Vinaya School to the preceptorial hall of Baohua Shan, and from Jiaoshan Buddhist College to the meditation hall of Tianning Temple in Jinshan, completed Hsing Yun's training in Buddhist discipline and doctrine. The blend of masterly training and self-education helped him realize the equal importance of practice and understanding in the Mahayana spirit. Afterwards, with youthful ardor, he stepped into a tumultuous and desperate society and found himself embroiled in the survival of both his nation and his faith.

Chapter 3

Facing Turbulent Times

*A*fter graduating from Jiaoshan Buddhist College, Hsing Yun first became the director of Dajue Temple and then the principal of Baita Primary School. Stepping beyond his monastic Buddhist background and into the pulse of society, Hsing Yun crossed into the threshold of a great epoch.

It was a maddening time. The belligerence of warlords, the aggression of the Japanese, the strife between the Nationalists and Communists, and the suffering of the common folk outraged him as it did the thousands of other young patriots. Accompanying his outrage over these injustices was a deep sadness that arose out of his Buddhist compassion. Of critical concern was the Buddhist religion itself, hanging precariously on the brink of extinction. Hsing Yun recognized the crucial need for reform and regeneration. "Don't expect Buddhism to grant you any favors. Think only of what you can do for Buddhism!" That was the birth of a body of thought, which would continue to evolve in the years to come.

Buddhism in China, Its Ups and Downs

Indian Buddhism was introduced into China during the reign of Emperor Ming [58–75 C.E.] of the Eastern Han Dynasty and flourished for the next 400 years in the Sui and Tang Dynasties. Mainstream Buddhism during this period was socially-oriented.

Many eminent monks were active in both political and literary circles. Some were highly regarded in the imperial court, such as Tiantai School's Master Zhiyi [538–597 C.E.] in the court of Emperor Yang of the Sui Dynasty, Faxiang School's Master Xuanzang [602?–664 C.E] in the court of Emperor Taizong of the Tang Dynasty, Huayan School's Master Fazang [643–713 C.E.] and Chan School's Master Shenxiu [605–706 C.E.] in the court of Empress Wu Zetian of the Tang Dynasty. Other monks befriended literary luminaries such as Bai Juyi [772–846 C.E.], Wang Wei [701–761 C.E.], Li Ou [772–841 C.E.], and others.

The Buddhist community attempted to reach the general public by way of literature, drama, and art, and in so doing enriched the cultural legacy of the era. Through financial assistance and other charitable deeds, religion and livelihood were further interwoven. Such services included the establishment of *the inexhaustible treasury*, which was a banking system offering interest-free and contract-free loans,[17] *clinics* that provided medical services for the ill and the poor, and *fields of compassion*[18] to help the needy. These efforts to meet the needs of the community were extremely successful during the Sui and Tang Dynasties.

However, the tide had turned drastically by the Song [960–1279 C.E.] and Yuan [1279–1368 C.E.] Dynasties. Political persecution and the rise of *lixue*[19] doomed the prosperity Buddhism had previously enjoyed. Intellectuals drifted away from the monastics, and monastics themselves drifted away from secular life altogether. Zhu Yuanzhang [1328–1398 C.E.], the founding emperor of the Ming Dynasty, had been a Buddhist novice monk in his youth. He fully recognized this all-embracing faith,[20] its popular appeal, and its valuable influence on society. Concerned that religion might instigate division instead of cohesion, he took action to control it by allocating vast mountain properties to the monasteries, and relocating the monastic population to these designated areas. From that point, Buddhism made a distinct departure from society, and its interaction with the general public swiftly declined. Behind the closed mountain gates, Buddhism assumed the guise of a conservative and reclusive religion. Clearly, its integration with Chinese culture was waning.

Venerable Master Lianchi [1532–1612 C.E.][21] of the Ming Dynasty wrote in *Leisurely Writings by the Bamboo Window* about the corruption within the sangha that so anguished him: "Some act like geomancers, like prognosticators, like physiognomists, like alchemists.... Some hold up their record of donations with arrogance and pride.... Some pose as fortunetellers, carrying around a mere copper piece, beating it with a bamboo stick to predict the future...." Monastics degraded Buddhism by behaving as roving practitioners of the occult or simple paupers. Fearful of the disintegration of Buddhism, Master Lianchi lamented, "This is the absolute worst in the Period of Declining Dharma!"

Without cultural support, the once hearty pulse of Buddhism became faint, and monastics shifted their focus to performing funeral services. The religion totally dissociated itself from the general populace and the literati detached themselves from a degraded and stagnant sangha. Ironically, the occasional monastic who expressed concern for worldly matters or possessed a reputation akin to that of the literati was criticized as being overly secular. Venerable Master Taixu, who lived at the turn of the century, was among those who were victimized by this common misconception of Buddhism, one that is unfortunately still believed to be true.

The initial founding of the Republic of China within Mainland China was accompanied by a movement against Confucianism engineered by young intellectuals who had very little knowledge of Western thought. Buddhism also received a public beating during this period. These intellectuals criticized the clay Buddhas and country monks as feudalistic, misguided, and superstitious hybrids, and they viewed monastic ceremonies with disdain. "Down with the temples and up with public education" was a common slogan, reflecting a mindset used to promote national salvation. In 1927, warlord Feng Yuxiang, nicknamed "the Christian General," ordered the annihilation of Buddhism in Henan Province. At his command, monastics were exiled or viciously murdered. Likewise, the provincial authorities of Zhejiang wanted to eliminate the sangha, and the central government's Minister of Internal Affairs, Xue Dubi, proposed that monasteries be converted into schools. The entire nation was inflamed by anti-Buddhist sentiment. This was one of the most painful and devastating eras in the history of Buddhism in China.

Master Taixu, the Legend

In this time of crisis, the young sangha saw flickers of light in the perilous darkness. It rekindled their hope in their religion and validated their patriotism. Venerable Master Taixu [1889–1947 C.E.] was the beacon at the forefront who led the way.

Many of Hsing Yun's teachers at Jiaoshan had studied under Master Taixu, and Hsing Yun read his works extensively. The desperate young sangha at the time was particularly impassioned by his call: "Every citizen is accountable for the rise and fall of a nation; the sangha is accountable for the rise and fall of Buddhism." Master Taixu redirected the teachings of Buddhism from the passivity of reclusion to its integration into society. Spearheading massive reforms within the Buddhist hierarchy, monasterial assets, and doctrinal teachings, he urged that "worldly matters be viewed through a spiritual lens and tended to accordingly."

In restructuring the Buddhist hierarchy, Master Taixu urged that the dormant sangha be revitalized, by training every monk to be a skilled instructor or Dharma teacher and every nun a qualified teacher or nurse. In reforming doctrinal teachings, he encouraged people to substitute the fatalistic belief that "life is suffering" with a positive attitude, which affirms that life is valuable. He envisioned the reliance on the monastery be replaced by a self-sufficiency that is attained through individual effort and cultivation.

Master Taixu also created the contemporary format of Buddhist education. In 1918, the groundbreaking of Minnan Buddhist College caused uneasiness across the nation. Unfortunately, the relationship between the school and the monastery, where the college was housed, was plagued by conflict that both parties had difficulty resolving. After ten years of irreconcilable tension, the partnership dissolved. Several attempts were made to reconnect, but these endeavors were never systematized.

With astute observation and analysis, Master Taixu knew that Buddhism could not exist without a united China. In the pursuit of national unity, he called for monastic participation in anti-Japanese activities in the divided and desperate country. "The nation, society, and all living beings are one," he advocated.

Despite condemnation and accusations of betrayal from the senior members of the sangha, the younger monastics rallied to support Master Taixu and hailed him as the savior of Buddhism in modern China. In 1946, Hsing Yun found himself in the master's Chinese Buddhist Association Staff Training Class. A classmate demonstrated his loyalty, proclaiming, "Should Master Taixu ask me to tread in boiling water or walk through fire, I would not ask why."

The Written Word, the Tool of Reform

While stationed at Baita Primary School as the principal, Hsing Yun cared for the young and spent long hours pondering how to carry out Master Taixu's ideal of a new Buddhist faith. Like Hu Shizhi [1891–1962 C.E.],[22] who maintained that "China's doom was poverty and ignorance," he realized that the written word was the tool of reform and a bridge to the public. He soon embarked on a number of literary creations: *Raging Billows*, a monthly publication he founded with classmate Master Zhiyong that ran for more than twenty issues; *Xiaguang Fukan*, a supplement he edited for the newspaper *Xu Bao*; and extensive essay contributions to local papers in Jiangsu. His compositions generated a considerable readership among the youth. Barely twenty himself, Hsing Yun was ready to take Buddhism to new heights by urging that the conventions of Dharma services be revised and monasterial management be reorganized. While he was writing profusely, he was also absorbing mountains of knowledge by voraciously reading the literature of the 1930s.

After Japan surrendered, China struggled to gain stability and momentum once again. However, before stability could be attained, the nation became embroiled in yet another civil war. Hsing Yun was compelled to cease his endeavors and his studies. When Master Taixu passed away in 1947, his calls for reform were silenced. At the time of his death, Master Taixu never imagined that, years later his ideal would be launched from Taiwan by the renewed efforts of a young monk he had met only a few times.

Nanjing fell into the hands of the Communists in 1949, and the Nationalists were about to lose Jiangnan. The number of wounded multiplied and the country agonized every day. Members of the sangha, under the guidance of Venerable Master Leguan, began to organize medical relief groups. In honor of their monastic vow, they strove to provide services for all living beings.

The Dharma Lineage Is Preserved

Hsing Yun's close friend, Master Zhiyong, had tried for approximately two months to bring a 600-member medical relief team to Taiwan. On the tacit agreement not to perish together, Zhiyong decided to stay behind and defend Buddhism in China, while Hsing

Yun led the relief group to Taiwan.

With a heavy heart, Hsing Yun returned to Qixia Temple to bid farewell to Master Zhikai. His plan to spread the Dharma in Taiwan delighted his master, who gave him immediate approval. The night before Hsing Yun's departure, the master prepared a sumptuous meal in the refectory to honor his beloved disciple. But when dinnertime came, neither had the heart to raise his chopsticks. Speechless, their eyes were riveted on one another. Both men were moved to tears.

Back in Nanjing, Hsing Yun learned that a Taiwan-bound vessel would soon be leaving Shanghai. Without delay, he took the night train to Changzhou. In the still darkness of the Buddhist college, he roused his schoolmates—some of his acquaintance and even those who were not—from their slumber, and invited them to accompany him to the brave new world of Taiwan.

Over a hundred had pledged to follow Hsing Yun but only seventy—including Masters Yinhai and Haolin who now reside in the United States—actually boarded the vessel in Shanghai. With a vow to preserve the lineage of the Dharma, he and the others sailed across the vast sea. The voyage would chart a new course in Hsing Yun's life. It would also draft the next chapter in the history of Buddhism in China.

Part Two

CROSSING THE SEA, LIGHT IN HAND

Hsing Yun, in his thirties.

At the front gate of
Leiyin Temple, 1953.

With fellow monastics who crossed the ocean to Taiwan.

Traveling by truck, the Master leads Buddhist youths to the countryside to propagate Buddhism, 1957.

Promoting the reprinting of the Buddhist Tripitaka in Changhua, 1955.

108 participants of Lei-yin Temple's first Refuge Taking Ceremony, (March 29, 1953).

Presiding over the Amitabha Buddha Dharma Function at Ilan Buddhist
Chanting Association, 1956.

Venerable Master led the Ilan Buddhist Chanting Association to the countryside to propagate Buddhism, 1953.

Young adults of Ilan Buddhist Chanting Association followed Venerable Master into the countryside to promote Buddhism, 1955.

Chapter 4

The Tangshan Monk
Sets Sail

Near the end of the Ming Dynasty, immigrants from Fujian and Guangdong Provinces carried their Buddhist faith with them as they set sail for Taiwan, which was then under Dutch rule. When Zheng Chenggong [1624–1662 C.E.][23] assumed leadership of Taiwan, Buddhism was beginning to gain attention. His son Zheng Jing, a devout Buddhist, erected the Mituo Temple, and his mother invited the sangha to care for Kaiyuan Temple.

By the Qing Dynasty, more of the sangha had followed in the same footsteps as the early immigrants from Fujian and Guangdong. Taiwan witnessed the birth of numerous Buddhist temples throughout the country. Many temples over 100 years old are still standing, including Zhuxi, Fahua, Chaofeng, Lingyun, and Lingquan.

The occupying Japanese practiced a form of Buddhism in which the precepts and rules of discipline were less strict. This influence resulted in many Taiwanese monastics abandoning celibacy and vegetarianism. Some monastics altered their practice by wearing their cassocks only within the temple walls. Together, with practitioners from sects such as Longhua and Xiantian who were not required to take tonsure, it was often difficult to distinguish between those who were monastics and those who were not. The irregularity and non-uniformity of the monastic lifestyle and appearance caused many misconceptions about Buddhism.

Just the Shirt on His Back

The civil war ended in 1949. Shortly thereafter, a million more Chinese followed in their forefathers' footsteps and crossed over to the enchanting isle of Taiwan. The youthful Hsing Yun was among them. The notion of spreading the Dharma in Taiwan was a new prospect to him. He had heard little of the island, which remained as remote to him as that depicted in archaic texts. He had been told tales of the rich and powerful who had fled China and ended up destitute and homeless in Taiwan.

Like the other passengers from Tangshan[24] scurrying east, Hsing Yun began life in Taiwan with nothing more than the straw sandals on his feet and the shirt on his back. The only baggage he had was misplaced, and he offered his robe to a fellow monastic, Venerable Zhuyun. Locals took one look at his sandaled feet and stared in astonishment—a monk with shoes! Embarrassed, he went barefoot like everyone else.

His group of companion monks quickly disbanded. Like the others, Hsing Yun, then only twenty-three, was on his own. While seeking shelter in Taipei, he was repeatedly told for two days that the monasteries there were either "full" or unprepared to accommodate travelers from outside the province. At one point, a venerable monk spoke with uncharacteristic coldness, "How are you qualified to be here?" The night was cold, a storm was raging, and Hsing Yun was hungry. He stumbled into the knee-deep rain-water and soaked his only change of clothes. Finally, under the big bell at Shandao Temple, he curled up for the night.

The stranger in the strange land did not speak a word of the local dialect. However, the next day he decided to look up an old classmate at a monastery in Keelung. By the time he had arrived, it was past one in the afternoon. When those in the monastery asked if he had eaten, a visibly embarrassed Hsing Yun replied, "No, I haven't had a morsel of food to eat or a drop of water to drink. Not since noon yesterday!" Just as his classmate was about to show him into the kitchen, a desperate and sorrowful voice cried out, "We can barely feed ourselves. I'm sorry, we simply can't help you. Please seek help elsewhere." Everybody had difficulty just surviving, and lending others a hand was a terrible hardship. Hsing Yun understood their plight, looked around, and realized he must keep traveling. He turned to go, but was stopped by his friend. A pot of porridge had been cooked for him. His friend had paid for the rice out of his own meager earnings. As Hsing Yun held the bowl in his hands, he could not stop them from trembling in hunger.

After finishing the meal, Hsing Yun thanked his host and bade him good-bye. He intended to go up to Mount Guanyin in Chengzi Liao, but rain had flooded the road, leaving him stranded at the station, famished and shivering. Only someone who has experienced such incredible hardship and helplessness can identify with the plight of this lonely, young monk.

At Long Last, Yuanguang Temple

Ultimately, it was the compassionate Venerable Master Miaoguo of Yuanguang Temple in Chungli who gave Hsing Yun a place to stay. With the utmost gratitude, Hsing Yun toiled hard to reciprocate this kindness. Each day, he drew 600 pails of water out of the bottomless well for the over 80 inhabitants living in the monastery. Before daybreak, he would tread through the shadows on the moonlit dirt road, pushing a handcart, traveling nine miles to the market. Amidst the breezes blowing through the boughs, the idyllic peace over the land, the dogs barking from afar, and the clatter of his own wooden clogs, he would silently recite the name of Avalokitesvara Bodhisattva. When he reached the market, the vendors were still asleep. He would knock on their doors, make his daily purchases for the monastery, and then take the same dirt road back, chanting "Avalokitesvara Bodhisattva, Avalokitesvara Bodhisattva…"

In the monastery, few were as young and robust as Hsing Yun. He performed each task with energy and attention, including cleaning the latrines and helping to wrap and bury the bodies of the deceased.

Despite the enormous amount of chores, Hsing Yun never deserted his reading and writing. Once, he earned a small sum helping out in a chanting service. With the money, he hastened to buy himself new stationery. He was elated! Many a time, fellow monastics and devotees found him writing and thought he was neglecting more important tasks. He still recalls the concerned reaction of an elderly devotee, "Master, you must go and work, or else you'll starve!" During the same period, he took three months off to tend the woods around Fayun Temple in Miaoli. There on the grass he crafted *Singing in Silence*, edited a monthly magazine called *Life*, and wrote radio scripts.

Hard to Tell the Buddhas and Deities Apart

A daily routine of physical labor and basic chores was a natural way of life. Most people dared not venture beyond dreams of domestic well-being and a simple livelihood. As a visionary, however, Hsing Yun knew there was much more beyond complacent living. His dynamic and devoted will to advocate Master Taixu's Humanistic Buddhism in Taiwan never subsided. He remained persistently enthusiastic in spreading the Dharma. This great vow was not easy to put into practice, especially in the volatile cultural context of Taiwan forty years ago.

Scholars of Taiwan's religious evolution have long maintained that polytheism was the natural answer to a life at the mercy of the elements: typhoons, earthquakes, and threats of similar magnitude. There was simply nowhere to hide, except, perhaps, in the asylum of the Daoist temples that were rapidly being built. Many of these temples had eaves bedecked with ornate figures from Chinese mythology. Deities such as Mazu,[25] Lu Dongbin,[26] the earth gods, rock gods, and tree gods were depicted in conjunction with Buddhist motifs and symbols. The blending of rituals, archetypes, and architecture from both Daoist and Buddhist traditions made it difficult to distinguish a Daoist temple from a Buddhist one.

In some respects, Buddhist monasteries in Taiwan differed significantly from the landowning, self-sufficient establishments in Mainland China. Within the Taiwanese system, temples were constructed and sustained by donations from devotees and contributions made to the monastics. However, because Taiwan was experiencing an economic plight, substantial monetary gifts were nearly impossible. For an extended period, the meager finances in the Buddhist community could only provide for the basic necessities of life. Any idea of progress had to wait.

In addition, the monastics of the time were not well-educated. Most were competent in chanting the sutras and performing services to deliver the dead from hell, but teaching the Dharma was an advanced skill not yet possessed by many. During this era, misconceptions abounded perpetuating the notion that Buddhism's only social service involved tending to the deceased. There appeared to be very little intellectual value in the religion, and many of the well-educated were apathetic.

With devastating effects, a wealthy and overbearing American presence in postwar Taiwan brought Catholic and Protestant influences to the cities and villages. President Chiang Kai-shek and his wife[27] became converts, as did other famous political leaders and public figures. While Christianity was blossoming, Buddhism was wilting. Many people vividly recall the events that spiraled Buddhism into disaster: the violation of temple sanctity, the transformation of Taipei's Shandao Temple into military re-cruiting offices, and the degradation of the main shrine of Yuans-han's Linji Temple when it was turned into Dr. Sun Yat-sen[28] Me-morial Hall. A similar invasion of Buddhist sacred space occurred when the 100-year-old Dong Benyuan Temple in Taipei almost became a mosque. This intrusive plan was the authorities' attempt to welcome their royal friends from the Middle East. However, the temple was saved from demolition when a sizeable mosque was erected elsewhere, with government funding.

Incarcerated Three Times

The Nationalist government had barely gained any stability in Taiwan. Uncertainty was in the air. Newcomers from the Main-land were viewed with suspicion. Intelligence gathering and se-curity measures were of high priority. Many people, including monastics, suffered great persecution.

Hsing Yun has been incarcerated three times during his life-time. The first two times happened when he was directing Baita Primary School. During the day, the Nationalist military hunted for Communist guerillas, and at night the Communist guerillas assaulted the Nationalist military. Night or day, Hsing Yun was nabbed by both parties and subsequently pressed for enemy intel-ligence from both sides.

In 1949, rumors circulated that 300 monastics were sent to infiltrate Taiwan. Hsing Yun, along with Venerable Master Cihang—who later founded Mi'le Neiyuan[29] Temple in Hsichih—and other monastics from the Mainland, were jailed for alleged espionage. For twenty-three days, they were bound and shackled and mercilessly shoved around. There was not even room in the cell to lie down. Eventually the group was rescued from confine-ment by Sun-Chang Ching-yang, Wu Ching-hsiung, and other dev-otees.

Shortly after his imprisonment, the police acted on anonymous reports alleging that Hsing Yun was receiving radio broadcasts from the Mainland during the day and disseminating pro-Communist literature at night; he was under surveillance around the clock. However, a year passed and suspicion dissolved. Those sent to follow him were affected by his teaching and actions, and soon became his followers.

During the period of "white terror"[30] in 1952, Hsing Yun accepted a teaching appointment offered to him by Venerable Master Daxing at Qingcao Hu Buddhist College in Hsinchu. He found himself having to apply for a leave of absence with the local sheriff whenever he left the college property. Years later in Kaohsiung, Fo Guang Shan again faced new allegations, this time for allegedly storing over 200 rifles. By then, Hsing Yun possessed a clearer understanding of the times and its circumstances, enabling him to successfully communicate and negotiate with those in power.

A Rising Star

Taiwan began to benefit from the eminent presence of Buddhist monastics arriving from China. The true splendor of Buddhist doctrine was unveiling before society. Indeed, Buddhism was gaining strength. While all of this was happening, Hsing Yun emerged from his ordeals unscathed. The influence of his traditional Buddhist education filled his heart with the belief that "Buddhism depends on me." The young monk, noble in heart and disciplined in mind, would soon shine his light to the far corners of Taiwan, and beyond.

Hsing Yun developed a tremendous number of affinities during his two-year stint at Yuanguang Temple. He was Master Miaoguo's true protégé, and his earnestness and diligence endeared him to many. Grassroots support for this monk from China was mounting. He still talks about a gracious elderly lady who used to

sneak him a bowl of noodles: "Each time I saw her deeply wrin-
kled hands reaching through my study window with the steaming
bowl of noodle soup, broth spilling on the sill, I was touched beyond words!"

As the pulse of Buddhism gained strength, Master Miaoguo's
knowing hand guided Hsing Yun more deeply into Taiwanese society, and showed him how to walk alongside the devotees. With
keen and compassionate observation, he nurtured a profound
knowledge of the place and its people.

Chapter 5

Ilan, the Cradle

The Buddhist scene in Taiwan resembled a barren plain, where the foundation for spreading the Dharma and liberating living beings necessitated the right circumstances, courage, wisdom, and perseverance. Settling into his position in Ilan, in northeastern Taiwan, Hsing Yun was equipped with all four attributes.

Going to the City in the Mountain

The next chapter of Hsing Yun's life began in 1952, when he encountered layman Li Juehe during an executive election of the Chinese Buddhist Association.[31] Li was anxious to find a monastic willing to teach Buddhism in his hometown of Ilan. But Ilan was a poor and remote city. The Taipei-Ilan Highway was sharp and winding, with perils at every turn. The five-hour train ride from Taipei included uncomfortable, risky travel through numerous sooty tunnels. A few Dharma teachers would visit distant Ilan only once, opting never to brave the filthy and dangerous journey again.

Undaunted by the potential problems, Hsing Yun eagerly volunteered his service. At the end of the year, he set foot in Ilan for the first time. From then on, he never spoke of leaving. The community's immediate appreciation of Hsing Yun quickly blossomed into reverence and the willingness to be wholehearted followers.

In those days, going to a place like Ilan took great courage. Hsing Yun's bravery was born out of an earnest determination to spread the Dharma, accompanied by a peaceful acceptance of life's conditions—even when they were as dreadful as those in Ilan.

Geographically, Ilan is situated on a delta. Overlooking the Pacific at one end, the city is blockaded from the vast plain in the northwest by mountains at the opposing end. Life was insulated and the people were introverted. Hsing Yun's destination was Leiyin Temple in Beimen. Built during the reign of Daoguang [1821–1850 C.E.] of the Qing Dynasty, the former residential structure with its traditional courtyard was destroyed by a typhoon in 1963. Locals, headed by Hsing Yun, endeavored to rebuild it; construction was completed in 1978. It was here that Hsing Yun's career as an influential leader and teacher began to take shape and truly took flight.

Treading the premises of Leiyin Temple for the first time, Hsing Yun discerned why the place failed to retain other teachers of the Dharma.

He remembers leaving Taipei early that day and reaching Ilan shortly past noon. Crossing the temple threshold, he first laid eyes on three military families squatting inside. The shrine was there; the cushions for worship were not. They had been turned into pillows used for sleeping. Clothes and footwear were scattered all over. A stove blocking the latrine was still smoking; it had to be removed to gain entrance into the latter.

Hsing Yun let his eyes roam awhile until they alighted on an elderly bhiksuni, Abbess Miaozhuan, who was chanting sutras to relieve the suffering of devotees. When finished, she emerged with the query: "Are you the monk coming to lecture?" "Yes," he responded. Another half an hour passed before she returned with a cup half-filled with tea that had already turned cold.

Finding a Niche in the Shrine

Without delay, Hsing Yun embarked on his life's work. The devotees were receptive to his teachings, so he stayed. He found a niche in the main shrine. It was windowless and the ceiling was low. Once inside, he could not stand up straight, but he was content.

The people who were there in those days might still remember that they had to pay for the installation of every light bulb in their household. To minimize expenses, he hung the bulb before the Buddha in the day and dragged it as far as he could to the door of his living quarters so he could read at night. The cord was short, so he read and wrote at the threshold—the buzz of the mosquitoes kept him company until daybreak.

His soupspoon was made of scrap lead, so light that he found himself chasing it after the wind had picked it up and taken it for a fluttering dance. For the first six months, he slept on the floor. Finally, the devotees chipped in for a prison-manufactured bamboo bed and chair. The bed squeaked with every toss and turn, but still, Hsing Yun was content.

The entire community was poor, and Hsing Yun was not excluded from such hardship. However, life's limitations never concerned him nearly as much as the obstacles surrounding the development of Buddhism as a whole.

The conditions of the time were not very conducive to spreading the Dharma. Taiwan was still reeling from half a century of Japanese rule: not only were the people socially repressed and educationally deprived, but they lacked a correct view on religion. Also, in its reclusivity, Ilan was paranoid about anyone and anything from outside its boundaries. Needless to say, the every action of this young monk who had suddenly arrived from the Mainland was under close scrutiny. Some even challenged his wit and endurance with a few rude tests.

Master of Beimen

Buddhist lectures at Leiyin Temple were often disturbed by the clamor outside. Quick-witted, Hsing Yun would turn off the light, leaving only the spark of incense lit before the Buddha. The rowdy gatherers, shocked by the sudden darkness, would grow silent. It was then that they saw the magnificent figure of Hsing Yun and clearly heard his lectures. In this "silence," many hostile people changed their arrogant attitudes and came to accept the Buddha's teachings.

Another time, Hsing Yun was propagating the Dharma at a bustling night market in Ilan where seven avenues converged and a diverse group of people congregated. In the midst of his lecture, he was pelted with stones from all different directions. Afterwards, it was discovered that the violent disruption was instigated by a group of Christian zealots. Hsing Yun's forming of the Buddhist Youth Choir also came as a shock to many Buddhists, and some of the more conservative ones went so far as to threaten his life. In those days, every little thing had everyone on pins and needles.

Hsing Yun remained peaceful despite the continual threats. The people of Ilan bore witness to his energy and bearing, his maturity and wit, and his knowledge and charm. Some did not know his name, but to them he was the Master of Beimen. The older devotees certainly remember how he used to look. Ayao Gu, now over eighty years old, is among Hsing Yun's earliest follow-ers. "He was so endearing!" she grins, revealing her gold teeth.

Naturally, the handsome young monk with the charismatic presence was of enormous interest to the girls. *Shigu*[32] Hsiao Pi-hsia, who has followed the Master for almost four decades, recalls the time he went over to the office where she worked to make a phone call. Immediately, communications all over Ilan shut down because all the phone operators—their supervisor included—went to catch a glimpse of him! Today, most of the employees in that office are Hsing Yun's followers.

First Experimental Site for Humanistic Buddhism

Life may have been tough for the folks of Ilan, but once they had experienced the benefits of their Buddhist faith, Hsing Yun realized they would in turn become the supporting pillars of Buddhism. He was prepared to help Ilan become the first site to practice Humanistic Buddhism.

Because of the prevalent illiteracy of the 1950s, he employed the most accessible method for attracting devotees, which was calling on the name of the Buddha and chanting sutras. *Nian Fo Hui* (sutra-chanting services) were formed so that devotees would learn to recite the Buddhist texts. These services were a legitimate and effective form of public education. A formal lecture hall was added to Leiyin Temple in 1956 to accommodate the needs of the increasing numbers of attendees. At its inauguration, many highly cultivated masters, including Master Lcan-Skya,[33] came to offer their congratulations.

The chanting services paved Hsing Yun's way into the arena of regular lectures. To announce a forthcoming lecture, a devotee would carry a board through the streets with the inscription "Please heed the sutras," while another would be the crier, beating a hand-drum. The site of the chanting services was virtually the birth-place of Buddhism in Ilan. Beimen's bus stop still reads "Nian Fo Hui."

Sower of Bodhi Seeds

Inspiring and cultivating the interests of the young Buddhists would be next. Although he was not a natural singer, Hsing Yun formed a group of gregarious songbirds–the first-ever Buddhist choir in Taiwan. The lyrics he penned were then set to music by Yang Yongpu. The children flocked in. They brought their own chairs and poured tea for one another. Not long after, Hsing Yun offered a creative writing workshop. He treated every submission with the utmost attention and respect, and had the young intellectuals enthralled. Venerable Tzu Hui, a first-generation disciple reputed for her literary talents, was candid about her initial intention, "I went to the Master to learn writing, not Buddhism!"

In one article, Venerable Tzu Hui reflected on the mood shared among her peers at the time:

> The chanting sessions in Ilan included a range of projects to guide the young.... I have no words to express the grace in his demeanor, the depth of his thought, the extent of his knowledge. I was simply touched... We used to place our writings in a drawer beneath the altar in Leiyin Temple. We would retrieve them the next morning when we turned in another batch. Our papers were always meticulously critiqued, and we could not wait to exchange them. Everyone would be so excited to look at the comments on their papers. After a while, the Master would round us up for an overall critique, and we would be taught the techniques of composition.

Bodhi seeds of Buddhism were sown among the little ones, too. Specialized groups were formed for those attending junior and senior high school. The teachers among the followers would provide subject tutorials for the underprivileged children. To the disbelief and delight of many parents, these young people became living examples that "children of the Dharma never go astray."

Cheng Shih-yen, educator and best-selling author on Chan studies, was a student in one of these tutorials. He recalls how the Master went to great lengths to devise the most attractive projects for the kids, how well he understood them, and how he would pat them on the shoulder and sit them down to chat. The children would eagerly fly to his side after school. Members of the student body, Cheng recalls, walked tall with pride. Years later at Fo Guang Shan's first International Chan Conference, Hsing Yun ran into this child from the tutorial who was now an adult, and said fondly, "O the willow seed carelessly planted is actually turning into a shade tree now! I'm so glad to see you again!"

Roots of Compassion

Viewed from the standpoint of modern marketing, Hsing Yun possessed a keen sense of the activities that would be most appealing and appropriate for the general public. He cultivated opportunities that would benefit and please a diverse range of people. Early training in Buddhism brings out innate insight and compassion, he believed. Preschool and primary level classes soon expanded into Sunday schools complete with all kinds of contests in the arts. Bodhi seeds, indeed, must be sown in the young.

Venerable Yi Kung, who holds a master's degree in Indian philosophy from Tokyo University, attended one such class for children. She took tonsure two years after graduating from the university and has followed the Master for two decades. She tells of frequenting Leiyin Temple with her two sisters at age four or five, and being drawn solely to the delicious snacks–Buddha or no Buddha! She realizes now, how well the master grasped the concept, "To share the Dharma with people, we must first draw them in by tending to their physical needs!" For the promise of a gift, like a steamed bun, a peach-shaped longevity bun, candied crispies, or a "Buddha's Hand" made of flour, the bouncy little girl would settle down to chant the sutras for the entire length of a burning stick of incense. In time she began to resonate with the Dharma. "A lot of us probably became Buddhists while munching on a little 'Buddha's Hand!'" Venerable Yi Kung laughs heartily.

Hsing Yun touched the average devotee with his sincerity and diligent service. He conducted seven-day chanting services, set up the lecture hall, cooked the vegetarian meals, and waited on tables. Of course, he also played all the Dharma instruments during chanting. And, whenever the pet monkey of a nearby kindergarten scampered off, somebody would invariably yell, "Master! The monkey's run off! Catch the monkey!" He would lay down whatever he had in hand to go help retrieve the mischievous creature.

Ilan, Where the Heart Is

There seemed to be no limit to the Master's generosity and energy. He would buy several hundred issues of the *Life* magazine he edited and give them away. For *Awakening the World*, he actually went out soliciting subscribers. Income from his writing was channeled into the purchase of silver chains with srivatsalaksana[34] pendants, which he hoped young devotees would wear with pride, and notebooks and pencils for the students and the children's classes.

In 1958, a lantern parade was held to honor and celebrate the growth of Buddhism. It was the Buddha's birthday. Tibetan Buddhists under the Dalai Lama's leadership were rising against Communist oppression. Hsing Yun decided to echo their cry, and gather all of his followers for a special event. Every district in Ilan was represented by a float. The parade of lights ran thirty miles, and three-fifths of the populace attended the celebration. With bright colors and countless participants, the parade demonstrated the power of unity; Buddhists had their first taste of solidarity.

During the course of twelve years, the alien monk and the city among the hills had become inseparable. "Coming, no one is there to greet me; going, no need to bid me goodbye. That's the feel of home," he says. No matter how far he roams, or how much time passes, his heart is always in Ilan.

Hsing Yun truly reserves a special affection for Ilan. At Yuanming Temple in Chiao Hsi, he finished writing the *Biography of Sakyamuni Buddha's Ten Great Disciples* at the speed of 10,000 characters per day. Even now, he misses the restful walk along the brook at the end of each day!

It was in Ilan that Hsing Yun nurtured most of his first generation of disciples: Hsin Ping, Tzu Chuang, Tzu Chia, Tzu Hui, Tzu Jung, and other venerables who form the nucleus of Fo Guang Shan.

The most dedicated devotees of Fo Guang Shan also came from Ilan. One such follower is Weng Songshan, founder of the China Buddhist Art Center. The former painting apprentice reciprocated Hsing Yun's support in helping him learn to carve Buddha statues thirty years ago with a generous donation to the Fo Guang University Foundation. He also thanked the Master for the opportunity to make such a gift.

Leiyin Temple, the Beginning

Without Leiyin Temple, Fo Guang Shan would not exist; without Fo Guang Shan, there would not be over one hundred branch temples around the globe,[35] the thousand disciples, and the million devotees. Enshrined in the temple is Vairocana Buddha.[36] Leiyin Temple was where it all began. It was the spark that ignited the fire of Humanistic Buddhism.

The source of one of the century's supreme masters and the impetus for Fo Guang Shan's impressive flourishing—that is Ilan. To call Ilan the cradle for the modernization of Buddhism in Taiwan would not be an overstatement.

Chapter 6

Master of Innovation

*S*akyamuni Buddha attained Buddhahood at the age of thirty-five. Venerable Master Xuanzang journeyed to India to acquire the Buddhist sutras at twenty-six. By the age of thirty, Hsing Yun stood at the threshold of his mission to modernize the spread of Buddhism and had positioned himself to take some creative risks.

Introduced from India into China over 1,000 years ago, Buddhism was an Eastern religion that did not actively engage in converting people, which made for passive Buddhists when it came to spreading the Dharma. Although devotees were welcomed, they were not actively sought. But times were changing and the age-old religious experience had to change, too. Hsing Yun considered how technology, politics, the economy, society as a whole, and even the makeup of the congregation could be integrated. How could orthodox Buddhist doctrine and this developing state of affairs connect? And who should help Buddhists awaken to the causes and conditions of this new age? The difficulty with Buddhism does not lie in abstract semantics Hsing Yun realized, but in adapting the spread of the Dharma to the times and following causes and conditions to explain them.

No stranger to the dynamics of modern media, Hsing Yun decided to systematically employ it to propagate the Buddha's teachings in Taiwan.

The Written Word, His Beloved Medium

Throughout his career, Hsing Yun has never ceased to call upon the wisdom of the written word as a vehicle for the joy of the Dharma. The written word is his beloved medium. Early in his days at Jiaoshan Buddhist College, he collaborated with classmate Master Zhiyong in founding a monthly newsletter called *Raging Billows*, and edited *Splendid Light*, a supplement to the newspaper *Xu Bao*. He also wrote for local papers in Jiangsu. When he arrived in Taiwan, he quickly assumed publishing commitments with the magazines *Awakening to Life* and *Life*. During 1957-58, he took over one journal and started another, *Awakening the World* and *Buddhism Today*, respectively. In 1979, he founded *Universal Gate*, a magazine that is leading the way in Buddhist publishing. After fifteen years and over two hundred issues, the originally fifty-eight page black-and-white production has evolved into a glossy magazine of high quality in content, design, production, and distribution, read by Buddhists and non-Buddhists alike. According to the Annual Report, the expenses for advertising and the revenues from publishing have not only evened out; they have even yielded a surplus.

Though he was never schooled in writing, Hsing Yun has fared well as an author and maintains an unbridled passion for the printed word. To him, the pen is the duster with which he clears away the mind's defilements and obstructions. He composed *Singing in Silence* while sprawled on the ground in the woods of Fayun Temple. In 1953, *Discourse on Avalokitesvara's Universal Gate Chapter* was his first work to be published. Special mention must be made of *National Master Yulin*, a best-seller that was made into a movie and later a television series in 1993.

This particular story came about while Hsing Yun was traveling across Taiwan on speaking commitments. He and his friend, Venerable Master Zhuyun, spent a night on a farm in Yu-chih,

Nantou. Given the courtesy of a spot closest to the toilet in the farmer's room, the pair found the stench of the nearby commode unbearable. But not wishing to be ungrateful for their host's thoughtfulness, they resolved to tough out the night. "Hey, Zhuyun, tell me a story. I can't sleep," confessed Hsing Yun. Master Zhuyun was the consummate storyteller.

"Let me tell you about Master Yulin[37] then." By the time he finished, morning had broken. "I won't let your efforts go to waste, Zhuyun!" promised Hsing Yun.

Returning to Leiyin Temple, he painstakingly wrote down the story against the sewing machine. Writing under the pen name Mojia, he was soon regarded as an emerging new talent. Once, a friend suggested that Hsing Yun should consider becoming a professional writer: "With that pen of yours, you should just become a journalist!"

Hsing Yun's brainchild, the Fo Guang Publishing House, has been energetic in publishing Buddhist-related titles. Genres range from biographies and literary pieces to articles on doctrine and etiquette. In recent years, audiotapes, CDs, and videos have been produced. Most important are the *Fo Guang Tripitaka*, the award-winning *Fo Guang Encyclopedia*, and the English translations of sutras. Hsing Yun's monthly journals, which appeared in *Universal Gate* magazine over a four-year period, have been published in a set of twenty volumes. They are thought to be an excellent way to connect with his disciples and followers worldwide, as well as an effective means of spreading the Dharma. Fo Guang Shan is currently collaborating with UC Berkeley to computerize the Buddhist Tripitaka.

In his own words, "Through the prajna[38] of the written word, not only are those of us in the here and now able to connect with the thoughts of the Buddha, but beings living millennia from now and light-years from here will be able to realize the wondrous meaning of absolute truth!"

Going the Electronic Way

In keeping with modern advancements, new electronic technology has become a tool of Dharma propagation. As early as in the days of Ilan, there was the Buddhist choir. Then came the radio programs, *Voice of Buddhism, Sound of Awakening the World, Gate of Faith, The Wondrous Use of Chan,* and *Wisdom of Life.* The latest addition to this list is special programming for Chinese-speaking audiences in Los Angeles, California.

The following works have also been made into television broadcasts: *Sakyamuni Buddha,* 1972; *Sweet Dew,* 1979; *Gate of Faith,* 1980; the award-winning *Venerable Master Hsing Yun's Buddhist Lectures,* 1983; *The Sixth Patriarch's Platform Sutra,* 1985; *Hsing Yun's Chan Talk,* 1987; *A Verse Per Day,* 1989; the award-winning *Hsing Yun's Dharma Words,* 1991; *Hsing Yun Speaks a Verse,* 1991; and *Hsing Yun Says,* 1994. These programs are on all three channels in Taiwan—often simultaneously.

Music from the Heavens

The earliest form of Buddhist music was *fanbei*: *fan* being the music of Mahabrahma,[39] and *bei* being clearness and purity. *Fanbei* is truly music from the heavens. In quiet moments, the heavenly music can expand and elevate people's minds. *Fanbei* was first used in preaching, and also employed in praise of the Buddha. Musical instruments that the Buddhist devas are depicted with include the *pipa*, the *zheng*, and the *qin*,[40] all instruments that have been adopted in Chinese music.

Hsing Yun cut the first-ever Buddhist ten-inch records in 1957. Six in all, they included some twenty songs. Wu Juche, who was teaching at the polytechnic college in Taipei, was offered a key role in producing them, despite the fact that he and Hsing

Yun had not even met before the project. The two had no dispute whatsoever about popularizing and humanizing this time-honored faith. Wu applauded Hsing Yun's originality and offered his help without reservation. The half-dozen records that resulted, struck a chord with wide audiences in Taiwan and all over Southeast Asia.

Three decades later, a 200-member choir from Fo Guang Shan Buddhist College gave a historic Buddhist chanting performance at the National Music Hall in Taipei. The event helped lift Buddhist music to an unprecedented status.

The growing popularity of karaoke and KTV[41] has sparked notions of presenting the various Buddhist hymns in a similar format. Hsing Yun wants Buddhist chanting to fill every household. From radio to TV programs and records to karaoke, Hsing Yun has emerged as a modern master of Dharma propagation.

Alongside the Simple Folk

In 1954, Hsing Yun began a series of lectures on the Tripitaka in Taiwan.

Tzu En, a devotee, tells of his experience in following the Master into the countryside:

> We would bike when the distance was manageable. As the youthful monk crisscrossed the countryside, his thirty or so equally youthful followers tagged along. In the evening breeze, we would race against the setting sun. The Master would either lead or follow behind everyone. When bikes broke down or there was an uphill ride, we would all dismount and walk our bikes together. When a typhoon struck, we would just bask in the Dharma rain. On our return, we would sing the Master's "Song of the Dharma Preacher" aloud and make our way back to Leiyin Temple.
>
> We would take the train when the destination was far off.

We had to scramble for the train, which ran infrequently in those days. Later on, however, the people manning the various stations along the Ilan route had been so moved that they made sure all of us were on board before the whistle blew.

As the day of a Dharma function approached, locals would parade through the streets sounding a gong and announcing: "Our Dharma is coming!" When the day finally came, throngs of people carrying statues of deities would lead the way. One such event drew a crowd of 5,000 in the tiny town of Yuli in Hualien County. Whether it was out in the open, inside the small town theater, or on the ground reserved for drying grain, Hsing Yun and his young friends busied themselves setting up the microphone, extending wires, screwing in light bulbs, putting up posters, arranging seats, and ushering in the audience. The young preachers then took the podium. Simultaneously, in both Mandarin and the Taiwanese dialect, aided by a slide show, they would read from the scripts their master had perfected for them. By the end, the crowd would be overjoyed.

For the next thirty years, Hsing Yun lectured in towns and villages, schools and factories, national museums and memorial halls, art centers and sports stadiums. As the venue and the audience grew in size, time stood witness to how the compassion and wisdom of the Buddha could reach far and wide through the efforts of this master.

Across the Oceans

Hsing Yun began moving his stage across the oceans about a decade ago. He visibly stepped up his teaching, especially in Hong Kong. Late in the summer of 1993, he made his way into a jampacked Hunghom Coliseum, which seats 20,000. For three consecutive days, he spoke on the topic of "The Study of Prajna Wisdom and the Nature of Emptiness in the Diamond Sutra." Media coverage was overwhelming. Each evening the coliseum filled well before the lecture was to start. Upon hearing that some people could not get into the arena, Hsing Yun arranged with Venerable Tzu Jung and stadium officials to have a 100-inch screen set up for those unable to gain entrance. During the two-hour lecture, the minds of those in attendance, seated or otherwise, took a refreshing shower in the Dharma rain.

Like many Catholic and Protestant preachers, Hsing Yun has been speaking in prisons for years. His lectures in Taiwan prisons are by formal appointment from the Legal Department. A few of his disciples and followers also lecture in prisons on a regular basis.

When he was last in Hong Kong, he spoke at Stanley Prison for the third time. Full of compassion, he talked to murderers, robbers, and drug dealers who were serving time in isolation. "These walls are nothing to be afraid of. Real incarceration is within the mind," he told them. On that day, the Buddha must have seen the thirty or so incarcerated men as the living beings they were, and not as the deadly menaces perceived through the eyes of others. The group quietly listened to Hsing Yun's counsel to seek the Dharma for an end to their violent ways. Many were brought to tears when, during the refuge ceremony, the Master sprinkled their heads with sweet dew to dispel suffering and bring about repentance.

Hsing Yun has an unwavering dedication to the revival of Buddhism and a sensitive touch on the pulse of Taiwanese society. The construction of Taipei's Pumen Temple in 1978 launched another series of Dharma activities: namely, "The Gathering of Bright Lanterns," "The Gathering to Reciprocate Parents' Kindness," Dharma meetings for women, and Chan and Pure Land Practice. The cross-island alms-rounds function, a contemporary version of a time-honored monastic tradition, and "Buddhist Family Visits," are regarded by some as a form of direct marketing in the spread of the Dharma.

Following the Master

Hsing Yun's projects have received their share of support and criticism. He has been condemned as garish and revolting, and feared because of his charisma and popularity. But as time has passed, his strategies have not only proved effective but have been adopted by monastics of other monasteries. Though some have tried, no longer can anyone deny that he is a significant modern Buddhist leader.

Once, a student, marveling at Hsing Yun's eloquence, asked him, "Master, how come you always have so much to say?" This has not always been the case. During his early years in the monastery he never crossed paths with a stranger, and if he had, would not have known how to talk with one. Ten years of his life revolved wholly around teachers and peers, and his first public lecture at Leiyin Temple was a petrifying experience for him. The whole time, he had to hold the edge of the table in front of him to hide his shaking knees. Offstage, he found himself drenched in sweat. As appearances increased, however, so did his confidence and carriage.

In the beginning, his lectures did not draw a large audience. To disciples, he confesses the most embarrassing moment of his life—when, forty years ago in Ilan, he went onstage to find not a single body below. "The time and date were correct, I mumbled to myself. I waited and waited. Finally a handful of latecomers sauntered in. I began somehow. By the end of the lecture, the crowd hadn't gotten any bigger."

Now, he speaks eloquently. Guests at Fo Guang Shan desiring to hear him speak need only allow him the benefit of composing his thoughts during the five-minute walk to the Guest House to hear his inspiring words. For over ten years, he has needed only to look over television scripts thirty minutes before shooting. His record of a hundred episodes shot in a day without a single retake still amazes people.

Giving Society What It Needs

Sometimes, people leave traditional Dharma lectures saying how wonderful they were, while others are admittedly perplexed. It is easier to speak on the Dharma in ways that few can understand; it is much more difficult to speak with a clarity that all can grasp. What good is a lecture if the audience does not leave with new insight?

To explain Hsing Yun's popularity, Academia Sinica Social Researcher Song Guangyu gave this analysis: "Conventional wisdom states that all a Dharma lecture needs is a building big enough to house a few rows of seats. Hsing Yun transcends this kind of static thinking. He sees the needs of people and makes the Dharma accessible to them."

Those who have been to one of his lectures praise how the sound effects and stage designs are employed for maximum religious expression. "The curtain rises to reveal five images of the Buddha set on a crimson carpet with an azure backdrop. Four groups of attendants bearing flowers, candles, fruits, and tea walk solemnly through a mist created by dry ice. The deep resonance of a single drum marks the procession. The lighting turns magical. Fifty cassock-clad monastics appear with Dharma instruments in hand. It's all so arresting."

With the mood established, Hsing Yun takes center stage and delivers his speech. It has been said that an audience was so moved during one of his thirty-minute lectures, they broke into applause seventy-two times.

Monastics usually teach one sutra at a time and expound on each word and phrase. This can take months. Venerable Master Zhiyi[42] of the Tiantai School, teaching the *Sutra of the Wondrous Truth of the Lotus*,[43] spent ninety days on the character "*wondrous*" in the title alone. Modern life is too filled with work and social obligations to allow for such expansive analysis. Yet bits and pieces of lectures here and there serve us no better as Buddhists.

Aware of the tension between society's desire for thoroughness on the one hand and the pressures of time constraints on the other, Hsing Yun's lectures represent his mastery of innovation. On any single topic, his listeners can gain a better understanding of the Dharma within just a few hours. Topics always pertain to some aspect of everyday life and human psychology. Examples of his lectures include "Prescription for the Heart," "How to Increase One's Happiness," "Living and Religion," and "Ten of Life's Common Concerns."

Greatness of Wisdom and Completeness of Harmony

Though Hsing Yun still speaks with a slight country-boy Yangzhou accent, his charisma is undeniable. In everything he does—whether he is proving a concept with an anecdote or using a concept to discuss some subject matter, whether he is directly pointing to an answer or using implications—he always manages to do it just right. Few ever walk away feeling untouched or unconvinced.

Longtime follower Chang Pei-keng of the Chinese-Tibetan Cultural Association of the Republic of China looks at his teacher as a walking Buddhist lexicon and a human compendium of modern humanities and sciences. "The Master's state is the state of *prajnaparamita*,[44] that of the greatness of wisdom and completeness of harmony. He weaves an array of knowledge seamlessly in conversation; he cross-references without deserting the theme; he always sets off from the Dharma, traverses the ocean of knowledge, and returns home to the Dharma. With such ease he maneuvers through a field of information and knowledge!"

Some years ago, after being invited to Japan, he gave a talk on "The Message of the Twenty-First Century." After the lecture was over, a middle-aged woman came up to Hsing Yun and expressed utter amazement at her sudden comprehension of the Dharma. She told him that after attending more than 200 lectures and spending more than 10 years reading through Buddhist literature, his speech finally opened her mind. In another case, an astounded academic noted the complete absence of any mention of the word "Buddha." The manner in which Hsing Yun spelled out ways to purify the mind so helped his audiences they were ready to regard him as a living Buddha.

Adapting to Conditions

Hsing Yun skillfully adapts the contents of his lectures to meet the needs of his audience. Once, at the invitation of a dance troupe, he brimmed over with stories about devas dancing about, scattering flowers, flying thorough the heavens, and making offerings to the Buddhas. Then he focused on Buddhist chanting and songs of praise. To the spellbound musicians and dancers, he presented song and dance as another vehicle of the Dharma.

In another instance, Hsing Yun spoke on "Buddhism and Chinese Literature." He took an assembly of literati through an entire course in the translation of Buddhist texts: how Buddhism came to China, how Buddhist textual translation enhanced the Chinese literary vocabulary, how many literary works came to have the imprint of Buddhist thought. His audience came to realize that the Master had trodden down the same path that they were treading on.

He even discussed "Religion and Strategy" with Director-in-chief of the Warfare Strategy Association of the R.O.C., General Chiang Wei-kuo. Citing personal experience in the understanding of the Dharma and the living of life, he spoke in depth about various methods of practice. His listeners were truly captivated by his words.

With scientists, he debates the scientific viewpoint of Buddhism; with economists, how material value is explained from a Buddhist conception; with engineers, monasterial architecture. His methods of teaching and inspiring are such that people from all walks of life are led to the Dharma. Like Master Taixu's blackboard, which was once feared as a form of wizardry, Hsing Yun's innovations and reforms have been called deviant, even monstrous.

Unfazed, he says: "Modernization is a form of exploration. It entails betterment, anticipation, adaptability, and promotion. As nations, societies, and religions evolve, they must seek progress. That quest for progress and the will to be in agreement with Buddhist doctrine, combined with the right teaching skills, will result in timely and versatile representations of the Dharma, and ultimately facilitate an understanding of Buddhist teaching. In fact, since the days of Sakyamuni Buddha, this is what Buddhist preaching has always sought. During the Buddha's lifetime, the Dharma was passed on through speech. Then there were pattra[45] sutras, engraved sutras, and printed sutras after his entry into parinirvana. Now there is the computerized Tripitaka!"

The new generation of Buddhists is totally at home with markers and whiteboards, slides and projectors, and huge cinematic screens. Few have any qualms about the Buddhas enshrined in the halls of government, or the sounding of drums and bells in the city or the countryside. Hsing Yun's innovation and foresight have helped make possible the modernization of Buddhism and the spread of Buddhist teachings to every corner of the world.

Part Three

NURTURING AND CULTIVATING THE SEED OF BUDDHISM

With Venerables Tzu Hui and Hsin Ping (left) at the construction site of Fo Guang Shan, after overgrowths of bamboo were cleared.

Groundbreaking ceremony of Dongfang Buddhist College, 1967.

Hsiao Ting-shun looks back to the old days, when Fo Guang Shan was still a wasteland waiting to be developed, 1968.

Though not born a surveyor, the Master was involved in every aspect of Fo Guang Shan's construction.

Meeting with the Sangharaja of Thailand, (May 1, 1989).

With Chiang Ching-kuo, head of R.O.C.'s executive council at
Fo Guang Shan, 1972.

Hsing Yun listens intently as Taiwan's Internal Affairs Minister, Hsu Ching-chung gives a speech at the opening of Fo Guang Shan's Great Compassion Hall.

With Chen Lian, head of Fo Guang Shan's Supervisory Council.

Presenting his calligraphy "Answering the World Without Fear" to Taiwan's newly-elected President Chen Shui-bian during his visit to Fo Guang Shan Taipei Vihara, 2000.

President Chen: "If we abide by Master Hsing Yun's concept of 'Where there is Dharma, there is a way,' we will succeed in anything we do."

Receiving an honorary doctorate degree from the University of Oriental Studies, U.S.A., 1978.

With friends in the media industry (from left to right), publisher Gao Xijun, editor Wang Lixing, and media executive Wu Shi-song.

Presiding over the Triple Gem Refuge and Five Precepts Ceremony for all ethnic groups at Hsi Lai Temple.

Fo Guang Shan
Fo Guang Yuan
Cultural Exhibi-
tion Hall, 2001.

Always happy to see young ones taking part in Buddhist activities,
Sangha Day.

The Master handing out envelopes of money to the poor in
Bodhgaya, India.

His Majesty King Bhumibol Adulyadej (right) of Thailand receives the Buddhist Visiting Party inside the Royal Palace. Right to left: Ven. Pai Sheng, Ven. Hsien Tun, Venerable Master, Ven. Ching Hsin and others, (June 28, 1963).

Nobel Prize Selection Committee Member Dr. Savders calls on Venerable Master at Fo Guang Shan, March 11, 1981.

Meeting with Li Xian-nian, Chairman of Chinese People's Political Consultative Conference (CPPCC), (March 29, 1989).

Meeting with Ven. Dr. K. Sri Dhammananda at Mines Wonderland International Conference Center, Malaysia, (December 29, 2001).

Chapter 7

Heading South

A good walker must walk further; a good swimmer must find a larger ocean to swim in. Though Ilan was lovely and cherished, Hsing Yun realized the need for a great and resourceful expansion. He chose an unlikely tract of hilly and scrub-covered land on the outskirts of Kaohsiung.

According to Buddhist doctrine, all things arise from causes and conditions. Hsing Yun began by exploring one aspect of Kaohsiung's potential and ended up with a multifaceted endeavor dependent upon conditions of all forms. The most important cause was the determined and courageous Hsing Yun himself.

His relationship with Kaohsiung took root when he was excused from his commitments at Leiyin Temple to make frequent excursions to Kaohsiung to teach the Dharma. He was twenty-six at the time. He soon received the avid support of devotees who entreated him to build a temple. A place of worship and a cultural service center were constructed, followed by Shoushan Temple in the heart of Shoushan Park. He then found himself commuting regularly between the north and south, Ilan and Kaohsiung.

Monastics Are Instructed

Hsing Yun knew temples and monasteries alone could not revive Buddhism, purify minds, or transform societal tendencies.

But a Buddhist education could. "It must always be a priority to nurture new leaders in Buddhism, for then can they preach the Dharma into the future," he thought.

The class of 1964 was the first to attend Shoushan Buddhist College inside the temple. From the small group of twenty or so, annual admissions quickly mounted until the temple became overcrowded. To Venerable Tzu Chia, a graduate and director of Fo Guang Shan's Cultural Department, it seems like yesterday that she and her peers studied in the evenings within the confines of the hall of relics, and it is almost unbelievable how wonderfully the college has grown. Meanwhile, in making plans for a modern institution of multiple functions—educational, cultural, and religious—Hsing Yun followed the monasterial pattern in which he matured, and positioned the college for the anticipated boost in enrollment.

Many people rallied in support of his aspirations. Chengqing Lake, where the Grand Hotel now stands, was the choice site. Purchase of the property was made possible by the sale of the building that housed the Buddhist Cultural Service Center.

Maybe the causes and conditions for Fo Guang Shan had long been determined, or perhaps it had something to do with Venerable Master Hsing Yun's unique perspective and personality. Regardless of the reason, as the contract to buy the land was readied for signing, a disciple's words changed everything. The history of Fo Guang Shan would tell a different story if not for Venerable Yi Yen's observation: "The lake is a tourist hot spot. Our temple will surely follow in that trend. People are going to stream in, sightseeing while paying homage to the Buddha. President Chiang Kai-shek might even be an occasional guest."

That statement bothered Hsing Yun. He did not want the temple to become an addition to the lake. He hoped visitors from near and far would come with joined palms and hearts full of devotion to the Buddha. He dropped the plan. The decision was not nearly as appreciated then as it is now. Through the years, Fo Guang Shan has attracted thousands of people from Taiwan and abroad who have come and paid homage. Some people have even developed scenic spots in the vicinity. The president did not come, but one of his sons came three times and at least once while he was president himself.

While Hsing Yun pondered the next move, a debt-laden Chinese couple from Vietnam appealed to Hsing Yun, informing him that their vast, hilly property in Mazhu Yuan (Bamboo Grove), Tashu Hsiang, Kaohsiung, was up for sale. They pleaded for his help without which, they said, suicide would be their only recourse.

Hsing Yun was deeply moved by their plight. And in considering the terrain, he reflected on how the most extolled Buddhist monasteries in China are deep in the mountains. As the saying goes, "of all the celebrated mountains under heaven, most have caretakers that are monastics." Mountains like Ermei, Wutai, Putuo, and Jiuhua[46] are all in China. It was time to pick up the torch and erect another monastery, this time in the mountains of Taiwan.

Advancing as Others Retreat

Hsing Yun was firm. He wanted to see the land firsthand. More than thirty years have since passed, but he can still recall what he did the day he first visited the site of Fo Guang Shan. A hired bus took Hsing Yun and a few devotees for an hour's journey along a rugged road. Upon arrival, they found a treacherous thicket-covered land stretching as far as the eye could see. They were stunned; no one would leave the bus except Hsing Yun.

"Forget it Master! Who'll bother coming up here to pray? Except you, that is," mumbled the group.

"All right, all right," he replied, losing none of his enthusiasm. "I guess I'll go myself."

He took his cane and vanished into the thorny grove.

Some were awestruck by his determination; others clearly thought the whole episode was a waste of time.

An hour elapsed. Finally, he emerged–weeds and red dirt on his collar, and a broad grin on his face.

"My apologies! I've made you wait too long!" he said as he wiped the sweat off his forehead.

He still teases some of the older devotees who went along that day, "You said that no one would care to climb this mountain. Haven't you been doing exactly that all these years?"

When asked about his intentions, he answers that the raw, untamed mountain offered opportunity. The monasteries that existed in Taipei at the time were run by monastics many years his senior. Hsing Yun, then in his thirties, had virtually nowhere to go to be on his own. Furthermore, the location allowed more liberty from the distractions of politics and socializing, which might keep him from his true task of education and spreading the Dharma. There was no strife up on the mountain. It would be perfect for starting from scratch.

The Pioneering Days

Those were pioneering days. Only a few devotees supported his decision. Hsiao Ting-shun, a follower who joined Hsing Yun at Shoushan Temple and one of the key figures in the construction of Fo Guang Shan, says that no other experience in his lifetime has meant as much to him. Hsiao used to ride a motorcycle up the untraveled path with the Master clinging to his back, traverse three hills, and go on foot for another two hours before making it to the construction site (where the Buddhist college now sits).

"There was little we could do but stick to the geographical contours," recounts the shy former carpenter. I would snatch a piece of bamboo and sketch in the dirt. The two of us would think hard, and plan out where to dig and where to build.

"We would be drenched with sweat one moment and dry the next. Discussion went on nonstop. We often didn't sleep until the wee hours of the morning and would rise to work again at the break of day.

"The land was far from flat. I've lost count of the thousands of truckloads of dirt that it took to level it.

"Resources were limited. When it ran out, work would come to a halt. Truthfully, all we wanted was a small place. We would have been satisfied with a few parking spots before the mountain gate. That was good enough to start."

Decades of southern sunshine have tanned Hsiao and seem to have energized him. With the completion of his latest project, the Triple Gem Shrine, the rapport shared between Hsiao and the Master has become especially close. Hsiao, who is unassuming and short on words but delivers when it counts, sums up his experience in this way: "We didn't make a lot of money working with Fo Guang Shan, but I have received a lot of joy. Each time somebody speaks well of Fo Guang Shan, I feel that this life of mine has been very worthwhile."

Consider the Ways of the Ant

Abbot and Director-in-Chief of the Religious Affairs Committee,[47] Venerable Hsin Ping, was the first among the monks to join in the construction. He was stationed in a shack in the bamboo grove with no electricity. To fetch water, he had to descend the mountain to a brook half an hour away. At night, he had to patrol the grounds in pitch-darkness. The hills were so steep the bulldozer could not climb them by itself, so the students in the second and third classes at the Buddhist College had to literally push it along. The hourly rate for the machine was exorbitant considering living costs at the time and Fo Guang Shan's financial circumstances, so Venerable Hsin Ping's most pressing charge was to ensure that the machine was put to full use. "Not a single dollar from the devotees shall go to waste," he used to say.

Venerable Tzu Jung had come to Kaohsiung from Ilan with the Master. She was there throughout the construction process as well. She tells of the time, "The roof of Dragon Pavilion on East Hill was being laid when midway through the process, the worker mixing the cement left for the day. We didn't want the pouring suspended for fear that the roof might crack and leak in the future. The Master led a group of us, and we picked up where the man left off. We worked into the night with only the headlights of two motorcycles lighting the way. Venerable Yi Yen was up on the steep roof to smooth out the cement that kept sliding down. She exerted herself so much in pushing the cement back up again that her hands started to bleed."

The most frenzied time was when a typhoon caused a tremendous downpour, which washed away the upper dam of the Guanyin Release Pool.[48] Hsing Yun plunged into the clay-red rapids, and the others followed. First rocks, then their own bed quilts were passed along to block the opening and blanket the earth. They struggled together until the storm mercifully gave out, and light appeared from behind the clouds.

Hsing Yun looks out from the balcony of the Founder's Quarter and remembers, "We were like ants moving Taishan.[49]"

From Non-being, Being Springs

Chronologically, the first phase of construction of the Fo Guang Shan complex included Dongfang (Eastern) Buddhist College, Great Compassion Hall, Guanyin Release Pool, Dragon Pavilion, and the image of Maitreya Buddha.

The second phase saw the completion of Great Compassion

Nursery, Pilgrim's Lodge, the Great Welcoming Buddha, Fo Guang Vihara, and Dajue Monks Residence (a living quarter for monks).

During the third phase, the Main Shrine, Pure Land Cave, Pumen High School, Longevity Park (a cemetery), and an exhibition hall were finished.

In the fourth phase, Bamboo Grove (a guest house), Ksitigarbha Hall, Samantabhadra Hall, Daci Nunnery (living quarter for nuns), and a service center for devotees were built.

The latest additions include the Devotees' Center, the Hall of the Gold Buddhas, the Hall of the Jade Buddhas, and Tathagata Hall.

The Great Welcoming Buddha, standing a lofty 105 feet, beckons to those on their way to Fo Guang Shan. It is the sixth largest image of the Buddha in the world.

Literally with his bare hands, Hsing Yun has created a Buddhist sacred site of world renown. Truly, from non-being, being springs.

Seen from any viewpoint, there is a precision and harmony about every element of Fo Guang Shan: the grandeur of the architecture and openness of the temples, the moving artistry of the Buddha images and layout of the courtyards and gardens, even the decorative touches of the halls and chambers. It all reminds one of the saying, "One flower, one world; one leaf, one Buddha."[50]

With his ideas sketched on paper, Hsing Yun met with Hsiao Ting-shun who in turn transferred the plan onto the dirt with his bamboo stick. It was in this way that Hsing Yun irrigated a wilderness and raised a sacred dwelling place. In the building of Fo Guang Shan, architectural expertise and construction committees were never a factor. Just how did he do it? "I'm certainly unlearned in architecture," he says. "From the Mainland to Taiwan to the rest of the world, I've walked many miles and seen many structures. In each and every case I observe and I contemplate. I ask myself if I would have executed a design for a property differently if I were in the architect's shoes. By the time conditions are ripe for a temple or a school, construction plans have long been in place. That practically eliminates the prospect of complications." The answer to his success is simple: "One must pay attention."

Many-Splendored Land

The exterior design of Fo Guang Shan is modeled after classical Chinese palace architecture with numerous Buddhist motifs added. Its interior provides for the technological sophistication needed in a variety of functions. The complex has a state-of-the-art multimedia audio-visual center, a conference hall with simultaneous interpretation equipment at every seat, a lecture hall with a capacity of 2,200, and a first-rate internal and external communications network. Fo Guang Shan is the first computer-managed monastery.

Devotees and visitors alike, may savor a relaxing cup of Fo Guang tea, take pleasure in a restful moment in the shady pavilion, enjoy the amenities of the guest house, drop by the service center for a tour, or consult the monastics on various issues.

Traditionally, monasteries have been the picture of gloom and doom. The bright and airy Fo Guang Shan has turned that all around. It is the expression of its leader's disposition and personality traits, and an embodiment of his concepts and reasoning. Critics have called Fo Guang Shan wealth-oriented. There are certainly business people who would like to know its secret to success. It simply lies in thirty years of earnest devotees and visitors who gather every weekend to partake in and contribute to the Dharma. They come from all ten directions.

Fifty Lasting Firsts

The achievement of nurturing over a million devotees and

over a hundred branch temples aside, Fo Guang Shan has fifty lasting firsts in Buddhism.

These first-time achievements include: the first Buddhist choir, Dharma radio programs, music recordings, television appearances, Dharma lectures in the halls of government, monthly reprinting of sutras, public discussion sessions, children's classes, Sunday school, a ten-thousand-Buddha hall, preschool education workshops, the offering of bright lanterns,[51] slide shows used for propagating the Dharma, Buddhist wedding ceremonies, the Indian Cultural Research Institute, college-level summer camps, a Buddhist city college, a mobile clinic, a public library, a home for the terminally ill and lodging for their families, hardbound Buddhist books, devotee uniforms, monastic hierarchy, cross-country teaching, religious souvenirs, a student body, devotee study programs, Sangha Day, a temple housed in a high-rise, alms-round Dharma functions, Dharma transmission ceremonies,[52] short-term monastic retreats, teaching to the militia, a devotee service center, thanksgiving Dharma functions, and annual meetings for devotees. Also within the list of firsts are: International Buddhist examinations,[53] triple practice sessions in the Chan, Pure Land, and Tantric Schools, "Return to the Epoch of the Buddha"[54] functions, a museum and exhibition hall, home visits and service, an art gallery, the *Fo Guang Tripitaka*, the *Fo Guang Encyclopedia*, teaching on the outer islands of Taiwan, a world organization (Buddha's Light International Association), and a 200-member pilgrimage to India.

With these fifty-firsts in Buddhism, the media and his devotees credit the Master's wise leadership. They all say, "Had there been no Master Hsing Yun, there would be no Fo Guang Shan." However, the Master himself believes that Fo Guang Shan has become what it is today because of "the glory from the Buddhas' blessings and the achievements of the public. The benefits should

belong to the monastery and merits should belong to the devotees."

Rather than bask in the ready-made success offered by the
beautiful reflections of Lake Chengqing, Hsing Yun picked an
unlikely spot in Kaohsiung County that now enjoys the beautiful
rays of Buddha's light. Not surprisingly, real estate values in the
vicinity have soared; public utilities have been updated; highways
have been added; employment has multiplied; and schools have
been built. Neighborhood and village get-togethers and festivals
are now a regular attraction. Each year opens to an endless string
of community activities, which take advantage of the amenities of
Fo Guang Shan. To Kaohsiung, it is not only a religious landmark—it is also a basic promoter of community spirit and a dynamic cultural institution.

The view of Fo Guang Shan is awe-inspiring: the five peaks
undulating like the petals of an orchid, the tidal sea of lush green
woods, the statue of the heaven-touching Buddha, the parade of
halls, the overpowering heights of its structures, and the juxtapos-
ing eaves. It is a place of beauty, which presents twentieth-centu-
ry Buddhism not only as a religion but also as a culture, an educational opportunity, and a charitable endeavor.

Chapter 8

Epoch of
Buddha's Light

*L*ooking toward the Great Welcoming Buddha at Fo Guang Shan, one sees the picturesque backdrop of the shimmering Kaohsiung-Pingtung Brook. Since its inception in 1967, Fo Guang Shan has come a long way to become southern Taiwan's most unique landmark and one of Asia's most sacred Buddhist sites. Yet, based on the Buddhist concept of formation, abiding, destruction, and emptiness,[55] Fo Guang Shan must not be measured by the splendor of its external form alone. Fo Guang Shan's reason for being lies in the principle and practice of Humanistic Buddhism.

Coming out of the Mountain Gate

Spreading Humanistic Buddhism is the primary object of Hsing Yun's life work. From Master Taixu, he learned that monastics must come out of the mountain gate into society. Fo Guang Shan became a testing ground for this principle.

He defines this theme in one of his lectures:

To isolate the Dharma from daily life is the worst failing of Buddhism today. The most seasoned believer cannot seem to get rid of greed, anger, and ignorance,[56] and the most learned in the doctrine are still bothered by gossip about ideas of right and wrong.

Once Buddhism breaks away from real life, the Dharma

stops serving our needs and ceases to be our guide; once it fails to enrich the content of our lives, its existence becomes meaningless. The Buddha's teachings are for the improvement of life, the purification of mind, and the uplifting of character. It is a Buddhism which is pertinent to life and living that I want to spread.

Living Buddhism depends on how well our everyday life corresponds with the Buddha's teaching, whether we are sleeping, talking, walking, or doing anything else. The Buddha spoke about the resolve of the mind. To apply that teaching, we must resolve our minds about the way in which we conduct our daily lives, the way in which we give, and, overall, the way we practice Buddhism. Sleep done with intent becomes more restful; food eaten with attention becomes especially tasty; a road walked with resolve becomes smooth before our very eyes; a problem tackled with determination turns into a delightful challenge.

The resolve of the mind is an aspect of Dharma teaching useful in harmonizing all levels of human relations. It is not simply philosophical rhetoric. The Dharma is to be exercised and fulfilled as thoroughly as possible. There is no way that life and the Dharma can part company.

The Guiding Principles of Buddha's Light Members

"Give others confidence; give others joy; give others service; give others hope"—those of Fo Guang Shan live their faith by this guiding principle. What many businesspeople hold as a maxim, "plan for the future" and "develop consensus," Hsing Yun has long put into practice. He has spoken on what it means to be a Buddha's Light member while explaining these concepts many times.

Above all, a Buddha's Light member is fully engaged in

daily matters. Dismissed as passive and out-of-date, Buddhism has been on the decline for many decades. In looking for liberation from existence, it has habitually overlooked issues arising from life. How can Buddhism be accepted by society if it departs from the realities of family life, the workplace, and local and national concerns? The Buddha's Light member seeks to master living within the mundane world while spiritually transcending it.

Secondly, a Buddha's Light member assists first the living and then the dead. One of the greatest misconceptions about Buddhism is that it is primarily a religion that chants for and delivers the dead. Although they do not oppose Buddhist services for the purpose of gathering merits for the deceased, Buddha's Light members believe the living, much more than the dead, need Buddhism, and will therefore carry it from the temple into homes and communities.

The Buddha's Light member first tackles life before he tackles death and rebirth. While it is true that the ultimate goal of Buddhist practice is liberation from death and rebirth, to merely yearn for a good, clean life of spiritual practice tucked in the mountains safely away from the distractions of modernity is unrealistic. Virtuous and eminent masters of the past all began with the resolve to serve all sentient beings. Some promised to shoulder people's burdens like an ox throughout many lifetimes; others vowed to serve and suffer through endless years. Chan Master Baizhang Huaihai [720-814 C.E.][57] initiated a rule of productivity at his monastery—no work, no food. Today, a similar rule may guide one's life—prepare appropriately and live well. Then one may talk of extinguishing the cycle of rebirth.

Finally, a Buddha's Light member is like a humble pine that withstands the tests of time for a thousand years or like a plum tree that gracefully bears the weight of winter's snow and ice. Only the patient shall know success; only the humble shall truly be great.

Culture Is the Vehicle of the Dharma

Fo Guang Shan is built upon four essentials: "Spreading the Dharma through culture, nurturing talent through education, benefiting society through charity, and purifying minds through cultivation." Fo Guang Shan is no longer just a reputable temple in Tashu, Kaohsiung. It represents thirty years of unstinting effort by a thousand-member sangha and a million-devotee populace around the world.

Alms-round donations commemorating its twentieth anniversary have funded the Fo Guang Foundation for Buddhist Culture and Education in underwriting national and international Buddhist scholarly conferences. It has also financed the publication of the Buddhist journals *Benevolent Teachers, Blessing*, and the weekly *Buddhist News*, as well as gifts of books to libraries, schools, and prisons. A decade was spent researching, annotating, and indexing the *Fo Guang Tripitaka*. In 1989, the *Fo Guang Encyclopedia* was awarded the publishing industry's Golden Cauldron Award in Taiwan. The *Buddhist Historical Chronology* was named the most distinguished textual reference volume. The three monumental works of the Tripitaka Editorial Committee are collectively heralded as the "triple gems" of Buddhist scholarly research.

Awakening the World is a free publication provided to a readership of 100,000 in 42 regions and nations. Published three times monthly since 1957, the publication continues to function as a bridge of information for Buddhists worldwide. *Universal Gate*, which offers a mixture of popular articles and literary pieces, has a global circulation of approximately 30,000. Launched in 1979, this polished Buddhist magazine is the only advertising-based product with financial self-sufficiency, using computerized management and distribution networks.

Hsing Yun is an accomplished and dedicated author, editor, and speaker who has ensured that his disciples, like himself, are properly groomed for literary endeavors. Venerables Tzu Hui, Tzu Chia, Yi Kung, Yi Yu, Yi Sheng, Yi Chun, Yung Chuang, Yung Yun, and Man Kuo represent three generations of published writers. Sales of Hsing Yun's four-volume lectures have never slumped, nor have the sales of his other titles: *Biography of Sakyamuni Buddha, National Master Yu Lin, Hsing Yun's Chan Talk, Hsing Yun's Dharma Words,* and *Cloud and Water: An Interpretation of Chan Poems,* among others.

Fo Guang Cultural Enterprise Co., Ltd. has, during four decades, put out hundreds of serial titles, encompassing sutras and discourses, scholarly journals, literary anthologies, biographies, and doctrinal commentaries. The latest ventures are children's books, comics, cassettes, and videos–all attempts at giving orthodox Buddhism a contemporary appeal. The publishing house, together with *Fo Guang Scholarly Journal* and Fo Guang bookstores, form a diversified vehicle for teaching the Dharma.

Together with the Buddhist exhibition hall, art gallery, and exhibits of Dunhuang[58] paintings and Buddhist art, these vehicles demonstrate Fo Guang Shan's awareness of cultural importance and the many ways in which Buddhist faith can be expressed.

Education Is the Nursery of Talent

From Shoushan Buddhist College, established in 1964, to the current three-tiered sangha education program (see also Chapter 9), applications for admission have continually been on the rise, as are the credentials of the candidates—about a third of whom have a university education. Many candidates, with years of professional work experience, return to school with aspirations to learn the Dharma.

Ilan's Tzuai Kindergarten was the first Buddhist kindergarten in Taiwan, with graduates totaling over 30,000. Three more schools have followed: Tainan's Tzuhang Vehicle, Shanhua's Tzu-hui and Compassion, and Fo Guang Shan's Pumen. Zhiguang is a secondary-level business school. Last but certainly not least, Pumen High School, located at Fo Guang Shan, has gone from an enrollment of 91 students in 1977 to 1,600 today, and has emerged as one of the most outstanding private institutions in Taiwan. Hsi Lai University in Los Angeles, California, is a small institution of higher learning with a brilliant faculty and an international student population. It is also positioned to become a future hub in international Buddhist academic exchanges. To top off Hsing Yun's passionate dedication to education, the new Fo Guang University is scheduled to accept applications to its graduate school in 1995.

The establishment of a Buddhist city college at Puxian Temple, Kaohsiung, in 1983, sparked similar projects in continuing education at other branch temples. The city college offers three-month courses in Buddhist studies to suit the needs of working people, allowing them to take classes after work. This format remains both in-depth and broad-based and takes the Dharma further into society.

A variety of specialty classes also have been arranged in response to increasing social diversity and devotees' requests. There are courses in vegetarian cooking, calligraphy, and tai chi, as well as opportunities to participate in choirs and orchestras.

Charity Is the Vehicle of Benefit

Few are familiar with the history of Fo Guang Shan's charitable activities, which though long-standing and encompassing, are not publicized out of respect for the recipients.

The Compassion Foundation, working to "benefit society through charity," conducts philanthropic and social welfare activities that stretch over the span of a human life. They include the Great Compassion Nursery for orphans, Fo Guang Retirement Home, Ilan Graciousness Home for the Needy, Fo Guang Walk-In

Clinic, mobile clinics, foundation fund for the sangha, home visits and services, regular functions to release live creatures, winter collection drives of food and clothing for the poor, and disaster relief. Fo Guang Shan has also allotted 2,000 cemetery niches to house the cremated remains of those selected by Kaohsiung's County Social Welfare Department at no cost to the families of the deceased.

One recipient of these compassionate efforts was Wang Xiaomin, who, thirty years ago, was hospitalized in a vegetative state following a traffic accident. When her treatment exhausted family resources, Fo Guang Shan took her mother and sister under its care.

Ilan Graciousness Home provides an example of the tenacity required when undertaking charitable ventures. It was formerly a Christian-owned charity that was experiencing financial strain. Hsing Yun took over the operation together with the fate of its occupants. The newly graduated Venerable Shao Chueh and Venerable Yi Jung volunteered their services and thereby consummated the bodhisattva way by devoting half of their lives to washing, feeding, nursing, and, eventually, laying to rest those frail and lonely folks. Both of them have received awards from the government of Taiwan, R.O.C. for their exemplary deeds.

Fo Guang Shan has also contributed to natural disaster relief funds around the world, be it in response to flooding by the Yangtze River in Mainland China or catastrophic typhoons across Taiwan. Fo Guang Shan has undertaken fundraising and relief efforts of enormous proportions.

Behind its low profile in charity is a profound consideration for the dignity of its recipients. The hundred-or-so children in Great Compassion Nursery are as sheltered as much as they are cared for in life. Hsing Yun calls them his princes and princesses, and insists they be fed and clothed like any other children and cherished like gems by those who attend to them. He wants them to feel respected and that they belong with him. To those who came without a surname, he gives his own secular name, Li. The nursery is off-limits to tourists. The children are raised out of the spotlight, with the intention that they not be hurt a second time. Amidst the sense of peace and security that prevails in the impeccable classrooms and dormitory, Director Hsiao Pi-Liang's tone is soft yet firm: "This is a home, so we don't showcase it. Since the kids call me Mom, for that alone I must give them a safe, cozy environment."

Some rough statistics indicate that over 30,000 low-income patients visit Fo Guang Shan's clinic annually. The mobile clinic's twenty-three ambulances travel through twenty-eight cities, more than fifty towns, and over one hundred villages to serve the sick in outlying areas. Six affiliated temporary lodgings in Longevity Park provide a kind of consolation for the families of the terminally ill. Burials, provisions, and medical relief are commonly provided.

Cultivation—The Means to Purify Minds

Thoughtfully organized Dharma functions, community cultivation, practice, chanting, and Chan meditation together form the well-rounded religious organization into which Fo Guang Shan has evolved. Devotees from around the globe attend repentance services, solitary retreats,[59] sangha-layperson joint practice, the Eight Precepts Retreat,[60] the Seven-day Amitabha Retreat,[61] pilgrimages to the founding temple,[62] pilgrimages to India, branch temple tours, and annual meetings for devotees. Led in the direction of the Buddha gate by causes and conditions of their own, those who aspire to let their good roots flourish discover a dwelling for their minds and a center for their faith.

Fo Guang Shan ranks high in devotee popularity, positive

social impact, and national reputation. When a monastic is casually asked by a Taiwanese citizen, "Are you from Fo Guang Shan?" it is because Buddhism, monasticism, and Fo Guang Shan are synonymous to most. The leader of this Buddhist order, which is growing in international importance, is Master Hsing Yun.

Prayer Beads Worn around the Pulse of Time
There are those who look at the eight schools in the history of Chinese Buddhism, and point out that Fo Guang Shan has the potential to become a new school—the Buddha's Light School. However, Hsing Yun has no intention or desire to be put on a pedestal as the founder of yet another school. He takes comfort in his endeavors over the past thirty years because Fo Guang Shan has already established such notable achievements. It is:

1. a contemporary religious body and system that promotes
   a. gender equality in career advancement
   b. harmony between monastics and laypeople
   c. solidarity in the foundation of religious undertakings
   d. notable cultural and educational achievements
2. an international Buddhist body and network, which includes
   a. the Buddha's Light International Association
   b. global branch temples
   c. international conferences
   d. nonsectarian communication and exchange
3. a society founded on Humanistic Buddhism, which is characterized by
   a. Dharma teaching for daily living
   b. the practice of Buddhism within the family
   c. its social application
   d. a variety of activities
4. a bridge between Mainland China and Taiwan, which en-

compasses
a. a joint Buddhist Association as the foundation
b. culture and education as the primary objectives
c. cultural undertakings
d. educational endeavors

It began from nothingness; it will end in endlessness. Hsing Yun's prayer beads are worn around the pulse of time. As he strides the path of worldly affairs, with his transcendent spirit, so too strides Fo Guang Shan. The far-reaching footprints of Fo Guang Shan will certainly show evidence of an important influence within the development of Buddhism in China.

Chapter 9

An Outstanding
Disciple of Buddhism

Ascend the realm of purity
To seek the Truth.
Enter the mountain of treasure
To learn the Dharma.

*W*hat propels Fo Guang Shan is the energy of those Hsing Yun took four decades to nurture.

His conviction that the future of Buddhism depends upon the cultivation of the young—to whom he will be handing down the light someday—stems from the integrity of his orthodox Buddhist background. Early in his teaching career in Taiwan, he came face to face with the low standard of education in the sangha. Memories of the semi-illiterate chanting by rote still haunt him. Forty years ago, if a high school graduate decided to become a monastic, the general public would greet him with astonishment, saying "Unbelievable! There is an educated person entering the Buddhist gate." Many monastics sought earnings from services conducted for the dead and rarely lifted a text or sutra to glance at, much less read. All were regarded as "withered buds and rotten seeds." Properly educated monastics were a rare breed.

Revival Begins with the Right People

As the revival of a nation begins with the right people, the rejuvenation of Buddhism, Hsing Yun knew, would have to start from the beginning with the creation of a pool of talent. In fact, when some of the young followers in Ilan had requested to be tonsured, he declined because he had no school for them. Not until the Buddhist College at Shoushan, Kaohsiung was built, were the young people able to stay. Many were then tonsured.

The class of 1968 from Dongfang Buddhist College (formerly Shoushan Buddhist College) was to Hsing Yun an unprecedented yield from years of labor in Buddhist education. This graduation in particular symbolized the crossing of Buddhism over the Taiwan Strait. This group of locals would take leading roles in the future development of Buddhism.

Hsing Yun saw in Dongfang Buddhist College a fertile ground in which to nurture the new buds of Buddhism. A blend of traditional spirit and modern information and methodologies was a concept that became the backbone of Fo Guang Shan's educational body. It was also later referred to and adopted by other Buddhist colleges.

Dongfang Buddhist College was a three-year program. Members of its prominent faculty included Fang Lun, who was a specialist in the *Buddhist Tripitaka*, Tang Yixuan, Venerable Huixing, and Venerable Zhuyun, among others. The array of courses offered included introduction to natural sciences, introduction to social sciences, introduction to philosophy, Chinese history, Western history, Chinese literature, Western philosophy, basic Chinese culture, foreign languages, administrative affairs, writing, and sutra-chanting.

The first group of graduates—twenty in all—are now heading monasteries, assuming teaching positions in various Buddhist colleges, lecturing on the Dharma, or researching Buddhist classics. The second and third classes totaled approximately seventy graduates. By then, Hsing Yun was concerned about the lack of usable space and began to look elsewhere. That, indeed, was the underlying cause for Fo Guang Shan.

Young Intellectuals Are Received and Guided

There is a saying that it is, "Better to lead an army garrison than a sangha." Venerable Master Cihang also once said, "If you don't like someone, just convince him to run a school." Such is the formidable task of Buddhist education.

Hsing Yun worked feverishly to provide for everyone who attended the Buddhist College—free tuition and books, room and board, clothing and other necessities. "You and your students are going to starve," some observers kindly warned him. "When you have nothing left, you'll end up losing your devotees altogether." Hsing Yun believed in what he was doing and pressed on. The first structure to be erected on the once thicketed land was the Buddhist College, west of Baoqiao (Treasure Bridge). With this structure, the building of Fo Guang Shan began.

To keep the institution going, Hsing Yun who had never favored specializing in services for the dead, would do so, sometimes through the night, to raise funds. At one point, the young woman in charge of academic affairs resolved to take tonsure and joined him in those chanting sessions. That was Venerable Tzu Chuang. The teacher, who managed student affairs and worked part-time in a bakery to acquire extra sponsorships, was Venerable Tzu Hui. The kindergarten teaching staff, Venerable Tzu Jung, Wu Pao-chin, Yang Tzu-man, among others gave up their salaries. Devotee Hsiao Pi-hsia sold her properties to finance the Foundation for Buddhist Culture and Education. Venerable Tzu Jung would later direct the charities of Fo Guang Shan and spearhead Buddha's Light International Association; Venerable Tzu Chuang would establish Hsi Lai Temple; and Venerable Tzu Hui would found two universities, Hsi Lai and Fo Guang.

The college-level Buddhist summer camp of 1969 was designed to bring young intellectuals out of the ivory tower of academia and down to earth to tackle life's issues. The proper seeds were being sown to ensure the vibrant growth in Buddhist academia years down the line. The top students included Fo Guang Shan's own Venerable Yi Kung, and Yi Fa, together with the gallant Venerable Zhaohui—now all pillars of the Buddhist community. The summer camp was the springboard that fostered a challenging environment where young minds responded to the call for a life of commitment and service.

Strength of Mind for the Effort of Education

Hsing Yun invested most greatly in cultivating the talents of the young, both in financial terms and, especially, in strength of mind. The odds against him were unimaginable. Just prior to launching the second college-level Buddhist summer camp for six hundred participants, the water tower broke down. Anxiously, Hsing Yun supervised the emergency repairs during the day and stood guard, ear against the tower wall all night, until the rumblings of the motor and moving water began at three in the morning.

He later confided to disciples that he had vowed that in the event the motor did not start up, his blood would be transformed into pure water to be consumed by the young students.

In the fundraising for the Research Department of the Chinese Buddhist Research Institute, Hsing Yun and his students rolled up their sleeves and put on their aprons to cook for devotees, hoping they would be pleased with the rice and noodles and would be generous in their support. His determination and sincerity struck a chord with those who had lent a hand.

Venerable Tzu Chuang remembers an extraordinary experience that seemed to suggest the manifestation of the bodhisattva.

It was the eve of another summer camp and funds were drained, with the delivery of provisions still up in the air. Just as she was beginning to wring her hands in concern, she saw an elderly figure coming through the arched entrance. It was a peasant woman, straw hat on her head and no shoes on her feet, who requested specifically to see the director. Venerable Tzu Chuang received her and treated her to soup and rice noodles, which she clearly enjoyed. Quite unexpectedly, she produced a paper-wrapped package and said, "Give this to the Venerable Master. You may do whatever you please with it." Then, she turned and was gone. Inside was a neat bunch of notes amounting to NT $50,000 (approximately US $1,868) in the then new currency of Taiwan. The emergency situation was averted, and to this day, no one has the slightest inkling of who she was or where she came from.

The Sangha Takes on a New Look

Hsing Yun contends that Buddhism, instead of being a moldy picture of frailty and boredom is contemporary, progressive, and vibrant. "Buddhism needs the young, but the young need Buddhism even more," he says. The Buddhist College at Fo Guang Shan is now inhabited by youthful, amicable, confident, and disciplined pursuers of the Dharma. Hsing Yun has given Chinese Buddhist monastics a brand-new air. If Shoushan Buddhist College was a delicate, budding plant in Buddhist education, Fo Guang Shan is a luxuriant, fruit-bearing tree.

At the summit of Fo Guang Shan's three-tier structure is the Chinese Buddhist Research Institute, which encompasses three-year research programs in Dharma propagation, sangha education, Buddhist doctrine, management of ceremonial services, and monasterial management. Research fellows with master's degrees and graduate students with bachelor's degrees are required to complete a thesis in Buddhist studies no shorter than sixty thousand words in length. Acceptance of the thesis by the examination panel leads to the conferring of a Ph.D. or a master's degree in Buddhist studies.

Fo Guang Shan Tzunglin University is divided into two branches of study. One branch is a center for global scholarly exchange and it produces a constellation of international teachers of the Dharma. The other branch is a four-year program with departments in sutra and doctrinal studies, management of ceremonial services, social application, and teaching within a cultural context.

Dongfang Buddhist College administers both a men's and women's two-year school. The curriculum is a blend of tradition and modernity, of practice and comprehension of the Dharma. From fundamental Buddhism to higher research, the educational programs form an integrated whole. Due to the demand for international Dharma teachers in recent years, attention has been paid to foreign languages and computer studies.

With eleven departments, twenty-eight classes, a faculty of two hundred, and a student population of approximately eight hundred, this Fo Guang Buddhist education system has made history by renewing the Buddhist academy that flourished centuries ago. From this point on, Hsing Yun will be looking in the direction of Nalanda's[63] record population of thirty thousand students.

Equivalent to the Confucian Sages

To cite statistics from 1994, Fo Guang Shan's sangha has surpassed 1,100 monastics. Of this number, 225 are bhiksus, 937 are bhiksunis, and 30 are of the *shigu* status. Annual increases average a hundred new members of the sangha. The majority are between twenty-one and forty years of age. Of these, approximately seventy percent are college graduates. Also, thirty-five hold master's degrees and three have doctorates. Most are from Taiwan. About ten percent are from France, Hong Kong, Indonesia, Malaysia, Nepal, Singapore, Thailand, Vietnam, the United States, and elsewhere.

The monastics of Fo Guang Shan pride themselves on their record of having many members of the same family tonsured under the same master. Venerable Tzu Chuang, her father Hui Ho, and nephews Hui Lung and Hui Chuan all follow Master Hsing Yun in the monastic life. There are sisters, like Venerable Tzu Jung and Yi Lai, and other siblings, mothers and children, all of whom address one another as Dharma brothers.

Hsing Yun was alone when he landed in Taiwan. Now, the sangha of Fo Guang Shan holds three generations, including himself. After the founder, the succeeding generations of bhiksus are named, in order of tonsure: Hsin (mind), Hui (wisdom), and Cheng (vehicle). The second generations of bhiksunis are named as follows: Tzu (compassion), Yi (reliance), Yung (constancy), Man (completion), Chueh (awakening), and Miao (wondrousness). The third and most recent generation is named Tao (Way). Historian Li Dongfang compares this lineage with the seventy-two Confucian sages.

3,000 Splendid Rules, 80,000 Minute Details

Hsing Yun has created a unique system with a capacity to minimize internal strife. The monastics of Fo Guang Shan, according to the Master's rule, do not take disciples or build temples of their own. All disciples observe the discipline of Fo Guang Shan and no one has a personal following. Venerable Tzu Chuang is the master of tonsure to the third-generation bhiksunis, and Venerable Hsin Ping (and after Hsin Ping's passing, now Venerable Hsin Ting), to the third-generation bhiksus. Hsing Yun is the master to the second-generation monastics, and grand master to the third generation.

Observers think this system, with its protective measures against internal division and even possible corruption, and its family-oriented sense of justice, is a worthwhile reference for similar institutions.

Producer Zhou Zhimin of the television program *Aixin* (Loving Heart) is among those in the media who have become great admirers of Hsing Yun's management methods. She relates an incident that illustrates the strength of the sangha under Hsing Yun.

In late 1979, I was working on an episode entitled "Buddha's Light throughout the Universe"…On the sixth day of the Chinese New Year holidays, holiday revelries were still going strong when I, along with four of my colleagues, went to Fo Guang Shan. What transpired within the first half-hour we were there was absolutely eye-opening. I first showed Venerable Tzu Hui a proposal for our program. After just fifteen minutes, Venerable Tzu Hui presented me with a detailed schedule indicating where to work, with whom, and how. Even a theme was included for our convenience. It was so complete, we couldn't find a flaw even if we had tried. Over the next two days we adhered to the timetable presented to us and the shooting was smooth sailing all the way.

This instance mirrors Hsing Yun's personal style: planning, open discussion, delegation of responsibilities, monitoring of progress, reflection on the process, and projection into the future—a complete and all-encompassing approach in which not a step is skipped or an effort wasted.

Many share the observation that the branch temples of Fo Guang Shan, and its monastics for that matter, engender a different feeling than most Buddhist establishments. The monastics have about them a composure and propriety which are uniquely Fo Guang Shan's. Indeed, every move or gesture they make reflects the "Three thousand splendid rules, eighty thousand minute details." These bhiksus and bhiksunis are not only well versed in the multiple chores and skills of a conventional monastery but are also equipped with the knowledge and capacities needed for writing and theorizing, monasterial management and accounting, social work and teaching, and dealing with computers and other day-to-day technical and mechanical needs. Combining the Dharma as the essence and world knowledge as the tool, is the way to liberate all sentient beings.

Ingenuity Regenerating Itself

Hsing Yun thinks that the talented must be nurtured. Therefore, Tzu Chuang, Tzu Hui, Tzu Jung, Tzu Chia, Tzu Yi, and other monastics were sent to Japan, despite the shortage of funds. Many asked him to think twice: "What a loss of brainpower if they don't return! And if they do, how will you lead the highly-educated?" "Even though it will be difficult financially, it won't be a problem," Hsing Yun replied. "Once they come back, they can do a lot for Buddhism."

As their master anticipated, Venerable Tzu Hui, an education major, took over Fo Guang Shan's educational body in its entirety; Venerables Tzu Chia and Tzu Yi directed the compilation of the *Fo Guang Tripitaka* and the *Fo Guang Encyclopedia*; Venerable Tzu Chuang, who specialized in architecture, masterminded one branch temple after another; and Venerable Tzu Jung, who majored in social work, specialized in organizing, executing, and supervising large-scale events.

Hsing Yun could now rest assured that his torch was passing into the right hands. He was able to step down, and he did. He has since been sailing the four seas sharing the Dharma. In the meantime, Fo Guang Shan continues to thrive.

Over the past ten years, in order to elevate the quality of education for education for disciples, Hsing Yun has vigorously selected disciples for study aboard. Presently in Japan are Tzu Yi, a doctoral candidate, along with Yi Yu, Yi Hsin, and Man Ting, among others. Hui Kai is pursuing his doctorate at Temple University, and as is Yi Fa at Yale University in the United States. Man Guan, Chueh Fan, and quite a few others, are also attending universities and colleges across California. Yung Hsien and Chueh Hang are in France; Yung Yu and Yi Yi are at Oxford University in England; Chueh Cheng is at Sao Paulo University in Brazil; Yi Hua is at International University in India; Yi En is in Korea. Over one hundred in number, they each know why they are there and what they must do.

These disciples of Hsing Yun's are probably the most qualified ever in the history of Chinese Buddhism. Many of them are accomplished in the foreign languages needed to disseminate the Buddhist faith around the globe.

Life's greatest blessing would be the opportunity to read thousands of books, travel thousands of miles, do thousands of tasks, and liberate thousands of living beings. In dispatching disciples to go abroad and teach, Hsing Yun wants them to realize that "Fo Guang Shan is but a preparatory station, not a terminal, in the spread of the Dharma." Based on individual seniority, dedication, ability, and contribution, he maps out ways for them to further their studies and enrich their lives. Practically everyone has been out of Taiwan at some point. These monastics are a far cry from those who used to have only the oil lamp and *wooden fish*[64] for company and died keeping watch over a lonesome temple in the mountains.

Knowing a Gem When You See It

The sight of a youthful monastic in the old days would invariably invite a lament or two: "What a pity! To have renounced the world at such a young age!" There is nothing pitiable about joining Fo Guang Shan, where much is invested in training and the trained are allowed plenty of opportunity to grow. For, "being good at discerning the nature of all living beings and not ever being discriminative," Hsing Yun steers his disciples in their development based on their strengths and inclinations. In "accommodating them, shaping them, and employing them," he ensures that they become the best they possibly can be.

Among many others, the eloquent Tzu Hui, Tzu Jung, Hsin Ting, Yi Kung, and Hui Chuan have been sent to teach the Dharma. The literary Yi Sheng, Yung Chuang, Yung Yun, and Man Kuang run publishing. The academic Tzu Chia, Yi Chun, Hsin Ju, Yung Ming, Yung Chin, and Man Kuo compile the Tripitaka. The compassionate Hui Lung, Yi Jen, Yi Pin, and Yi Lai champion charitable causes. The serene Yi Yen, Hui Jih, and Chien Kuan concentrate on their practice. The studious Tzu Yi and Chueh San further their studies, and drafting specialists Tzu Chuang, Yi Min, and Hui Li undertake all aspects of building temples.

Hsing Yun is like a miner and sculptor in the discovery of talents. "He knows us better than we know ourselves," disciples say, brimming over with gratitude and admiration. One time, while he was discussing the issue of examination and certification with a jeweler, Hsing Yun beamed, "Others know gems, I know people."

The young monastics of Fo Guang Shan did not take tonsure out of despair in love or in life. They did so with perfect willingness. With compassion—the love for all, not for one—they have come to serve sentient beings. While doing so, they radiate joy, perseverance, wholesomeness, and grace. Witnessing this, many people start to think differently about Buddhism.

Some years ago, parents were still overheard insisting that their newly tonsured sons and daughters return home with them.

These days, however, students of the Buddhist College arrive with their parents' blessings and take tonsure in their presence. The old way of "grieving for the son relinquished to the gate of the void" has given way to modern parents "cheerfully walking their child to the gate of the Buddha."

Author Hsiao Hung sees Hsing Yun in every one of his disciples. "They're so affable—like their master. Passing by, they join their palms in greeting. If the path is narrow, they step aside to let others pass first. One has to possess devotion within to display it without. It is not a mere act. It is simply the Master's virtues finding expression through his disciples."

Born to Be an Educator

The learned educator Cheng Shih-yen finds in Hsing Yun a natural educator with many concepts and theories that should be widely adopted in the field of education. In the past, Hsing Yun witnessed classmates who had acted out of line at Qixia Temple being ordered to pay homage to the Buddha or kneel before the shrine for the length of a lit incense. Thinking to himself that paying homage to the Buddha is such a thing of beauty, he did not believe it should take the form of a penalty. Today at Fo Guang Shan, serious misbehavior is punishable by "being sent to your room and disallowed to pay homage to the Buddha." Cooped up in their rooms with a chance to reflect, students usually have little problem recognizing their own follies. When permitted in the presence of the Buddha again, many prostrate in tears and kneel for a very, long time.

He emphasizes the education of the mind. He replaces condemnation with encouragement and chiding with caring. He often tells this story of Chan Master Xianyai to other teachers:

There was a novice monk who was prone to succumbing

to diversions beyond the confines of the monastery. Under the cover of night, he would jump over the wall and venture out. One night, while Master Xianyai was making his rounds about the temple, he came upon a stool by the corner of the wall—evidence of someone's attempt to sneak outside. He removed the stool and stood in its place, waiting there as the night wore on. At last, the novice returned from his merriment. Not knowing about the removal of the stool, he alighted squarely on the master's head, and hopped to the ground. When he stood up to dust himself off, he found to his consternation that he was face to face with the master.

"The night is deep and the dew is heavy," the gracious Master Xianyai said, as if nothing were awry. "Take good care of your body. Don't let yourself catch cold. Run on home and put on more clothing."

Not another word was uttered about the incident, and no one ever knew that it had occurred. However, from that moment on, there were no more nocturnal excursions among the hundred or so novices.

Nurturing disciples is like cultivating orchids—disciples have to be strengthened by the accumulation of learning. Aside from the master teaching his disciple the Dharma, the disciple must be able to receive the Dharma from his master. The caring and understanding bond between a master and his disciples strengthens the bond in the sangha community. Yi Kung feels that Hsing Yun is like a father, "To whom we can pour our hearts out." Likened to the wise Sariputra,[65] Yi Kung says, "The Master is the Buddha. I would not have become a monastic if not for him." Even the most obstinate have been touched by his compassion, attaining wisdom. Even the most incorrigible have been nurtured by his tender care, attaining a virtuous way of life. Yi Kung recalls the time she relocated to other quarters. The Master made certain she was given a larger room "because Yi Kung has tons of books," and a table lamp "because Yi Kung has a lot of reading to do."

Venerable Hsin Cheng, too, has his share of reflections:

> That year in Changhua I was hospitalized after a car crash. The Master came to see me. With sweat beading his forehead, he stood there, as if rooted beside me, looking with great concern at my bandaged leg and mouth full of broken teeth. I'll never forget the look on the Master's face, looking as though he had been injured himself.

With so many disciples, the occasional disagreement and discontentment is inevitable. But all of them have the thought, "The Master treats me the best. If I am wronged, everything will be all right as long as he understands!"

Like Friend, Like Teacher, Like Father

Disciples eagerly look for ways to reciprocate the Master's tender concern. They often follow him as he makes his rounds within the temple grounds or when he goes abroad on lecture tours. It is evident that the feelings between master and disciples are mutual. Whenever he appears fatigued or is delayed at mealtime, they kindly offer him a cup of tea, a meal, or a hot towel.

For years, Hsing Yun has been undergoing treatment for diabetes. Often, disciples will not leave his side until he is seen having taken his medication at the end of a meal. Each time the statuesque master boards or exits a vehicle, one of his disciples will lay a hand on the doorway, ensuring that he does not injure himself by hitting his head.

To the older disciples, he is both master and Dharma friend. To the younger ones, he is a father. "The Master is as magnificent as a mountain yet he is approachable," they all say. "He is rather like the air we breathe, fresh and vital. We cannot be without it."

On the subject of filial piety, Hsing Yun's sigh is clearly audible. "When parents are young and useful," he comments, "their sons and daughters fight for their attention—like a basketball. After middle age, their children push them around—like a volleyball. Finally, old and incapacitated, their children kick them away—like a soccer ball."

"I left home to become a monk at twelve. I have no children of my own, yet my disciples are more loyal and dutiful to me than any children I would have had. One day, I too shall be old. Yet it is obvious that they are going to hold onto me tightly, not letting go of me—like a rugby ball."

In his bid to create inexhaustible brainpower for the Buddhist faith, Hsing Yun has transcended the limitations of Fo Guang Shan. Projects such as the Chinese Buddhist Research Institute, regular international Buddhist conferences and seminars, the Annual International Buddhist Examination, the Fo Guang Foundation for Buddhist Culture and Education, and diverse sponsorships for international Buddhist scholarly research, all serve the same end.

"When nurturing the young, we should not fear that they will be stronger than us. We should not fear their independent thinking," he has said many times. He vows that after they have been trained, they will be gifts to society, to the nation, and to all living beings.

Modern Pioneers for the Buddhist Faith

Hsing Yun is fully aware of the widening gap between Fo Guang Shan's incredible growth and the training of its forces. Because experience is limited, mistakes will be made. However, he believes that nurturing the talented is a hundred-year long path, and after some time, things will improve.

Such a self-assured openness has created modern pioneers for Buddhism. The future of Buddhism will rest on the shoulders of the thousand disciples at the Buddha gate. While his contemporaries are piqued by imminent concerns over posterity, Hsing Yun is free from worry. Some say, "Twenty years from now, Fo Guang Shan will stand as the most powerful religious body in Taiwan."

Chapter 10

Traditional Monastery, Modern Vision

*I*f we were to consider Fo Guang Shan as an enterprise, it would be among the top one hundred organizations in Taiwan. Fo Guang Shan functions as a well-organized entity energized by human and financial resources. It inherited its spirit of antiquity from the traditional monastery of the Tang Dynasty[66] and combined this with the ideals of modern management. Overall, Fo Guang Shan embodies modern Chinese Buddhism just as it provides a valuable model for business management.

A Product of Teamwork

Organizational masterpieces are typically the brainchild of their founders. Fo Guang Shan is no exception. The development and operation of Fo Guang Shan arose out of Hsing Yun's vision.

In Hsing Yun's worldview, Buddhism is the enterprise of all living beings. Consequently, he sees Fo Guang Shan as a product of teamwork. The Religious Affairs Committee is vested with decision making powers in regards to the developmental direction and interdepartmental communication and coordination. The eleven committee members each serve a term of six years. A director-in-chief is elected from the committee to serve a term of six years as well. Presently holding the position is Abbot Venerable Hsin Ping.[67] Branching out from above is the abbot's office and the Domestic Supervisory Council. The council oversees ten management departments governing temple affairs, devotees and public service, charity, fringe benefits, construction projects, financial affairs, personnel resources, and systematic functions. The Religious Affairs Committee also handles the Education Council, Culture Council, Elders Council, the Office of Sangha Affairs,[68] the Fo Guang Shan Foundation for Buddhist Culture and Education, the Fo Guang Pure Land Cultural and Educational Foundation, the Compassion Foundation, the Fo Guang University Organizing Committee, Buddha's Light International Association, and others— totaling over 180 units.

With headquarters in Kaohsiung, Fo Guang Shan has a vast network of over a hundred branch establishments. A majority of these were founded by Hsing Yun himself. A handful of these temples voluntarily merged with Fo Guang Shan due to financial strain, internal strife, or the absence of a master.

Jile Temple in Keelung, newly renovated last year, is one such temple. The causes and conditions that bound the temple and Hsing Yun together through four decades date back to 1949, when he first set foot in Keelung. After stepping off the ship, he passed an old weathered temple. When Hsing Yun glanced inside the temple, a monastic returned his gaze—no words were ever exchanged. Thirty-two years later, the director of the Keelung Buddhist Association and Abbess Hsiu Hui of Jile Temple, whom Hsing Yun had met only briefly at that point in time, invited him to conduct a three-day seminar. Hsing Yun was told that Venerable Hsiu Hui had read his works and identified with the concept of Humanistic Buddhism. After three years, the eighty-year-old Venerable Hsiu Hui made a gift of Jile Temple and its surrounding properties to Fo Guang Shan.

Yuanming Temple in suburban Ilan, where Hsing Yun completed his *Biography of Sakyamuni Buddha's Ten Great Disciples* and his work on The *Sutra on the Eight Realizations of the Great Beings*, was another gift to Fo Guang Shan. In 1982, Abbot Chueh

Yi entrusted Fo Guang Shan with the temple just prior to his passing. Yuanfu Temple in Chiayi, erected at the turn of the twentieth century, was another temple entrusted to Fo Guang Shan.

Connected at the Core

Considering the hundred or so branches stemming from the nucleus of Fo Guang Shan, there is certainly a need for an intricate organizational structure. The first level of branch temples is under the direction of the headquarters, and includes major temples such as Taipei's Pumen Temple, Kaohsiung's Puxian Temple, Los Angeles' Hsi Lai Temple, and the Tokyo Fo Guang Shan Temple. Each is organized by its location in a metropolis containing a million or more inhabitants, its ability to hold Dharma activities for a thousand or more people, and its eight or more resident sangha members.

The second level includes branch temples, lecture halls, and viharas. Branch temples maintain an outward appearance of traditional temples, and lecture halls and viharas are nestled within the structure of modern buildings. Again, each is categorized by its location in a city of half a million or more in population, its ability to hold Dharma activities for five hundred or more, and its four to eight resident sangha members.

At the third level are the Chan and Pure Land centers. They are all located in suburban areas and must have the ability to hold Dharma activities for two hundred or more, with two to four resident sangha members.

Lastly, the preaching centers in more rural areas are run in an itinerant fashion by visiting monastics.

Financial independence of all branch establishments is required. Financial assistance, however, is often sought from the headquarters in cases requiring a major construction project.

The global setup of Fo Guang Shan is unprecedented in the

history of Buddhism. Similar to the Vatican, it is especially unique in the centralized training and delegation of its members. Although monastics from Fo Guang Shan are assigned to various positions abroad, they always maintain strong ties and communcation with the founding temple, which keeps the feeling of camaraderie alive.

The Organization

Two subsystems exist within the organization of Fo Guang Shan: the stages of seniority and administrative appointments.

The stages of seniority fall into five classes and fifteen grades. The first stage is the class of ethical practitioner, which includes six levels lasting a year each. The next three stages are: 1. Learning practitioner which spans another six grades or levels lasting three or five years each; 2. Cultivating practitioner in three levels lasting four years apiece; and 3. Teaching practitioner in three grades spanning five years each. The culmination is the class of master or elder. The administrative appointment pertains to the delegation of duties at Fo Guang Shan.

Hsing Yun has designed a management scheme of tremendous flexibility and versatility in which human resources are delegated in accordance with: academic credentials (from Fo Guang Shan Buddhist College, outside institutions, and individual study of the Buddhist Tripitaka), personal cultivation (character, conduct, and practice), and work experience (seniority and contributions to the monastery). This system is capable of promoting outstanding junior members to vital positions as well as bestowing recognition on senior and responsible members.

Undoubtedly, corporate executives are well acquainted with a system that maintains an orderly business by preserving seasoned workers, while igniting innovation by boosting promising newcomers.

In tackling the enormity of a personnel structure such as Fo

Guang Shan's, the order strives for placement of "the right person in the right place." Most monastics or sangha transfers come once every three years, usually during the first and seventh month of the lunar calendar. Before the transfer, individual preferences are submitted to the Religious Affairs Committee, which then evaluates them. Implementation of transfers corresponds with the demand by the relevant departments and units. Appeals are rescheduled for further discussion.

Regulated transfers result in managerial fluidity. No one hangs onto a position or grows powerful enough to abuse it. Promotions and transfers are defined as awards and penalties. Supply from a pool of talent is always ready, always fresh, and Fo Guang Shan's disciples are instilled with the values of cooperation and communication. This division of labor is best illustrated in large-scale functions. From the perspective of contemporary management, this is humanized management.

Devotees learn to "abide by the Dharma, not the person teaching it." This protects and maintains each temple. Exposure to constantly renewed leadership substitutes personal sentiment with an open and free system.

Economics

Hsing Yun is an example of a monastic who has never maintained his own personal temple, raised his own funds, or pocketed his own savings. Every penny, in terms of income and donations, is channeled to the individual temples for maintenance and other expenses. Financial and administrative authorities are distinctly separate within Fo Guang Shan; in the hands of junior executives lies the former, and the senior executives handle the latter. Everyone collects a monthly stipend on the basis of seniority and position: teaching practitioner, NT $400 (US $12); temple director, NT $300-350 (US $9-11); director, NT $300 (US $9); secretaries,

NT $200 (US $6); cook for the guesthouse, NT $150 (US $5), and so on. Daily necessities, room and board, and transportation, are all paid for by Fo Guang Shan. Salaried layworkers receive a monthly average of NT $3,000 (US $91).

Compared to standards in the business world, the budget allotted for personnel salaries is relatively frugal. Hsing Yun firmly believes that Fo Guang Shan has been built on the principle of selflessness. In the agricultural spirit of Chan practice, advocated by Venerable Master Baizhang Huaihai during the Tang Dynasty, "No work, no food" is alive and well.

Some critics say, "Don't go study at Fo Guang Shan. Fo Guang Shan students are forced to do hard labor," or they say, "Fo Guang monastics only do menial labor, instead of cultivating their true nature." To Hsing Yun, who was raised performing diverse chores, manual labor is natural. Once separated from fetching water and chopping wood, wearing clothes and eating food, the expression of the Dharma is lost. The essence of Chan, or meditation, is reflected in work. Without exception, the eminent masters throughout the ages built their character through devoted labor. The Sixth Patriarch, Huineng, carried rocks and pounded grain. Master Baizhang Huaihai hauled firewood and fetched water, and wearing a cloak of straw, Master Nanquan Puyuan drove cattle. In his first ten years of monastic life, Hsing Yun spent six years serving meals, two years fetching water, and a year and a half tending the shrine and working in the kitchen.

Even students attending the Buddhist colleges have obligations in addition to privileges. At Fo Guang Shan, the traditional monasterial daily routine complete with the punctuating bell, drum, and board is still intact. The wake-up signal is sounded at 4:20 a.m., followed by morning liturgy, and breakfast. Classes are conducted for three hours each in the morning and afternoon, and self-study is mandatory for two hours in the evening. The day closes

with the evening liturgy, meditation, and rest. Chores such as cleaning and cooking are included. For cooking, old-fashioned wood-
burning stoves are still used, because they are deemed indispensable devices in the training of patience and concentration.

Self-Sufficient Finances

In supporting its community of monastics and laypeople,
and initiating diverse projects in education, charity, and construction, Fo Guang Shan's financial burden is understandably cum-
bersome. To maintain self-sufficiency, Fo Guang Shan has established kindergartens and schools, published books and magazines,
and produced memorabilia and souvenirs. Though assailed for
"multifaceted commercialism," Hsing Yun is at peace with his intentions.

"Buddhists are not social deserters," he says, "Nor is there
any call to rely on contributions from society. It is appropriate for
us to trade our labor for our livelihood. In both personal practice
and in spreading the Dharma, we have to be self-sufficient before
we can serve the public. Most of all, Buddhism, having received
donations from society, must give in return. This is the basic reasoning behind the business ventures of Fo Guang Shan."

Indeed, the monastery needs donations to continue providing expanded services to people all over the globe. The two main
sources of income in a traditional temple come from conducting
repentance ceremonies and services for the dead, and from generous patrons. Hsing Yun believes that performing Dharma services
for the dead is established upon the mutual relationship between
monastic and devotee, and not predicated upon any sort of monetary exchange. While devotees make contributions to the temple,
it is only right for the sangha to provide Dharma services for devotee needs. Therefore, repentance ceremonies and services for the
dead at Fo Guang Shan and its branch temples are organized and

discreet.

Hsing Yun does not favor the practice of receiving donations from just a few patrons with hefty checkbooks. Unfortunately, lavish givers may also pose oversized ego problems and end up
doing more harm than good to the general harmony that permeates
a temple. That is why Hsing Yun prizes small sums from countless humble donors, over huge sums from a handful of generous
patrons. Small donations offered with loving-kindness engender
good affinities among followers far and wide.

"Most days most people don't mind small sums," he adds.
"When they do give, they certainly have no intention of seeking
control of temple affairs in return. An abundance of visitors at Fo
Guang Shan means more cherished friends and affinities that per-
meate lifetime after lifetime."

Drops in the Ocean

How are good affinities from far and wide accumulated?
First of all, those who contribute to the temple receive gifts "from
the Buddha." In a way, the mammoth Fo Guang Shan has been
built from offering little souvenirs to its devotees year after year.

In addition, weekly pilgrimage tours, though not exactly
profitable, have become extremely attractive to devotees as well
as non-devotees who spend two days and a night at Fo Guang
Shan. The tours are one of the most effective means of igniting
interest in Buddhism. Among many others, Venerables Yung Ping
and Yung Wen came in contact with Buddhism and, ultimately,
their own destiny into the sangha when they joined a pilgrimage
tour.

On the conviction that a great ocean begins with small drops,
Hsing Yun had the "Ten-thousand Buddhas Hall," a series of in-
door and outdoor statuaries, "The Hall of the Gold Buddhas," and
"The Hall of the Jade Buddhas." These dazzling features were

made possible by a collaboration of donors. Other spectacular features include 480 golden Buddhas surrounding the Great Welcoming Buddha, 8,000 images of Avalokitesvara Bodhisattva in the Great Compassion Shrine, 14,800 images of Sakyamuni Buddha in their respective niches in the Main Shrine, pillars, Chinese roof tiles, and relief sculptures; these artistic masterpieces provide devotees with an opportunity to pledge their donations. Each donor leaves Fo Guang Shan having deepened his or her affinity with the Buddha.

Other Dharma functions such as the Light Offering Service, the Chinese New Year's Festival of Light and Peace, and thousands of affiliate functions bring in tens of thousands of devotees and their contributions.

In the Red

Despite an appearance to the contrary, Fo Guang Shan is not an entity of great wealth. In the words of a temple spokesperson, "Fo Guang Shan is not wealthy, but it knows how to utilize financial resources—even those of next year, and the year after that." It is a center where resources are effectively and efficiently directed to the necessary departments.

Hsing Yun does not speak on matters of money unless compelled to do so, and often tells disciples to refrain from being overly concerned about them, saying: "If you know too much, you'll lose sleep over it."

Supported by neither a nation nor any financial consortium, Fo Guang Shan is accomplished in handling resources. However, it must be noted that, estimated at NT $150 billion (US $5 billion) in assets, Fo Guang Shan is far below the top-ten list of Taiwan's wealthiest religious organizations.

Both a Giver and Receiver

Hsing Yun is a monk who is unafraid of wealth, unafraid to create the conditions necessary to build wealth, and unafraid to utilize wealth. "I'm both a giver and receiver of wealth," he says, candidly discussing the prevalent view in Buddhist circles that poverty symbolizes cultivation and wealth is interpreted as a vulgarity. "Catholics and Protestants are lauded for their financial strength. Why should Buddhists alone shy away from money matters! However, wealth is a requisite unless one doesn't want to achieve anything. How best to put to use the devotees' good, ethical, and sacred wealth for the benefit of all living beings—that is what we should be concerned about."

For years, the media has painted a picture of Fo Guang Shan as a bustling place, lacking in spiritual tranquility, selling soft drinks and profiting from souvenir sales; a place of air-conditioned and carpeted guesthouses; and populated with monastics riding in sedans and making phone calls. Their conclusion, Fo Guang Shan is far too worldly, and Hsing Yun is just an enterprising monk.

Despite the criticism, many visitors of Fo Guang Shan have come away with something far more sacred and profound. Apart from areas open to the public where modern comforts are provided for the convenience of devotees and tourists, restricted areas exist where practice and cultivation are conducted. Wood-burning stoves are still in operation. Sleeping quarters, neither air-conditioned nor carpeted, are lined with boards in the traditional sparse manner. Monastics rise at 4:30 a.m. and retire at 10 p.m. They do not enjoy weekends or holidays, are never paid overtime, and wear the same clothing and two pairs of shoes year-round. Fo Guang Shan monastics live a simple life. They do take occasional automobile rides or make periodic phone calls. But then again, in an age of electronics and telecommunications, insisting that monastics should always travel by foot and that they remain ignorant of worldly affairs at all times would be ludicrous!

Hsing Yun admits he is powerless against the distorted rumors that circulate about Fo Guang Shan. He feels deeply for his disciples and followers. He urges them to continue to receive devotees and visitors with kindness and compassion, diligence and service, hoping that with a meal and friendship more resources shall be gathered for the care of the old and young, the running of schools and the preaching of the Dharma.

The System

Many believe that Taiwan has been faithful in propagating the tradition of Chinese Mahayana Buddhism. Moreover, under Hsing Yun's leadership, Fo Guang Shan keeps orthodox discipline and etiquette intact, while realizing the social traits of modern society and bringing its management system into Buddhism.

The Buddhist sangha always had this healthy system in place. The precepts and rules, for instance, were instrumental in ensuring monasterial peace. Similarly, the six points of reverent harmony[69] guaranteed monastic unity. There was monasterial order in Mainland China because there was a system. However, the same was not true in Taiwan. We had no system and we each went our own way.

Hsing Yun grew up in a traditional monastery and later traveled to various places in order to spread the Dharma. Through this practice, he cultivated both his magnanimous temperament and expansive knowledge. The Fo Guang Shan that he created is a current version of a traditional monastery in Taiwan. "A temple has to be like a temple, and a monk has to be like a monk." Tonsure has to follow a system as does the passing of the precepts. In 1991, Fo Guang Shan conducted a three-month Ten-thousand Buddhas Triple Platform Ordination. Receiving the complete Triple

Platform Precepts—the sramanera or sramanerika precepts, bhiksu or bhiksuni precepts, and the bodhisattva precepts—qualifies a monastic in the Mahayana tradition. Five hundred recipients attended the most systematically and meticulously executed ordination in Taiwan to date. Every single detail went by the book; work and rest, morning and evening liturgies, explication of the precepts, meditation, rehearsal, and labor. Abbot Kaizheng of Hongfa Temple called the event the most accurate and accomplished monastic ordination in Taiwan within the past four decades. Retired Abbot Pucheng of Song Kwan Sa of Korea found the sights and sounds to be invaluable references for Buddhist practitioners.

From Propriety to Professionalism

Everyone, though burdened with chores and duties, must adhere to the morning and evening liturgies, and never stop learning. Hsing Yun established Passing on the Light College for the specific purpose of continuing education and in-service training for monastics. Attendees take four courses per quarter for four years. In addition, a monthly letter comes from the Master himself inquiring about their progress. Typically, the letters are accompanied by concepts of Humanistic Buddhism, textual research, case studies, preaching methods, or learning experiences. Students are required to delve into these materials and submit reports on them. Examinations are held twice a year, and diplomas are awarded to those who pass. Failing an exam is not an unusual occurrence.

Fo Guang Shan's benefits system is about the most thorough there is, tending to everything from medical care, leave of absence, continuing education, and travel, to family visits, loans, and burials for parents.

There even exists a dining system called *guotang*. For each meal, everybody is required to line up, join palms, chant the Buddha's name, and wait for the sounding of the board before entering the dining hall. Seated, everybody begins with the five contemplations[70] and ends with the offering mantra[71] before they start to consume the two bowls (of soup and rice) and one plate (of vegetables) set before them. Eating in the deliberate manner of "a dragon swallowing a pearl and a phoenix nodding its head," no one is to glance around or talk. Everyone must completely finish his or her serving—a sign of cherishing one's blessings. At the end of the meal, the entire group leaves in single file while tables are quickly cleared.

Life on the mountain can be aptly described as flowing with conditions while remaining disciplined. No one will dispute the professionalism with which Fo Guang Shan conducts itself. It is Hsing Yun's influence at work.

Chapter 11

Dharma Realization Within the World

*H*e lives on the mountain but thinks of those below. Feet on the ground, he eyes the universe. From the temples, goodness overflows for the benefit of all living beings. Although the heavens are lovely, this world is lovelier.

Hsing Yun's lectures, writings, temples, disciples, his very person, and his devotees are all manifestations of the concept of Humanistic Buddhism.

Some researchers of Taiwanese Buddhism believe that Hsing Yun has set up a separate "Buddha's Light School," a new addition to the eight traditional Buddhist schools.

Though Hsing Yun did not set out to create another school, when his ideas and accomplishments are traced over the past five decades, it becomes clear that a coherent system has emerged.

The Buddha Was Human

Why is it called Humanistic Buddhism? The reason is that the founder of Buddhism, Sakyamuni Buddha, was not a deity, nor was he a savior. He was a real human being.

Sakyamuni Buddha, originally named Siddhartha, was born in 544 B.C.E. on the eighth day of the fourth month of the lunar calendar in Lumbini, Kapilavastu, India. Siddhartha's parents were Suddhodana, head of the Sakya clan, and his wife Maya.

Siddharta's mother died seven days after his birth, leaving him to be raised by her sister Prajapati. Amidst the adoration of his people, Siddhartha grew up to become the peerless leader his father groomed him to be. At seventeen he married Yasodhara, who in the ensuing year bore him a son, Rahula.

Yet, Siddhartha could not find the answers about the true nature of life and the meaning of the universe in his nobility or the affection of his loved ones. Eventually, he left his palace and went on a quest for truth. He became an ascetic, and for years, led a life of austerity. Finally, at the age of thirty-five, Sakyamuni seated himself on the diamond throne[72] beneath a bodhi tree, gazed at the stars above, and in deep and profound meditation became enlightened. Subsequently he began to turn the wheel of the Dharma[73] and founded a sangha. After teaching for forty-five years, he entered nirvana in a grove of Sal trees[74] near Kusinagara. Most Buddhist literature that exists is a record of Sakyamuni Buddha's teachings compiled by his disciples after he passed away.

Sakyamuni Buddha, as history tells us, was born and raised in this world, attained enlightenment in this world, and entered nirvana in this world. He tasted life's joy, anger, misery, and happiness. He experienced human birth, aging, sickness, and death. *Buddha* in Sanskrit means the "enlightened one." Sakyamuni *is* the Enlightened One. We are humans yet to be enlightened.

The Dharma as the Buddha taught it in his time, was primarily geared towards working, living, sitting, resting, thinking, and behaving in life. The result of his teachings is a human-oriented Buddhism. Hsing Yun applies the Buddha's teachings of 2,500 years ago to modern life, and in the process, he furthers the development of Humanistic Buddhism.

The Five Precepts, Cornerstone of World Peace
Once, when asked at a military academy about the tangible

contributions Buddhism can make to a nation and its society, Hsing Yun replied, "The Tripitaka along with its twelve divisions of sacred sutras are all beneficial to the nation and society. But the Five Precepts alone will suffice to govern a country and rule the world."

Specifically, freedom in the contemporary sense is that which does not interfere with the freedom of others. That is exactly what the Five Precepts teach. The precept against killing prevents us from infringing on the safety of others and encourages a respect for life. The precept against stealing keeps us from plundering the property of others and creates a respect for the rights of others. The precept against adultery stops us from violating others and is thus, a respect for virtue. The precept against lying keeps us from ruining the reputation of others and thus is a respect for morals. The precept against intoxication prevents us from losing our clarity and keeps us from becoming a danger to others. If we abide by the Five Precepts, respect one another, and fully enjoy freedom within legal bounds, the nation and society will undoubtedly be safe, harmonious, and joyful.

Though six decades have passed since the day he started school, Hsing Yun will always cherish the very first character that he was taught—"ren," meaning people. Throughout his life, Hsing Yun's respect for people has never diminished. Fo Guang Shan exists for the practice of Humanistic Buddhism. Those who join its sangha must share the consensus of awakening oneself and others, and of benefiting oneself and others. Journalist Wu Lingjiao once wrote, "Those who seek liberation from the cycle of life and death solely for themselves must not seek Fo Guang Shan."

Worldly Life Is Affirmed

In Humanistic Buddhism, the idealistic and realistic Hsing Yun sees an absolute affirmation of the value of worldly life. He also insists that joyful practice is actually more important than asceticism.

Hsing Yun does not think it realistic to be obsessed with the idea of liberation from birth and death, or to engage solely in solitary practice, turning one's back on worldly affairs, and living off the support of others. That, he says, would be a parasitic existence. "Practice, practice—that is all I ever hear about! *Practice* is becoming another word for laziness," Master Yin Shun once lamented. For, indeed, practice is neither a slogan nor a ritual. Practice is the real life application of the Dharma in the form of service and offering, diligence and patience.

"Tackling life is more important than tackling death," Master Taixu once said. One must understand living before seeking liberation from birth and death. Buddhism is to be applied to daily life because it is a religion for living.

Venerable Master Huineng of the Chan School spoke this verse in the *Sixth Patriarch's Platform Sutra*:

> *The Dharma is here in the world;*
> *Enlightenment is not apart from the world.*
> *To search for bodhi[75] apart from the world*
> *Is like seeking a hare with horns.*

In a nutshell, "the Dharma is but the innate goodness of human nature." There lies within every aspect of daily life, the potential realization of true wisdom. The following verse gives a metaphorical depiction of such a state:

> *Exhausting the days in quest of spring, nowhere to be found;*
> *Treading the clouds along the mountain range with sandals of straw.*

> *Returning, [I] chance upon plum blossoms, hold them to*
> *my nose;*
> *Only to be told that spring is already on each and every*
> *bough.*

Chan masters teach that practitioners who are in business follow a code of ethics, and neither swindle nor evade taxes. Those in the military should be valiant and guard their nation. Those in political office need to be loyal and accountable, and serve their hometown. Those in academia are called to focus on their studies and teaching. In other words, when all people fulfill their roles with devotion and integrity, the Dharma will be in every breath.

A Religion of Blessings

To Hsing Yun, modern Humanistic Buddhism is a Buddhism of sounds, colors, actions, and humor. "What I mean by Humanistic Buddhism is a life of joy and interests, of gratitude and well-being, of compassion and virtue. Such is the liberation for all as taught by the Mahayana, and the Way as learned from the Pure Land."

The *Amitabha Sutra* speaks about a world of utmost happiness in the West, where the ground is resplendent with gold chambers and ceilings are adorned with the seven gems, where water is of the eight merits, colorful birds speak the Dharma, and gorgeous flowers never wither. It is an indication that Buddhist practice does not necessarily mean eating poorly, clothing oneself in rags, or being forever deprived of daily necessities.

"If you seek joy after death, why not cherish your happiness and well-being in life?" Buddhism is not a religion of suffering, but one of blessing. Hsing Yun hopes that the beautiful and good side of this world will be cherished and defines the Pure Land on earth as:

Courteous, respectful, utter kind words;
Optimistic, content, joy abounds;
Reasonable, peaceful, freedom exists;
Compassionate, magnanimity, safety be celebrated.

Hsing Yun is probably one of the most listened-to storytellers alive. He skillfully uses social concerns and familiar everyday circumstances to elucidate the profound and wondrous teachings of Humanistic Buddhism.

On Wealth

Since many human beings are particularly attracted to money, Hsing Yun often speaks on the Buddhist view of wealth.

"Buddhism does not deny wealth," he says. Many Buddhists absolutely refuse to discuss the subject, stigmatizing "gold" as a "viper." Those practitioners certainly do not recognize *gold* as absolutely necessary to sustain practice or to spread the Dharma for the benefit of all living beings. However, the truth is that the wise cherish wealth and know the correct way to acquire it and use it, for when wealth comes in a proper way, abundance should be celebrated. Buddhists have no cause for resistance towards wealth.

Hsing Yun tells a story about a man who took great pains to store gold bars in his cellar.

For thirty-odd years the gold bars sat untouched. Then, one day, the man opened his cellar door only to discover that the gold had vanished. The shock of the empty cellar nearly killed the old man. Attempting to console him, a neighbor asked, "Have you ever spent any of the gold?"

"Absolutely not!" the man retorted.

"So you've never even touched any of the gold in all

these years?"

"No, never!" responded the old man.

"Well, don't worry then," said the neighbor. "Let me get some bricks, wrap them up and put them back in your cellar. The bricks can take the place of your missing gold! Why bother to mourn over something you never intended to use in the first place?"

Hsing Yun's story reveals an understanding that "possessing wealth is a blessing, and knowing how to spend wealth is wisdom." Neither one who devalues wealth, nor one who is a miser can be called wise. *Possessing* wealth is a pleasure, but being able to utilize it for the benefit of others is the *true joy* of wealth. Most of all, wealth appears in various forms in our life; stamina and health, thankfulness and contentment, a meaningful existence, peace and security for loved ones, a wholesome spirit...all are forms of wealth worth cherishing and cultivating.

On Destiny

Life is a transient experience. In a moment, some people may instantly ride the crest to success while others are plummeted into disgrace and destitution. In search of an answer to what the next moment might hold, people often resort to all kinds of fortune-telling practices or fengshui in order to predict their future. A favorable prediction will send some off walking on air, and an unfavorable one will shroud others in fear and dread. Humanistic Buddhism is empty of such predictions. Fatalism is not a view adopted in Buddhism. Our destiny is in our own hands, and far from being a fixed entity, can be altered.

This following story is an illustration of the Buddhist perspective on life and destiny:

A master who had attained arhatship realized in meditation that his favorite disciple had only seven days to live.

"Why does this lovely child have only seven days left in his life?" he thought. "What a misfortune! I can't tell him the truth. So young...how is he going to take such news?"

At dawn, the master set aside his heartbreak and summoned the little disciple, to whom he said, "My good boy, you haven't seen your parents in so long. Why don't you pack your things and go home for a visit!"

Innocently, the disciple took leave of his master and went home. One day went by, then another. A total of seven days passed but nothing was heard from or seen of him. Just when the master was mourning the loss of his disciple, the little novice showed up in his presence quite safe and sound.

Incredulous, the master took his hand, looked him up and down, and asked him, "How did you return? What happened in the last seven days?"

Perplexed about his master's concern, the disciple responded, "Nothing, Master."

Again the master quizzed him, "Try to remember what happened. Did you see anything? Did you do anything?"

"Oh, I came upon a pond on my way home and saw a group of ants caught in the water. So I picked a leaf and helped them back ashore."

The child's compassion at that moment—the master was relieved to learn–had sown such bountiful goodness, that in saving the ants' lives he amended his own destiny.

Though merely another parable, it once again shows how exhaustible fortune really is. Like a mountain of wealth stacked away, if it is abused, all the blessings in one's life may disappear. Conversely, regular contributions to a savings account will amount to a substantial balance in time. That is also how a life of misfortune may be turned around. In Humanistic Buddhism we are encouraged to rejoice in life, accept the future, purify our minds, change our ways, and create our destinies.

On Politics

Politics is an ultra-sensitive topic, especially in politically sensitive Taiwan. Yet Hsing Yun, with unmistakable integrity as to what he will and will not do, has long been speaking publicly on Buddhist political views. When cautioned by followers against the taboo—which most masters and monastics would rather avoid—he replies that politics are a public issue. As gregarious as humans are, no one is an island, and therefore no one can live above and beyond politics. The Buddhists of modern society vote, pay taxes, serve in the military when drafted, and live a life closely connected with politics. Since our lives are intertwined with political issues, a proper view of politics is absolutely necessary.

"I have renounced the life of a householder, but not the country," Hsing Yun often explains. He means that in accord with the concept of Humanistic Buddhism, monastics should also be concerned about the affairs of the state. Chanted monthly on the first and fifteenth, *In Praise of the Precious Cauldron* is "done with deep respect, praying for longevity for the republic, as long as heaven and earth shall last…"

Chan Master Changlu once prayed for "all countries to be at peace and all frontiers stilled, all arms dismantled and forces dismissed, all winds gentle and rains kind, all men and women both safe and joyous." Records of politically influential monastics are ample. Venerable Master Xuanwan of the Tang Dynasty, an imperial tutor, coached the heir to the throne in ways to rule his country and love his people. Xuanwan instructed the heir to practice charity, eliminate killing, respect nature, and observe vegetarianism.

In yet another example, Master Taixu countered Japan's accusation that China was corrupting Buddhism during the Sino-Japanese war by visiting the Buddhist countries of Burma,[76] Ceylon,[77] and others, and winning support for China in the process. Master Leguan called for monastic medic relief workers in resistance to the war as well.

Hsing Yun believes that Master Taixu's moderate and objective standpoint of "questioning politics without intervening" is the attitude modern Buddhists should take. He suggests caring about the well-being of the country, but not pursuing the glory and fortune of public office. Politicians are advised to emulate the Buddha's wisdom as recorded in the *Gradual Discourses of the Buddha* [*Ekottara-agama*]: refraining from corruption, anger, evasion, isolation, trespassing, selfishness, and so forth.

On Relationships

Relationships are the cause of all suffering in modern society. Too many lives spiral into tragedy because an ego is inflated, a battle of wills seems necessary, or cheating and bullying appear easier then dealing with the problems in relationships. Hsing Yun has lived long enough to recognize even the most subtle causes and effects. He views one's existence as the result of causes and conditions binding one to another. The affairs of the world are plagued with pain, sorrow, and anxiety stemming from our common incapacity to treat one another with kindness and cultivate *ourselves* with dedication. In fact, the strife between *them* and *us* is an epidemic even between loved ones.

In the *Hundred-Parable Sutra* there is a story about a couple squabbling over a piece of cake:

A man bickering with his wife over a piece of cake thought to himself, "Women just can't hold their tongues. I can beat her at that game!" He proceeded to suggest that the two of them should battle in complete silence, and if either of them uttered a sound, the other would get the treat. His wife acquiesced. In a mute stalemate the pair sat, with the cake placed between them.

Then a burglar came upon the scene. Naturally he had no way of making sense of the two rigid silent spouses. Taking advantage of the situation, he began to prowl about the premises looking for valuables. Still, the couple remained in silent combat. This so emboldened the intruder that he began advancing toward the lady of the house. A moment later, he was laying his hands on her. Remarkably, the husband was completely unmoved by what was transpiring before his own eyes. Unable to contain herself any longer the wife rose to her feet screaming, "Are you blind or something? Can't you see I'm being assaulted?"

Incredible as it might sound, her husband sprang from his seat, snatched the piece of cake, and started munching on it. "Hah, you've lost," he said in laughter. "The treat is finally all mine!"

To be as cold and calculating as the husband in this story—bearing a grudge when there is triumph, and disdain when there is loss, and allowing for boundless ignorance that triggers ceaseless defilements—is the source of strife and hostility in every form.

To resolve a multitude of relationship issues whether marital, friendly, sibling, or collaborative, Humanistic Buddhism offers an obvious and feasible solution: "You be big and I'll be small, you have a lot and I'll have a little, you be praised and I'll be scorned, you rejoice and I'll suffer." To illustrate this, Hsing Yun has another story.

There were two neighboring families: the Zhangs, who were incessantly quarrelsome, and the Lis, who appeared to be forever basking in peacefulness. In time, the Zhangs felt compelled to ask for advice from their neighbors.

"Why do we bicker from day to day while you seem so at peace with one another?" queried the Changs.

"You fight because you're all outstanding people," replied the Lis. "No one in our family is even good enough to start a fight."

"That sounds like nonsense! What do you mean?" asked the Zhangs.

"Well, take the breaking of a vase for example. You each think you should be the last to be blamed and that somebody else should be held accountable. The finger-pointing becomes increasingly vicious because you all insist you're in the right and everybody else is wrong," said the Lis.

"As for us, we would rather admit our own guilt than hurt another's feelings. Thus, the apology of the one who made the blunder is met with apologies from others who say, 'Surely it's not your fault, no, not at all. I was careless to have left the vase in that spot.' We always start by thinking we're in the wrong and holding ourselves responsible. We do not evade any issues. Harmony, therefore, is a matter of course."

On Responding to the Times

"An effective writer is capable of responding wholly to the times," humorist Lin Yutang once said. Likewise, Humanistic Buddhism, which is not only a concept but a practice, is sociologically significant. Hsing Yun *is* a religious master "capable of responding wholly to the times." Moreover, he acts in the moment with astuteness and intelligence, charting his own course.

To assuage the agony Taiwan suffered from the severance of

diplomatic ties with the United States in 1979, Hsing Yun conducted a Buddhist chanting concert to raise funds for a patriotic foundation. To elevate social values above existing trends, he organized a series of campaigns in 1992, which were designed to purify minds by means of the seven virtues. The seven virtues, alongside the basic Five Precepts, are the seven means of self-discipline in modern society: no smoking or drugs, no violence, no stealing, no gambling, no drinking, no indecency, and no quarreling.

To respond to the organ donation drive at Chang-Gung Memorial Hospital some years back, the gracious monk led many others to follow suit by pledging to donate his own organs. In regards to preserving the environment, Hsing Yun rallied public support by speaking up for the reforesting of Kaohsiung, conserving the country's water resources, recycling used paper, and protecting wildlife.

Perfecting a Person, Becoming a Buddha

Unlike some reclusive monastics, Hsing Yun adheres to the conviction that "the Dharma is for solving all issues in life," and that a Buddhist should exercise, without fail, every awareness and concern for various social changes. In recent years, whenever he has noticed a new social phenomenon, trend, or social problem, he endlessly ponders, "How can the principles of the Dharma be applied? How is the contemporary Buddhist to respond?"

Consider the controversy over abortion, which many religions still strongly object to even to this very day. Where, then, do Buddhists stand? Terminating a pregnancy is a violation of the precept against killing, Hsing Yun asserts, and retribution is inevitable. However, he points to circumstances such as medically confirmed fetal abnormality or pregnancy caused by sexual assault, under which childbirth will in all likelihood, encumber society enormously and sink the mother hopelessly into a life of torment. He maintains that, as long as the mother is ready to shoulder the retribution for killing, the ultimate decision to end the pregnancy is hers and hers alone. By the same token, Hsing Yun makes it clear that he believes crucial decision-making pertaining to euthanasia lies with those closest to the patient and must only be rendered with love and compassion.

Hsing Yun does not avoid touchy social issues such as divorce and domestic violence either. On such topics he comments, "You can find the basis for all solutions in the Dharma. I am merely applying it to fit the needs of the times." A Buddhism that fails to keep abreast of modern concerns or provide viable solutions to its problems resembles "a grown person stuck in children's clothing." He does not see how such an empty practice can last.

Hsing Yun braved insufferable misunderstanding and mortification through four decades of advocating Humanistic Buddhism. Time has honored his vision. Master Taixu prepared an outline for Humanistic Buddhism at the turn of the century, and Hsing Yun has succeeded in continuing the momentum. With his lifelong belief in the idea that "the perfecting of Buddhahood comes by means of perfecting the human," he has paved the smoothest and broadest way for Humanistic Buddhism.

Chapter 12

Good Affinities
around the World

*F*o Guang Shan's morning and evening liturgies always open with a passage in praise of the incense-offering:

> *Incense in the burner is lit now*
> *To permeate the dharma realms;*
> *From afar, the assembly of Buddhas have heard.*
> *How auspicious the clouds are, forming above*
> *And how intense the devotion is;*
> *The Buddhas appear wholly before all.*
> *Let us take refuge in the great bodhisattvas,*
> *[Let us take refuge in the great bodhisattvas,*
> *Let us take refuge in the great bodhisattvas.]*

This passage explains how the Buddhas, moved by the pervasive devotion of those who chant and pray, gladly protect and guide them, ensuring that blessings are shared with all living beings in the ten directions.

Surrounded by Good Affinities

People-oriented from an early age, Hsing Yun has made countless affinities with friends and devotees. As visible as the auspicious clouds, these affinities have been significant conditions in the success of Hsing Yun's career and in the creation of Fo Guang

Shan.

Statistics from the Taiwan Department of Civil Affairs indicate an average of about one temple or church per 1.54 sq. miles. Buddhist temples number 1,560 in Taiwan today. The Department of Internal Affairs estimates 4.85 million Buddhists, 3.63 million Daoists, 910,950 devotees of Yiquan Dao, 421,648 Protestants, and 295,742 Catholics in Taiwan.

Statistics from Fo Guang Shan show that over one million people have formally taken refuge in Taiwan under the temples of Fo Guang Shan. This means that one out of five Buddhists in Taiwan is a Fo Guang Buddhist. Notably, in the first half of 1994, over 10,000 devotees took refuge within the precincts of Fo Guang Shan, the temples in Taipei, and Hsi Lai Temple in Los Angeles. Moreover, some 200,000 donors contributed to the newly erected Triple Gem Shrine and the Halls of the Gold and Jade Buddhas; over 200,000 free subscriptions of *Awakening the World* are regularly distributed; overseas, Fo Guang Buddhists number around 200,000.

It is small wonder that with grassroots support and their subsequent social influence, Hsing Yun and Fo Guang Shan have both become esteemed in the eyes of political enthusiasts. Once Hsing Yun was appointed consultant for party affairs by Taiwan's current majority party, the Chinese Nationalist Party (Guomin Dang), and another time he was honored with the title of Member of the Central Committee at which he remarked, "As a committee member, I honestly don't know what I can do for the party and, in that regard, I certainly don't know what the party will want me to do!" The laurels are for the Buddhist circle as a whole, he insisted, not only for himself. In fact, all that he has ever accepted from politicians are gifts of tea during the Mid-Autumn Festival and the Lunar New Year.

Of course, some politicians appear more sincere than others. Most of the time, they display little affinity with the Buddha, yet close to election time, they begin streaming through the mountain gate. Invariably, they are after headlines in the media: "Hsing Yun Pledges Support for…" On occasion, political luminaries are seen seated in the VIP area during Fo Guang Shan activities. "By asking a mayor or county supervisor to come and address the crowd, it'll be easier for us to obtain access to necessary sites when we need them," Hsing Yun jokes.

Political Monk No More

Being dubbed a political monk was certainly no pleasure. Hsing Yun probes his heart and still remains nonpartisan among political circles. In fact, the government has had little or no part at all in the growth of Fo Guang Shan except for, perhaps, the ten-year delay in matters of official registration. Hsing Yun was a great sport about the delay saying, "Mayors serve terms of three or five years, this monk serves for life. The permit will come some-day."

Actually, "the political monk" was the moniker given to him by dissidents who were venting their wrath over Hsing Yun's friendliness with the Nationalists.

Those who have walked the path of contemporary Chinese history with Hsing Yun will never forget how the Nationalists fled the Mainland only to exercise another thirty years of despotism in Taiwan. Under those circumstances, no one dared to befriend the dissidents. Lacking social support, Buddhist groups were vulnerable back then. Like the rest of the population, the Buddhists, together with other religious bodies, had only the Chiang government to support and the Nationalist Party to vote for. That was the political environment and psychological milieu of that era. Why should Hsing Yun be singled out?

Presently, political conditions and personal values are different. When the Nationalist-backed Venerable Mingguang ran for a seat in the National Assembly several years ago, not a single person accused him of being overly political.

Concerning his label as the political monk, Hsing Yun has only this to say about his dilemma. "The media, not I, rant and rave over politics and sensitive topics like the future of the strait and the dissidents on the Mainland. If I don't come up with a response, I'll be deemed unaware and unconcerned. If I do, I am overly political."

Friends in Public Office

Political monk or not, the rest of the world has come to know and appreciate Hsing Yun on a much deeper level. He does not worry over such a title. "Defamation in it of itself is incapable of spoiling one's character," he says, "Unless the character is an unwholesome and hollow one. The way to confront slander is not to try to clarify oneself, but to quietly reject the conflict." With regards to some political figures, Hsing Yun does not shun them but rather treats them without discrimination. Perhaps, some come to him with dubious intentions at first. However, after having interacted with them for a period of time, Hsing Yun has made a number of close friends.

Vice Chairperson Wang Chin-ping of the Legislative Council and Legislators Pan Wei-kang and Shen Chih-hui are frequent visitors. Pan, the sole Buddhist in a family of Catholics, is so motivated by Fo Guang Shan's principle to "give others confidence, give others joy, give others service, give others hope," that she has adopted this principle as the foundation for her actions at work.

Also, Secretary-General Wu Po-hsiung of the president's office, Judge Lin Fu-tsun of the High Court, Mayor Lin Shui-mu of Keelung, and Chairperson Chung Jung-chi of the Provincial

Committee of the Nationalist Party, often communicate with Hsing Yun. To commemorate the passings of Presidential Political Advisor Chiu Chuang-huan's parents, Hsing Yun conducted funeral services for both. Former mayor of Kaohsiung County, Yu-Chen Yueh-ying, regarded him as her personal consultant in municipal affairs.

His friendship with Chen Lian, head of the Supervisory Council, is almost legendary. Chen did not learn about Buddhism until age fifty, but has since become a remarkably diligent and avowed protector of the Dharma. His family now shares the same devotion, and his eldest son Chen Yu-ting has entered the order at Lingquan Temple. Moreover, with the unanimous endorsement of his siblings, Chen moved the remains of his parents, former Vice President Chen Cheng and his wife, from Taishan to Fo Guang Shan three years ago. Hsing Yun assured the most dignified arrangements for the occasion. In last year's fundraising for Fo Guang University, the executive representative of the entire body of Fo Guang devotees literally packed two trucks of Chen's family antiques, paintings, and calligraphic pieces and sent them off to Fo Guang Shan for auction.

Friends in Business

Hsing Yun has more than a few friends in business. Wu Hsiu-chi of President Corporation has been a great friend for over three decades and a strong supporter of Fo Guang Shan. Chang-Yao Hung-ying, whose semiconductor business Hsing Yun named "Light of the Sun and Moon," played a key role in the founding of Hsi Lai Temple, Los Angeles. Pan Hsiao-jui, owner of the Grand Formosa Regent in Taipei, supported the Master since the very beginning of Fo Guang Shan. "Making donations gives me the greatest pleasure," says Pan Hsiao-jui. Years of charitable endeavors with the support of his wife have endowed him with a benevolent face, which many people say resembles that of Maitreya Buddha.

Tseng Liang-yuan and Huang Li-ming, a couple in the construction business, fondly address Hsing Yun as "Old Papa" instead of master. Having striven hard to initiate fundraising for the new Taipei Vihara, they gave a hearty gift to the Master. They call themselves the gleeful, ultimate beneficiaries.

Friends in the Cultural Circle

Some of Hsing Yun's best friends are from the cultural circle. "In the early years, there were very few individuals who had the motivation to lend a hand in Buddhist cultural affairs," he says. "Those who did shall forever be my guests of honor." Academics Chen Ku-ying, Yang Kuo-shu, Wei Cheng-tung, Hu Fo, and others share warm memories of the days they used to teach at the Buddhist college and, in particular, the amount of respect lavished upon them—a rarity today.

A writer and artist himself, Hsing Yun knows well how to appreciate like minds when he runs into them. He presided over the painter Li Chi-mao's wedding. Scriptwriter Sun Chun-hua's daughter, now Venerable Miao Jung, is a disciple. Through various fundraising art auctions for Fo Guang University in the past two years, he has been able to build unprecedented affinities within cultural circles.

Writer of popular thrillers, Szu-ma Chung-yuan, a friend of twenty years, describes Hsing Yun as "insightful and visionary, positive and pragmatic, modern and unconventional." Szu-ma also calls him historically innovative in the spread of the Dharma and the expansion of Buddhism. Other literary figures include Chao Ning, who took refuge under Hsing Yun and was given the Dharma name Puguang, and veteran author Liu Fang who, though Hsing Yun's senior in age, calls him Master with unquestionable readiness.

Essayist Ying Wei-chih once dined with Hsing Yun at Pu-men Temple. "Monastics receive their sustenance from all ten directions, as the saying goes," joked an apparently satiated Ying afterwards. "This pen-wagging bunch received ours from eleven today!" Members of the media—Li Yu-hsi of the *Ming Sheng Daily*, Lu Chen-ting of the *Central Daily News*, and Su Cheng-kuo of the *Chinese Times*—initially visited out of curiosity but could not leave without bowing their heads in awe.

The entertainment industry also has its fair share of follow-ers, namely Kuo Hsiao-chuang; Chen Li-li; Cheng Pei-pei; Tien Wen-chung; Wang Hai-po; Kou Feng, producer of the miniseries "National Master Yu Lin" for television; Yang Ching-huang and Kuang Ming-chieh, who played the leading roles in the series; and many, many more.

Friends in Need of a Friend

Those around Hsing Yun marvel at what a good friend he is. Li Zijian, a painter from the Mainland who found himself in the United States with virtually nothing, was given assistance and pro-vided with a residence. Li was assured that his creative endeavors would not be interrupted and that his wife and child would be able to join him. A year later, Li reciprocated his patron's kindness with close to a hundred works collectively titled "This World Needs Love." Further aided by Hsing Yun, Li's work was exhibited at Hsi Lai Temple, Fo Guang Shan, and Taipei's city art gallery, and Li is currently taking his works across Japan, North America, and Europe.

Hsing Yun also came to the rescue of Gao Ertai and Pu Xiaoyu, both on the faculty of Nanjing University at the time of the June 4th Massacre in Tiananmen Square [1989], as both were forced into exile in the United States. The couple's fortunate encounter with him led to their eventual discovery of both physical and spiritual peace. They said that when they wandered to this foreign land, it was the Master who guided them so that they could find a new start in life.

Qian Jiaju, an economist of international renown from Mainland China who had spent a lifetime delving into materialism and Marxism, left for the same reason as Gao and Pu, and was also Hsing Yun's guest in the United States. After attending the Master's lecture on the *Sixth Patriarch's Platform Sutra* three times, he became a Buddhist at the ripe old age of eighty. As much mentor and pupil as good friends, the two are often heard addressing each other as "Elder Qian" and "Great Master."

Friends Are Forever
Wealth is not forever, friends are. All along, Hsing Yun has been surrounded by generous and undemanding friends. Chen Chien-cheng, a civil servant from Kaohsiung's Department of Financial Affairs, was in the audience on every occasion when the Master spoke, nodding in agreement as he listened. That nodding agreement has extended over twenty years now, from the early days in Shoushan Temple to the current days of Puxian Temple. The children and grandchildren of Hsing Yun's first generation of followers, some of whom were named by the Master himself, are becoming equally devoted. Lin Qisung, a devotee from an affluent background, is often spotted wearing an apron and a broad grin, working in Hsi Lai Temple's kitchen and serving meals in the dining hall during Dharma functions. At Fo Guang Shan, whenever there is the odd paint job to be completed, it is done under the auspices of Chang Tien-yung and Chang-Yun Wang-chueh, a couple who run a paint business. The pair hardly ever get to greet the Master in person, but year after year they have made their offerings, never faltering, never saying much. One of the most puz-

zling incidents of quiet devotion, however, was when an elderly devotee slipped a red envelope into Hsing Yun's hands at the end of a Sangha Day Celebration.[78] Later, the monastics discovered that the envelope was stuffed with bundles of jewelry. But the incident happened so quickly, Hsing Yun never got a good look at her face.

Just what transpired in Hsing Yun's life to transform the lone monk into the magnetic individual attracting so much kindly affection? To put it simply, devotees feel close to Fo Guang Shan. They need only ask to be aided and supported in their weddings and funerals. They are updated about Fo Guang Shan's monthly events by an ample supply of journals and newsletters. Devotees are taken care of, both physically and spiritually, by attending lectures, Dharma functions, chanting sessions, and workshops. They even receive occasional visits from the monastics when they are sick and more often when they are well and up for a friendly exchange. They are given the opportunity to pray for added well-being and to be rid of misfortune. Some of the older devotees are given birthday cards annually, always a week prior to their special day. What better connects people to one another than such affection and commitment toward harmony?

Lin Ching-chin, a follower for four decades, recalls how caring the Master was to him:

> I was in the army back in 1962 when the Master visited the Chinmen front. He brought along a package of Buddhist texts, which were intended for me. But his schedule was far too tight and I was stationed out in the islands. We didn't even get to see each other. So he had to take the books all the way home and mail them back to me again. I honestly have no words for how I felt when at long last the package reached me.
>
> After my military service, I was readying myself for fur-

ther schooling. The Master wholeheartedly supported me. I used to take advantage of the lecture hall when no one was chanting and work into the wee hours. Master would keep me company either doing his own reading or writing. At times he would treat me to the snacks given to him by devotees. "I don't snack at night," he would say, trying to ease my mind. I didn't fare that well academically but eventually I was accepted into a university. The Master was thrilled with my progress and gave me a copy of the *Far East English-Chinese Dictionary.*

Upon graduating from National Taiwan Normal University, Lin returned to Hsing Yun's side and spent the next decade helping him found Zhiguang, a school of commerce. He even helped transplant the shade-giving trees on campus. For a while, Lin suffered from a painful stomach ulcer, but he was never remiss in fulfilling his commitment. "I didn't bring shame on the Master," Lin voices his gratitude from deep within. He and his wife, both teachers, have been faithfully sending their monthly donation for the last ten years—a commitment very rarely upheld even between children and their own parents today.

Receiving with Wisdom

Director Kou Feng remembers how the Master once received him with the most profound wisdom, which, alongside his vast compassion, was instrumental in drawing countless followers. "There seems to be this fully packed bookcase in my mind," was the way that he described his inner sense of unrest to the Master. "I didn't think that in trying to reclassify my books, I would knock the bookcase over!"

"I'm troubled, too!" the Master replied with a dash of humor. "Except that you're deeply troubled and I'm only somewhat disturbed. You can't let go, but I can!"

Hsing Yun added, "I've a bookcase in my mind, too. Like yours, it is not in good order. If I could put it in order, I wouldn't be sitting here. I'd be sitting there!" Hsing Yun then gestured in the direction where the bodhisattva was seated in the shrine. What he intended to tell Kou was that one who is free from worldly cares is no longer an ordinary human but a bodhisattva.

Such is Hsing Yun's way:

> *Whether you awaken instantaneously or cultivate over life-*
> *times of practice;*
> *Never abandon concern for any sentient being.*
> *Flow with the world and care for all living beings;*
> *Always help them connect with the Buddha.*

"I won't desert anyone," Hsing Yun pledges. To him, nobility and commonalty are the same; everyone is one of the many. Best-selling author Lin Ching-hsuan still recounts the details of the hospitality that Hsing Yun extended to him long before his success. The Master literally went out of his way to greet Lin when he paid his first visit to Fo Guang Shan. Last year, Lin went on a lecture tour in the United States on behalf of Buddha's Light International Association. The Master, who had just returned to Los Angeles from Russia, made it a point to thank him in person. Lin arrived a quarter of an hour late for their appointment due to traffic. But the moment his car drove through Hsi Lai Temple's main gate, he could see a tall figure in the distance, cane in hand, waiting in the hot July sun. The sight was simply unforgettable.

Hsing Yun's sensitive consideration makes working with him a sheer pleasure. In fact, he always takes the initiative to have people comfortably settled before anything else. "To direct volunteers," he says, "One must first and foremost be a volunteer to the volunteers. Have stationary and seats in place before asking volunteers to write, have buckets and hoses at hand before asking volunteers to water the plants. Tell them where the faucet is, too."

Those gifted in the arts were exceptionally hard to come by during the early years in Ilan. When Yang Hsi-ming volunteered to paint the murals for the kindergarten, Hsing Yun was so thankful that he attended to him day in and day out, preparing brushes, paint, palette, rulers, as well as tea and snacks like an apprentice. When Chu Chiao became editor of *Buddhism Today*, he often had to work late into the night. Hsing Yun would be there for him as well, cooking noodles or bringing him a glass of milk to keep him going.

To this day, during those tedious drives on the freeway, Hsing Yun is the one who keeps the driver entertained—and awake—while others nap.

All Affinities Are Attributed to Buddhism

Though many have become devotees and supporters of Fo Guang Shan out of sheer admiration and respect for Hsing Yun, he attributes all affinities to the institution. "These are Buddhist devotees, not my personal followers. Don't ask them for favors or donations unless absolutely necessary," the Master tells his disciples. "Don't ever make financial deals with them. Don't lose your temper with them so that they lose their faith in Buddhism."

Hsing Yun continues to reiterate to his disciples and staff what good affinities mean to him. "Coldness towards devotees is coldness toward me and neglecting guests is injuring me."

On one occasion, Hsing Yun heard that a young monastic in charge of a branch temple complained that devotees were becoming less compliant and that many were unwilling to do manual chores. The monk's distress troubled Hsing Yun visibly. "If my disciples should think such absurd thoughts," he said in shame, "I would have them mop the floor and scrub windows for ten years! Although it's great that devotees wish to help, it's just as well that they don't help at all, for they've come to pay homage to the Buddha, not to work!"

Preaching Amidst the Secular World

Many a time, the Master has taught his disciples that, in the Chan School, a monastery is compared to the plants in a grove. Just as a single plant cannot make a grove, nothing works unless done harmoniously. Practice cannot be isolated, but must be carried out in such a manner that it deepens one's connection and opens one's heart to the world. Hsing Yun's recognition of the potency of the people is really the backbone of his acute sense of popularization, possibility, and public relations in the spreading of Buddhism in modern society.

The traditional Buddhist temple was generally either deep in the forested mountains or at the end of a blind alley, and always a picture of somberness. Devotees either could not find it or would not dare to make the difficult journey. The monastics hardly ever stepped outside the monastery grounds, and they often appeared stern and uncaring. Fo Guang Shan and its branch temples have changed standards and created a distinctive, pleasant, and upbeat temple image. As well as being places of worship, they function fully as premises for socializing and study. Some visitors even come away with a sense that any place can be ground for preaching. A few of the lecture halls are even upstairs from so-called "beauty parlors" and the like. About these institutions, Hsing Yun says with a laugh, "It's hell below and heaven above. Let's hope the people will get promoted."

The newly opened branch temple in Taipei is right by Sungshan Train Station. Parking space is plentiful. The five stories below the fourteenth floor house the shrine, conference room, meditation hall, dining hall, reception room, audio-visual room, gift shop, and art gallery. Directions outside the elevators are precise and clear, and the volunteer guides are very helpful. Plenty is always going on, and visitors are more than welcome to participate. In a little over a year the temple has gained the notable favor of devotees in northern Taiwan.

> *Wherever red dust[79] rolls,*
> *Bodhi is taught.*
> *Wherever the heart is pure,*
> *Meditation is complete.*

Hsing Yun looks to the day when there will be no shortage of temples to visit so that Buddhism may truly take root in the lives and minds of all.

Affinity Before Buddhahood

Hsing Yun's affinity with millions of devotees and friends from all walks of life was not cultivated in a single day. In the minds of these people, the Master's deep yellow robe and towering figure are "awe-inspiring to view and heartwarming to be near." And to them, every move he makes reflects a childlike purity.

"Affinity with fellow humans comes before the attainment of Buddhahood." Fo Guang Shan today is best summed up in the verses that Hsing Yun composed for its main shrine:

> *Coming from the ten directions,*
> *Going to the ten directions,*
> *In the ten directions, all endeavors shall be completed;*
> *Thousands of people cultivating,*
> *Thousands of people contributing,*
> *For the hundreds of thousands, affinities shall be made.*

Part Four

SPREADING THE DHARMA TO LIBERATE ALL BEINGS

Handing down the abbotship of Fo Guang Shan to
Venerable Hsin Ping, 1985.

Visiting the ancient piramid while propagating Dharma in Egypt.

Hsing Yun enjoys the sights of Holland with devotees.

A grand welcome by the locals while visiting Ladakh, India.

The Buddhist Visiting Party of R.O.C. departs for South-East and
North-East Asia, 1964.

Master: "Protecting lives is better than releasing them after their
capture."

Reaching out to refugees in northern Thailand, 1988.

The Dalai Lama visits Hsi Lai Temple, 1989.

Never one to emphasize self-importance, he ensures that all living beings are content.

Meeting with His Holiness Pope John II for a Cross-Century Religious Dialogue, 1997.

Presenting flowers to victims of the Nanjing Massacre, 2000.

Developing good affinities with the children of Cambodia, 2002.

Director of Thailand's Puttamonton Dr. Amnaj Buasiri invites the Master to plant a bodhi tree, signifying the planting and growth of Mahayana Buddhism on the land of Theravada Buddhism, 2002.

Attending the groundbreaking ceremony of Kaohsiung County Chen Fu Shan Community, 2003.

Chapter 13

The Passing and Receiving of the Baton

*A*s the months and years have passed from the pioneering period, Fo Guang Shan has grown from infancy to assume the vigor of young adulthood. Hsing Yun, parent-like, thought the time was ripe for it to move forward on its own. He was determined to pass the abbotship on to Venerable Hsin Ping, his first disciple among the bhiksus, on the eighteenth year of Fo Guang Shan's founding.

A Historical Moment

September 22, 1985 was a moment of historical transmission at Fo Guang Shan. As day was breaking in southern Taiwan, there was already a sea of devotees gathering in front of the Main Shrine. Plainly clothed seniors, casually dressed youths, and formally attired men and women waited quietly, all kneeling with palms joined. In reverence, they heeded the sounding of the bell and drum and the chanting of a dozen young monastics before the Buddha, all eagerly awaiting what would be the grandest Dharma Transmission Ceremony in the history of Buddhism in Taiwan.

At ten o'clock sharp, with the sun shining brightly and thousands of devotees watching, Hsing Yun, accompanied by senior Venerables Yueji and Wuyi as witnesses, unrolled the Dharma scroll and started to read aloud the names of all the ancestral patriarchs of the Linji School. He then handed down the abbot's cassock and alms-bowl, the constitution and rules, the jade scepter, the Dharma staff, and the whisk—all emblems of the abbotship. Upon receiving these, Venerable Hsin Ping pledged the following before the crowd:

> *The Master's heart shall be my heart; the Master's resolve shall be my resolve.*
>
> *[I shall] abide by the monasterial rules and ancestral directions to spread the Dharma in benefit of all sentient beings.*
>
> *Receive people from all ten directions and spread the spirit of Fo Guang Shan.*

At that, the sound of music rose and thousands of doves flew skyward. Those in the crowd below were warmly receptive of the new abbot, and yet they felt reluctant to part with the Master.

Accompanied by the new abbot, Executive Director Venerable Tzu Hui, and over one hundred abbots and abbesses of the branch temples, Hsing Yun bade farewell to the Buddha in the Main Shrine and then took the path down the hill. As he walked on, he looked at the familiar objects and scenes around him.

Meanwhile, along the 0.6-mile path between the Main Shrine and the Non-Duality Gate, emotional devotees lined up. Many were very moved and pleaded:

"Master, take care!"

"Master, come back soon!"

"Master, don't forget about us!"

Waving good-bye, Hsing Yun held his smile to the end. Hard as it was to let go, hard as it was to walk on, one must walk on. With that, he vanished beyond the Mountain Gate.

Handing Over Duties

Hsing Yun had given the public only a month's notice prior to the actual transmission. But for those at Fo Guang Shan, it was an expected move, not a surprise. The new abbotship meant a transfer of duties, not a change in an established system.

Hsing Yun was not only the advocate of Fo Guang Shan's system, but also its facilitator. Clause twenty-two in chapter four of Fo Guang Shan's constitution states clearly: "The abbot of Fo Guang Shan is the director of the Religious Affairs Committee, serving a term of six years, with one reappointment by popular vote, and under exceptional circumstances, a second reappointment by two thirds of the popular vote." Hence, toward the end of his second term, Hsing Yun was already searching for a successor both from within and from outside the community. By the time he had completed his third term, his resolve to step down was unshakable. Venerable Hsin Ping was the unanimous choice to be the next abbot. Furthermore, monasterial supervisory laws require the presence of an executive director, a position that Hsing Yun had also assumed while holding the abbotship. Venerable Tzu Hui was appointed to take his place.

Venerable Hsin Ping, at fifty-eight years of age, had been a follower of the Master for three decades dating back to the Master's time in Ilan. He was tonsured in 1961, received the precepts under Master Daoyuan of Haihui Temple, Keelung, in 1963, and went on to attend Shoushan Buddhist College and the Chinese Buddhist Research Institute. In the early days of building Fo Guang Shan, Hsin Ping was stationed in the construction quarters. In 1973, he was named the head of Hsing Yun's male disciples. Admired for his melodious chanting and his kind, easygoing manner, Hsin Ping was the most beloved of the leading monastics.

Venerable Tzu Hui, age sixty and also from Ilan, hails from a prominent family. Acclaimed in Buddhist circles for her excellent capabilities, she played her role as executive director as no one else could. She began following Hsing Yun when he first set foot in Ilan forty years ago and has since been his personal interpreter in the Taiwanese dialect. She has certainly bridged the gap between Buddhism and the people of Taiwan. Venerable Tzu Hui graduated from Ilan's Lanyang Secondary School for girls with high grades and from Japan's Ohtani University with a Master of Arts degree in Buddhist Studies. She has also studied at Kyoto University in Japan. For many years, she has been on the faculty of the Chinese Culture University.

Rule of Law, Not of People

To clarify his intentions, Hsing Yun wrote this verse just before he handed over Fo Guang Shan at the age of fifty-eight:

> *Those of Fo Guang Shan are heading west,*
> *While Mojia[80]heads east.*
> *Coming and going in the same manner,*
> *In this world, the mind is always free even if the body is*
> *busy.*

Hsing Yun understands the affection of his disciples and devotees, but his mind remains calm. He firmly believes that only a well-developed system can ensure the continuous existence of a religious organization. At the Dharma Transmission Ceremony he stated frankly the four reasons for his stepping down:

- Rule should be established by law, not people
- No one is deemed indispensable
- Stepping down is not considered retiring
- Replacing previous leadership with new leadership reinvigorates Buddhism.

"I'm merely shedding the load of official commitments," he added. "A monk will always be a monk. I have no way of resigning as the Master!"

Probably the only thing that troubled him, other than the passing on of the baton and renewal of the system, were the astronomical debts that were now laid upon his disciple's shoulders. Hsin Ping, though, never spoke of these to others, nor did he say much about the burden. If many mouths had to be fed, he would do whatever he could to ensure that each one was sated. That was the resolve for which he was most celebrated.

For Fo Guang Shan, the transmission was representative of the new superseding the old, helping to make it a modern Buddhist institution. For the rest of the Buddhist circle in Taiwan, however, it was like a gigantic rock hurled into an otherwise calm lake. The rippling effect left a long, lasting impact.

First-Ever Term Set for Abbotship

Transference of the abbotship is a matter of course in the Chinese Buddhist tradition. The transmission can go by lineage; it is deemed the handing down of the Dharma. When transmission is done by inviting an eminent master from the outside to take over the abbotship, it is called the "monastery of the ten directions" or "passing on to the sages." For the time being, Fo Guang Shan has followed the lineage tradition. But then, who can tell what may occur in the future? And, why did its first transmission cause such a sensation?

In a rhetorical article published in *United Monthly Magazine*, Buddhist scholar Yang Huinan lauds the Master's decision and hints that others should follow suit. He further points out that the term system might not exist in the traditional Chinese Buddhist monastery, but the abdication of the abbot was not unusual, especially in an established monastery where transmission is an integral part of the operation.

Buddhist and Daoist temples and monasteries during the pre-Nationalist era were, at best, dubious in identity. Properties were never defined, the rich and powerful would assume propriety and run the sangha, or the abbot would simply refuse to let go. As writer Li Ao once put it, the elders in China would not only refuse to hand over the baton but they would also have the younger generation "batoned"! Current government monasterial supervisory laws, though tough, have ironically been the factor behind many conflicts between the laity and sangha. More often than not, an old abbot's death within his term sparks triple-party contention over monasterial properties among his disciples, his secular family, and the director of the temple. Litigation, fistfights, and other less honorable incidents make glaring headlines. In the end, monasterial serenity is no more.

Yang believes that Hsing Yun's abdication set the first-ever term for monasterial abbotship and pointed to a brand-new direction in monasterial management. "Those abbots who harbor the intent of being there for thousands of years," Yang writes, "will have a lot to fidget about from now on. Should they follow what is right willingly? Or should they hold on to their titles until death? Hsing Yun! O Hsing Yun, what a portentous example you have set!"

As it turned out, Hsing Yun succeeded in setting the tone for the ensuing abdication of a number of elderly monastics, like Songshan Temple's Master Linggen, Huayan Lianshe's Master Nanting, and Huiri Jiangtang's Master Yin Shun.

Living the Spirit of Passing the Baton

As Fo Guang Shan continues to flourish, Hsing Yun's disciples uphold the conviction of "success is not about the individual" and take pleasure in their supporting roles. The senior monastics, in particular, are seen manifesting their master's baton-passing spirit and are willing to take a back seat to their up-and-coming juniors.

Venerable Tzu Chuang, known for her industriousness in the founding of branch temples, turned Pumen Temple over to the younger generation of monastics ten days after its opening and proceeded on to another construction project. Venerable Yi Kung's continuing education at Tokyo University was arranged by Venerable Tzu Chuang, who also accompanied her there. When asked why Yi Kung was sent to such a prestigious institution while she herself had attended the less prestigious Bukkyo (Buddhist) University, Venerable Tzu Chuang simply replied, "That's the spirit of Fo Guang Shan."

One year, by coincidence, all the abbots and abbesses left their posts at the branch temples in Southeast Asia and Japan to join Hsing Yun on a lecture tour in Hong Kong. "Wouldn't the thought of being overthrown from your abbotship on your return faze you?" Hsing Yun asked Hsin Ping, smiling. "It's one of the worst military maneuvers, you know, for the entire leadership to be away like that."

"In that case," Hsin Ping replied, also smiling, "let's build a second Fo Guang Shan!" Everyone who heard the exchange laughed. It was evidence of the absolute desire of the Master to let go and the readiness of his successor to lead and delegate. No matter who is at the helm, everything shall proceed according to the system.

Truly Letting Go

Hsing Yun spent the first six months after he had stepped down in isolation in the United States, to enable a smooth transition. Over the past ten years, Hsing Yun has truly *let go*. Now he leaves the entertaining of guests at Fo Guang Shan to the abbot and all the construction and activities at branch temples to their respective abbots or abbesses. Whenever he is asked for his opinion, he always inquires, "Have you consulted the abbot first? What does he think?" He is neither compelled to intervene nor is he keen on giving advice anymore–a definite show of confidence in the system and its operation, and a show of support for the new leadership. "I can't stand people putting down the bowl but not the chopsticks," he notes. "Stepping down, one must absolutely let go."

Official titles mean little to Hsing Yun. Even though he is now relieved of all of them, he still works just as hard. "Editing journals, helping in the kitchen, and everything in-between," he says, "I promise to give it my best effort." One Lunar New Year, devotees were again expected to swarm Fo Guang Shan. A plot at the foot of the hill was allocated for parking so that devotees would no longer have to pay to park nearby. It was New Year's Eve, and everybody was busy with assigned tasks. Hsing Yun also requested that the abbot give him a job: painting in the lines in the new parking lot. By six in the evening, dinner was ready but he was not. He quickly lay down his work and went over to greet the hordes of newly arrived guests. Afterwards, he snuck back to the parking lot and picked up where he had left off. Not until four o'clock the next morning did he, together with a couple by the name of Tsai, finish eighty new spots for buses and eight hundred for cars. As devotees started to take up those spots one by one, it was at last time for Hsing Yun to go to sleep.

In another instance, the exhibition hall was vacated following the very first auction of calligraphy and paintings to raise funds for Fo Guang University. In the middle of the night, Hsing Yun and a handful of disciples rushed to the scene and set up another display so that visitors would have something fresh to look at the next day.

"Give a small chore to the competent," he explains, "and it

will be maximized; give a big task to the incompetent, and it will be diminished." Undeniably, he is a monk of the utmost competence.

Retreating as Advancing

Freeing himself from duties, the Master had plans to meditate and teach, to read and write. But the discerning had no problem predicting that, barely sixty and with his stamina, Hsing Yun could not possibly retire like that. Chang Peigeng, Secretary-General of the Chinese-Tibetan Cultural Association of the Republic of China and a follower who is two years his senior, shares that opinion. "He knew too well," Chang observes, "that no matter what he did at Fo Guang Shan, he would still be an abbot. He needed urgently to peck through the shell. By leaving the abbotship, he was in fact embarking on a new journey in his life." Hsing Yun's performance during the past decade has confirmed that view. He has emerged from his cocoon to create a global career in Buddhism as well as a radiant second spring in his own life. When asked to whom Fo Guang Shan now belongs, his answer is, "Fo Guang Shan is not owned by any one person, but it is yours to keep if you have it in your heart…I honestly don't feel as though Fo Guang Shan is mine. Rather, I feel the world, the universe are mine to keep, for I can lay it all down. In so doing, I can pick it up again."

Hsing Yun uses this Buddhist verse to illustrate his sentiments ten years after his abdication:

> *By hand, I plant an entire field with green rice seedlings,*
> *Lowering my head, the sky appears in the water.*
> *Purification of body and mind is the path,*
> *Stepping backward is actually moving forward.*

Chapter 14

Like Clouds and Water

*T*he most well-known masters in *Biographies of Eminent Monks* are categorized according to their cultivation, learning, preaching, asceticism, and so forth. Hsing Yun will be highly ranked among the preaching masters.

Buddha in His Mind, the Way beneath his Feet

With the Buddha in his mind and the Way beneath his feet, Hsing Yun has endured the unendurable in spreading the Dharma for the liberation of all sentient beings. When he took over the editing of Venerable Master Dongchu's *Life* magazine in the early years, he often traveled on foot to Sanchung rather than spend a dollar for public transportation. Sometimes he would oversee the formatter and printer at work for hours on end without eating anything the whole day. The unthinkable happened, when at the age of twenty-eight, he began to travel across Taiwan with his followers to promote the reprinting of the Tripitaka. To protect the valuable but heavy sound equipment from being bumped or broken, he carried it on his own lap all the way eastward. Consequently, he suffered a case of arthritis that almost cost him his legs. Another time, while en route to Kaohsiung to spread the Dharma, as the train conductor came around to collect tickets, he discovered that his ticket was nowhere to be found and he had not even a dime to pay for a new one. Instead, he had to hand over his fountain pen in lieu of the fare. Obtaining basic material needs was difficult enough at the time, let alone having to contend with the even more daunting task of breaking through the insulation and inflexibility that shrouded society at the time. Hsing Yun's resolve to spread the Dharma and liberate all sentient beings was to be challenged again and again.

Public gatherings under martial law were always mistrusted. In the shade or in front of the stage, men from the National Intelligence Bureau would lurk, chewing over each word for suspected treason, or breaking up the gathering on the pretext of a failure to pre-register the event. The speaker, though, soon learned that opening with praise about the leaders of the government would ensure the absence of prospective disruptions. Officials were equally suspicious of all campus activities, possibly an aftershock from the student movement that preceded the Communist era on the Mainland. Needless to say, Hsing Yun's Buddhist summer camps for college-level students in the 1960s were harassed, and attempts to speak on campus often barred. An already publicized engagement at National Taiwan Normal University was rescinded at the last minute without any explanation whatsoever. Many times, he demanded to know why Catholic and Protestant preachers were permitted on school grounds yet not the Buddhists, but he was given no more than a cold shoulder in response.

Prisons, too, were out of bounds. As much as the Buddhists longed to reach out and bring peace to those in confinement, political dissidents included, the conditions were not right. Similarly, the hope to preach to the armed forces and the police remained a dream. The government largely controlled the media, which did not appear to be any more accommodating. A day before *Gate of Faith*, the first national Buddhist telecast that was set to go on air in 1980, Hsing Yun learned that the visual part of his five-minute prologue would be deleted, leaving just the audio. The reason for this: monks were not allowed to appear on-screen. Trying to appeal his case with a cross reference to monks portrayed in the popular soap operas, he was denied on the grounds that he was not an actor playing the role of a monk.

Political, economic, and social progress within Taiwan has enabled the master preacher to spread the blossoms of Buddhism with perseverance and patience. Today, Fo Guang Shan and its branch temples are landmarks of Buddhist worship. Hsing Yun now takes the podium in the halls of government and other equally majestic venues. Twenty-odd years since its inception, the Buddhist summer camp for college-level students has received into the arms of the Buddha tens of thousands of youthful intellectuals, and in the process, produced the most promising talent for Buddhism. Invitations and pleas from academia are endless. Hsing Yun has also taught a course on religion and life at Tung Hai University, established and chaired a research center on Indian culture at the Chinese Culture University, and is responsible for the popularization of Buddhist studies among the new generations of intellectuals in Taiwan.

Buddhism in Prison Walls and among the Armed Forces

Speaking behind prison walls and among the armed forces is now routine for the monastics of Fo Guang Shan. The Department of Legal Affairs has conferred on Hsing Yun, the official title of "educator of morality." He has spoken at almost every prison in Taiwan. "Prison is really the best place for practice," he often tells those serving sentences. "Take advantage of your time here to repent with deepest sincerity. What freedom of mind it is to be able to regard your sentence as a practice in isolation!"

Once a timid young man came to see Hsing Yun. "Master, do you remember me?" he stuttered. "I was serving time five years ago when you came to speak. What you said turned my life around."

Another time, the Master received a red envelope on which was written: "An offering for the Master. In prostration, your disciple who has relinquished the wrong way for the right."

Spreading the Dharma among the armed forces, though relatively late in blooming, has been just as fruitful. The green light was not given until Hao Po-tsun took office as Chief of General Staff. Hsing Yun took the forces by storm when he toured the frontlines of Chinmen and Matsu in 1989 and was thereafter asked to speak by the Ministry of National Defense as well as the die-hard Department of Central Intelligence at a range of events.

With rapid growth in social diversification, freedom of expression, and the Buddhist populace, the media too, has rushed to amend their policy in favor of Buddhist content and the appearance of monastics. All three television stations in Taiwan are now more than glad to include Buddhist programs. Contrary to those times in the past when this monk bought air time for huge sums of money and the stations were thankless, they are now in hot pursuit of Hsing Yun and more than willing to reimburse him handsomely for every three-minute appearance.

Never Leaving for the Day

The Master's Dharma teaching has actually attained new heights during the ten years since he left the abbotship.

"The freeway is my bed and the car, my cafeteria," is how Hsing Yun likes to describe his style of travel. He used to set off from Kaohsiung just before dawn and return from his travels when the stars dotted the sky. In the sweltering heat of last July, he traveled all around Taiwan in three days: from Ilan, through Hualien, Taitung, Pingtung, Kaohsiung, Tainan, Changhua, Miaoli, Hsinchu, and Taoyuan to Taipei. He gave a total of eighteen lectures and greeted twenty thousand devotees. When the much younger members of the media touring with him were about to call it quits, the Master was apologetic. "I'm sorry to have caused you so much stress," he said to them. "I've been long accustomed to this. The body is tired but not the mind!"

Another time, Hsing Yun returned to Fo Guang Shan from Taipei at one o'clock in the morning. He was there to conduct a memorial service commemorating the twenty-ninth anniversary of the passing of the late Vice President Chen Cheng at six a.m. He returned to Taipei at noon, and then presided over a committee meeting for a fundraising concert and informal talks on Chan over a vegetarian meal. At midnight he was at long last able to leave for the day. "It feels good to be off!" the Master said, heaving a deep sigh. "Without any overtime compensation," his disciples chorused.

No time for idleness—that practically summarizes the Master's daily life. Under almost no circumstance will he take time off, for others would be let down. His right femur was fractured in a bathroom fall in 1991. He was hospitalized and underwent surgery in which the bone was set with four steel pins. A lecture scheduled a week later for a literary society was canceled, only to be reinstated three days later. Newly discharged from the hospital, he took the podium in a wheelchair on that day and spoke for a full hour. Many were moved to tears at the sight of his paleness and frail health. People were overheard saying, "Even if he hadn't uttered a word, this is simply the very best lecture ever. What cultivation!"

Around the Globe Two and a Half Times in a Year

Chasing the wind; racing the sun—that metaphorically describes Hsing Yun's life as a roving monk who takes the Dharma to the ends of the world.

According to his journal, it is estimated that Hsing Yun travels about a hundred miles each day and around the world two and a half times each year. In the summer of 1993 alone, he went to Russia, New Zealand, Australia, Hong Kong, England, Germany, Brazil, France, the United States, and Canada, across four continents in a single month. He is probably the most frequent flyer among Buddhist monastics. President Shih Yung-kuei of China Television, a longtime friend, once joked, "Looks like you don't need a passport anymore!" A couple of devotees once gave the Master two dozen pairs of reading glasses, pledging that each would be kept at a different location for his convenience.

Although the sun has its daily recess, this wandering monk does not. Adaptability must be instantaneous wherever he goes. Each year he averages a thousand lectures, conducts refuge ceremonies for some eighty thousand people, receives about a hundred twenty visiting groups and receives guests over a thousand times, writes about a million words, and records three hundred telecasts. "I seem to have some kind of micro-adjuster inside," he says of his own flexibility. "My mood and attention are automatically capable of attuning to changing time and space."

Let us tag along on one of his trips! The instant he sets foot in the airport, he is swamped with requests to chat or to have a photograph taken. Should a group show up for the latter, he holds his pose until everyone, even the occasional overzealous young female devotee, comes away with a satisfactory personal portrait with the Master. On-board the aircraft, the crew, as well as fellow passengers, take turns sending hearty regards. Once on the ground, he is swamped again—virtually buried alive in leis and bouquets, blinded by the flashing of cameras and deafened by greetings of well-wishers. Security is understandably tight throughout. Then he is sped on to the next public speech, the next reception of guests, the next lecture, the next conference. Every moment is occupied, and he does not seem to have a second to catch his breath. Finally, when all is finished, he takes leave of each place—only to have the crowds of devotees swarm around him again, though this time in the form of farewell.

Keeping Busy Is Cultivation

Venerable Tzu Chuang remembers the record Hsing Yun set, of visiting thirteen temples in Malaysia in one day. Guests were at the door first thing in the morning. Lectures were delivered non-stop. Later, devotees would not let the Master return to his hotel alone. The venerable herself did not get to speak with him until two or three in the morning. There were crowds to welcome him, to see him off, to dine with him, to bid him goodnight. He could barely find time to excuse himself to use the restroom. To ensure that others received joy, he joined them and ate one generous meal after another.

"All too often I just sleep with my robe on," he says. "And, waking up, I am lost as to where I am." Some blame it on what they perceive to be oversized ambition. Those who know him well, know that it is spirited resolve:

> *Let me borrow the past month, the past day*
> *To pay back this month, this day;*
> *Let me borrow the next month, the next day*
> *To make up for this month, this day.*

Despite the strength of his eloquence, Hsing Yun is nearing seventy and weakening physically. He gets tired and needs a break more frequently. Yet there is so much to do and so little time. "It's easy for me to go away and practice in solitude," he says. "But there is so much Dharma teaching waiting to be done. How can I take a break? Disciples look up to me as their role model. Should I recede, they would all follow suit!"

Let us look at a breakdown of his daily schedule: speaking

(lectures, classes, teaching, entertaining), eight hours; writing, four hours; travel, four hours; sleeping, six hours; eating, washing, and miscellaneous, two hours. As driven as he is, some might ask, how does Hsing Yun find time to practice? "Serving all sentient beings," he says, "satisfying the needs of all sentient beings, solving the problems of all sentient beings–keeping busy is cultivation. Anyone looking for leisure may find it in the grave."

Time Management

With keeping busy as the norm, time management is essential. In fact, Hsing Yun is proud of his punctuality, which was inspired by a passage learned in childhood from a textbook at a nearby English school: "Off to school in shirts and shorts, [let us] always [be] on the dot." The Master always wakes up on time for the earliest morning engagement, and he always leaves ample time for any appointment. Most unfathomable of all are the sessions he records for telecast, during which he maintains perfect timing in each of the four-minute shoots, has never had a retake, and never needs to be edited. To the awestruck crew it is as if "he carries a timer in his sleeve."

He is especially clever with planning and takes great advantage of intervals. The exceedingly harsh training he received in the monasteries—in which he would figure out how to ready his clothes, belongings, and bedding each night to enable himself to complete his toilet within three minutes the next morning—is the reason why, quite unruffled, he writes on planes, replies to faxed documents in vehicles, and chants the name of Amitabha Buddha as he drives by each power pole. With disciples rallying around, he reads documents, listens to reports, and gives verbal instructions simultaneously in order to make everyone happy.

The innumerable methods of practice always lead back to the path of the bodhisattva. A decade of traveling has scattered lotus seeds far and wide and sown infinitely good causes and conditions.

In 1988, Hsing Yun, together with a volunteer medical group, traveled into the remote mountains and barren regions of northern Thailand in order to reach out to the illiterate and neglected. He went from traveling in a large vehicle to a small one, then to a donkey, and even a borrowed military helicopter at times. To those refugees and their offspring of Chinese descent, he gave sustenance and medical care to their bodies, and the Dharma to eliminate suffering and cultivate joy in their anguished minds. Li Jianyuan, daughter of General Li Wenhuan of Northern Thailand's Third Army, was in the audience during one of Hsing Yun's presentations. She later visited Fo Guang Shan for three days and, on departing, became tearful. She said, "Master, what you did for us in Northern Thailand was give us another chance at life!"

Pearl of the Orient Awash in Buddha's Favor

The fruit of Hsing Yun's efforts is by far most visible in Hong Kong. The British colony is understandably peppered with Christian and Catholic churches, missionary schools, and hospitals. Indigenous faiths were once piteously undefined and best manifested in the immense following commanded by temples attributed to Huang Daxian and the like. The spread of Buddhism has been shouldered by a number of eminent masters. The endeavors of Masters Jueguang, Yongxing, Changhuai, and others in hospitals, schools, and senior homes are exemplary. But somehow, the average person remains woefully alienated from Buddhism.

Hsing Yun first taught Buddhism in Hong Kong seven years ago. Things have improved year by year ever since. These days, auditoriums are bursting at the seams. Officials at Hunghom Coliseum reserve three days annually for his Dharma lectures. The coliseum now proudly stands as "a pure lotus in the Fragrant Harbor." And, as always, his schedules are packed with requests for interviews from the media and the public.

The Master from Taiwan has helped to eradicate the erroneous public perception that monastics merely take without giving to society. Each year he actively participates in local charities by way of alms-round fundraising for the government, Tung Wah Group Hospitals, Po Leung Kuk,[81] and other institutions for the developmentally challenged.

As time goes on, more Dharma lectures by local masters are dotting public events, more notables openly acknowledge becoming Buddhists, and society has come to respect the sangha and the essence of Buddhism. The Pearl of the Orient is now awash in the favor of the Buddha.

Chiang Su-hui, Taiwan's Director of the Department of Information in Hong Kong and a resident of fifteen years, is sympathetic about the uncertainty of Hong Kong's future beyond 1997, and its people's quickened pursuit of spirituality. The timely entry of Hsing Yun into their lives and the stability and assurance he has given them are the reasons behind his soaring popularity among them.

As one of the major gateways for import and export trade between China and the rest of the world, Hong Kong has the best of both worlds, East and West. Hsing Yun has become dedicated to the city. With the fluctuating worldwide emigration of the people of Hong Kong over the last few years, Hsing Yun's impact, too, mushrooms in every corner: England, the United States, Canada, Australia, and even South Africa. He is extremely grateful to the people of Hong Kong. He believes that they have actually opened the way for spreading the Dharma across all five continents.

Merely a Monastic

As events of the decade continue their flow, the monastic who merely wanted to unload duties at the temple to focus on quiet cultivation, teaching, studying, and writing, has carved out a braver, newer world with remarkable causes and conditions.

The Dalai Lama once shared his sentiments about his Nobel Peace Prize saying, "I am just a simple Buddhist monk—no more, no less." Hsing Yun gave the same reply when asked about the transition from being the abbot of Fo Guang Shan to becoming a roving monk.

Endurance is reciprocation of the Buddha's favor; labor is for the benefit of all sentient beings. Each step of his feet leaves behind trails of lotuses, the rustle of his robe sweeps clean the path to the Pure Land. Like Master Xuanzang who traveled to India through 800 miles of deep sand on his white horse, vowing, "Better to perish taking one step west than to survive taking one step east,"[82] Hsing Yun is creating the latest chapter in the history of Buddhism through his own travels.

Chapter 15

Affection for the Isle, Heart for the Mainland

*W*ith Taiwan as the focal point, Hsing Yun's teaching tours in the past ten years have covered the world with the exception of the land he left behind four decades ago. On the Mainland, still under Communist ideology, religion is perceived as an antigovernment activity infused with superstition and backward practices. The government's preservation of a handful of monasteries and eminent masters is therefore only aimed at appeasement. On the other hand, the Nationalists, licking their wounds, had sworn to block all channels of communication with the Mainland. Consequently, not even the rapidly maturing Buddhist practice in Taiwan was able to find its way home. Not until the late 1970s did President Chiang Ching-kuo give his approval for family visits to the Mainland. In time, this triggered an economic and cultural exchange. These factors indirectly contributed to Hsing Yun's homecoming, and they also molded the position he would assume as the island and the Mainland started to "nudge" each other.

A Cough Drop, a Condition

Conditions can lead to such incredible happiness. The condition that led to Hsing Yun's homecoming was a mere cough drop. In 1986, during the sixtieth birthday gala for Thailand's King Bhumibol Adulyadej, Hsing Yun and Ms. Tien-Liu Shih-lun heard the severe hacking cough of a lady seated in front of them. She just happened to be the wife of Zhao Puchu, chairman of the Buddhist Association of China. Tien quietly pulled a cough drop from her purse and handed it to Mrs. Zhao. It pacified Zhao's cough in an instant and she was more than thankful.

Sharing the same roots, the encounter away from home touched off an instantaneous friendship between Mr. Zhao and Hsing Yun. That evening Zhao Puchu delivered an autographed copy of his works to Hsing Yun.

Zhao, over eighty years of age and highly ranked in public office on the Mainland, is an expert in Yuan opera and classical verse. He is one of the three foremost Chinese calligraphers of our time. A lifelong Buddhist, he has done his best to guard the Dharma even during the worst of times. Over the last few years, he has been especially dedicated to the revival and repair of severely damaged monasteries. One of Zhao's recent accomplishments is the construction of the towering bronze statue of the Buddha overlooking Lantau Island in Hong Kong. It is depicted on the front of the city's electronic subway pass and is viewed as Hong Kong's most updated cultural symbol.

Despite an age gap of twenty years, Zhao and Hsing Yun became close friends and agreed to meet again.

It happened two years later in California when Hsing Yun was working on two major projects at Hsi Lai Temple: 1) the Sixteenth General Conference of the World Fellowship of Buddhists and 2) the Seventh General Conference of the World Fellowship of Buddhist Youth. With a fondness for Taiwan and his heart in the Mainland, he struggled to bring both Buddhist organizations from Taiwan and Mainland China under one roof. He was hopeful that the ongoing conflict over Chinese representation[83] would end.

To avoid political overtones, Hsing Yun clearly stated in the invitation that each delegation would be representative of its organization, not its country. The only flags that would be flown were those of the United States—representing the host nation—and that of the World Fellowship of Buddhists. No other flags would be allowed. He also suggested that the titles of the Buddhist Association of Beijing, China and the Buddhist Association of Taipei, China, be used.

The ensuing negotiations, verging on collapse more than once, took a winding course before settling down to mutual acceptance of Hsing Yun's proposal. Setting aside their longstanding political deadlock, the two Buddhist organizations were finally able to compromise their differences and sit opposite one another at the conference table.

When news of the breakthrough was announced at the Opening Ceremony, it earned a standing ovation from more than five hundred delegates representing eighty Buddhist organizations in thirty countries. Representatives from Hong Kong and Southeast Asia also supported Hsing Yun's approach. Zhao subsequently invited Hsing Yun to visit the Mainland.

A Whirlwind Tour

This would be the first official visit by a Buddhist monastic to a country bound and shackled by materialist ideology for over half a century. How it was going to be justified to government authorities was the question. Lu Keng, a journalist much respected on the Mainland and in Taiwan and Hong Kong, returned to the Mainland to lay the groundwork. Finally in 1989, Hsing Yun led a Dharma Preaching and Family Visiting Group of the International Buddhist Progress Society to the Mainland. It started a whirlwind that swept across the land, and it opened the door to the bonding between Taiwan and Mainland China.

Academic consultants Charles W.H. Fu and Tang Degang, along with over seventy authors, journalists, and monastics, together with groups of devotees from the United States, Canada, and Singapore, formed a delegation of more than two hundred. Starting from Shanghai in the east, this group traveled to Tunhuang in the west, Beijing in the north, and Chengdu in the south between March 27 and April 25.

The U.S.-based author, Wang I-ling, records the *highly formalized*[84] official reception for the international Buddhist leader and his much-publicized tour:

> He shook hands and dined with every governor and mayor in every province and city he toured. No matter the time of day, droves of monastics and laypeople greeted him at train stations and airports. The red carpet was rolled out everywhere he went, and the bell and drum sounded as he visited each temple to offer incense and pay his respects to the Buddha. His motorcade was so popular that officials on bikes and on foot were needed to lead the way through the overwhelming crowds during the festivities at Longhua Temple in Shanghai.

Enraptured audiences listened to the Master's every word as he described the Chan mind and the nature of human beings. Also, at the joint invitation of Beijing, Qinghua, and Renmin Universities, he spoke at Beijing's National Library, causing a sensational and heartfelt response among those in attendance.

When they arrived in Sichuan, the name of the great monk from Taiwan was even on the lips of bustling shoppers.

"For years, the Nationalist government has been harping about fighting back," scoffed a reporter touring with him. "Today, against all odds, the Master has made it back!"

Indeed, Hsing Yun's presence as a speaker from Taiwan standing at the podium in the People's Hall was unprecedented. His trip restored faith and hope for Buddhists on the Mainland and impressed the Buddhist masters residing there.

A Breath of Fresh Air

Hsing Yun freely talked to the leaders of the Communist Regime, Li Xiannian and Yang Shangkun, about concerns over the pillage of religion during the Cultural Revolution. He requested that a religious policy be put in place and that monasterial management be returned to monastics. His plea was sincere: "As Communists, religious belief is not of importance to you, but it is to your benefit to at least understand religion."

To an appreciative Zhao Puchu, the visit was like "ten thousand miles of fragrant blossoms bearing succulent fruits." Abbot Xuefan of Qixia Temple in Nanjing was also deeply moved. He stated that, "[Hsing Yun's] rousing of the Buddhist morale from its long hibernation is exactly the breath of fresh air that Buddhism in China needs."

Hsing Yun impressed everyone. He was precise, thorough, erudite, and witty. Whenever he spoke to officials, Buddhist College students, or the public, his words of praise or advice were impeccable.

He also gave many generous gifts. To every monastic he encountered he gave a red envelope containing a monetary gift to foster good affinity and to many monasteries he donated his own literary works and sets of the *Fo Guang Encyclopedia*. He also presented a jade Buddha and two new cars to Qixia Temple and made a generous donation to the Gallery of Modern Literature. The Buddhist Association of China received a generous sum of money and a tour bus. To his hometown of Jiangdu and his master's hometown of Haian, he donated monetary gifts. And to schools and charities, he gave vehicles and ambulances for deaf and mute children.

Professor Wang Yao of the Dunhuang Research Institute and Central Institute of National Minorities in Beijing called Hsing Yun "the embodiment of altruism." "It's been one hearty embrace between the Master and the people of the land," Wang noted. He saw Hsing Yun's visit as a living symbol to a tormented, mortified nation that its innate spirit is alive and well on the international stage.

Dear, Dear Home

Finally, Hsing Yun returned to his hometown of Jiangdu.

Lu Keng, the publisher of Hong Kong's monthly magazine, *People*, stated that:

> It was the first time this journalist of fifty-one years saw a city empty itself onto the streets to salute someone. The rows lining both sides of the main street were three-people deep. Spectators were straining to see from buildings and people were perched in trees, all clapping and cheering. With this as a backdrop, Hsing Yun handed his mother a bouquet and grasped her hand.
>
> "I'm home!" He told her, and could say no more.
>
> "It's good to have you back!" she echoed. "It's good to have you back."
>
> Their tears seemed endless, faces reflecting what it had meant for them to be without each other. Mother and son then greeted the crowds from the balcony. A band of monastics delivered a trilling "Ode to Mother." Tang Degang and I recited congratulatory verses for the reunion.
>
> "I am Li Guoshen!" In plain Yangzhou dialect the popular religious leader reintroduced himself to his townsfolk using his hometown name.
>
> "Yangzhou has at long last come up with a truly fine human being!" murmured a teary elder.
>
> As Hsing Yun turned to depart, he was stopped by a well-groomed mother, who raised her baby to him. He bent to touch

the youngster's cheek with his own. At least twenty cameras must have captured that shot...

Despite her pride over brother Guoshen's achievements, sister Suhua, who now resides in Guangxi Province with her family, could not help but feel distraught by how long they had been apart. "I've turned gray," she said, as she strolled along the shaded path in Yuhua Tai Park in Nanjing, "and he's grown old, too. Still, he's but a child in my memory!" She has to fight back tears each time she relives their reunion.

On his return to Qixia Temple, the principal and teachers of the Vinaya college who had disciplined the fledgling Hsing Yun, received him with a ceremonial tribute. From his seat as the guest of honor, Hsing Yun rose to thank Qixia for its nourishment of the Dharma and benefit of cultivation. Weeping as he spoke, he shared a poignant moment with a muted gathering of disciples and devotees, "May the radiance of Qixia light up the future of Buddhism in China." Later he gave a lecture to the young monastics gathered there.

When he returned to Jiaoshan Temple, he joined those masters who had previously taught him how to pray and chant. He amused everyone with candid confessions of childhood follies and an occasional escape or two.

Far-Reaching Consequences

While aboard the yacht Emei along the Yangtze with Hsing Yun, Charles W.H. Fu, Professor of Religious Studies at Temple University, wrote about the revitalization of Chinese Buddhism and noted a revelation about the trip:

First, it indirectly indicates the stirring of Chinese Buddhism in response to external aid and timely conditions. Buddhist morale in the country has reached new heights as a result. The lift that Hsing Yun gave Buddhist circles was exactly what they needed. Buddhism was too economically suppressed to have bounced back on its own strength.

Second, it helps resume Buddhist cultural communication between the country and the rest of the world. While Buddhists from outside are astonished by the magnificent stone-sculptures of Dazu,[85] Sichuan, ancient monasteries, and other relics, Chinese Buddhist circles are being updated, through the gifts of publications, as part of the new progress of modern Buddhism.

Third, it helps resume Buddhist scholarly exchange between the country and the rest of the world. Hsing Yun's seminar with research fellows of the Chinese Institute of Social Sciences was the first one of its kind. Together they probed the extent of religious modernization, encouraged the interrelationship between religion and socio-economic developments, and urged scholars to overcome their prejudice and ignorance that "religion is merely superstition."

Fourth, it transcends the political reality between Taiwan and the Mainland. While the two continue to experience conflict over timeless political differences, a religious unification seemed the most likely, with Buddhist organizations serving as the ideal mediators.

Political enthusiasts in the media both in Taiwan and Hong Kong seized this opportunity to expound from different perspectives. They questioned the legality of his visit to the Mainland because of his status as a member of the Central Advisory Council. They speculated that Hsing Yun was playing messenger for the government of Taiwan and predicted that he would be bought by the Communist rulers. Aware of the generous donations that he had contributed, they accused him of trying to buy his way through the Mainland.

The Xu Jiatun Incident

All these speculations were mild in comparison to the disruption that was to occur one year later—the Xu Jiatun Incident.

Returning to Los Angeles, Hsing Yun and company stopped in Hong Kong to dine with Xu, who was then heading the branch office of the New China News Agency in Hong Kong. Xu, who now resides in the United States, is frank as he recalls their meeting: "I regard the Master as an eminent Buddhist figure, a high official in the Nationalist government, and a relatively significant target of diplomatic assimilation."

Jiangsu Province is home to both Xu and Hsing Yun. The former relates with fondness their first meeting, "Like old friends, we started to chat with the same regional accent." Hsing Yun then courteously booked their next appointment at Hsi Lai Temple, which Xu cheerily confirmed. Just prior to the June 4th Massacre, a thank you note reiterating the promised meeting reached Xu, who was somewhat tickled: "Hsing Yun's conspiracy letter is here."

Following the Tiananmen Square incident, the reformists were subdued while the government continued to rid themselves of dissidents. Xu, who had publicly sympathized with the student movement and never discouraged supportive demonstrations staged by his staff, was blacklisted for future retaliation. Dismayed over the lack of refuge offered within the system, he decided to take time off the following May and flew to the United States. He would accept Hsing Yun's offer to stay at Hsi Lai Temple.

Xu's disappearance shocked many on the Mainland, in Hong Kong, and in the United States. The people of Hong Kong had come to cherish and respect the man who had been at the helm of the city's branch office of the New China News Agency for seven years. Furthermore, the fifty-year Communist Party member was the highest-ranking official to flee since the flights of Wang Ming to the then Soviet Union in the 1950s and Lin Biao to Mongolia in the 1970s. The enigma of his whereabouts must have caused more than a few anxious, sleepless nights.

No one knew that Xu was at the temple until two weeks later, when Hsing Yun accompanied him on an excursion to San Diego and Las Vegas. Along the way, the two were spotted at a ghost town by tourists from Hong Kong. Before they knew it, their pictures were in the papers. The temple was bombarded with phone calls day and night asking about Xu.

As the situation became more urgent, Hsing Yun informed his guest, "Monastics don't lie. Since you're here with us, I can't tell people otherwise. Evading the calls won't solve anything either. We have to say something."

Xu subsequently gave consent for a press conference in which Hsing Yun and Lu Keng announced on his behalf, his four personal principles. They were: 1. no seeking of political asylum, 2. no violation of national security, 3. no interviews with the media, and 4) no contact with exiled members of the June 4th Movement.

Buddha Gate Open to All Those Who Suffer

When the issues were resolved regarding Xu, there were still many unanswered questions about Hsing Yun. How could a monk, supposedly above and beyond the three realms, become involved in such political turmoil? What was he after? Hsing Yun's attitude is one of "Let bygones be bygones." He has no regrets, for as the Buddha gate is one of compassion, it will be always open for those who suffer. "I've never treated Mr. Xu as a political personage," he says, "Just as someone in need."

Refusing to become embroiled in the strife of politics, Hsing Yun declined permission for a gathering at Hsi Lai Temple of exiled members of the June 4th Movement and the conducting of Buddhist services on behalf of the victims of the Tiananmen killings. However, the Communist government could not forget so easily. When Xu was officially expelled from the party the following year, he was also accused of being involved with subversive elements.[86] That was the extent of Hsing Yun's alleged guilt. Consequently, Hsing Yun was banned from the Mainland. The goodwill from his family visit and preaching tour vanished overnight. Buddhist circles on the Mainland remained quiet, and some hastened to disassociate themselves from Hsing Yun rather quickly.

The visitation ban lasted two years until Jiang Zemin annulled it. Hsing Yun was then allowed home again to see his mother, though not without the strictest protection[87]—a sign of sustained distrust on the part of the authorities.

Surprisingly, supportive affirmation of Hsing Yun during these troubled times came from Hong Kong, as it played a questionable role in the regards to its relationship with China. The Master placed just after Jiang Zemin and before Li Teng-hui in a public poll for the most newsworthy people.

Xu now lives reclusively in the United States. He often considers how much Hsing Yun has done for him, "For the entire time I've been here, the Master has consistently respected my privacy while attending to all my needs as far as personal health and daily life go."

Looking back, Hsing Yun's virtue and gallantry were undeniable to many. However, some cannot condone how he was dragged into political muddy water. The subsequent rift with the Communist government would considerably slow down the momentum from his first lecture tour and almost terminate all efforts to reinvigorate Chinese Buddhism.

Tangible Exchange

Hsing Yun has enjoyed attention in China like no other individual. His experiences in Taiwan will always be helpful should Chinese Buddhism be allowed to reinvigorate itself. Because of his popularity, the Communist government remains lukewarm towards him. It is clear to Hsing Yun that despite ostensibly opening the door to the outside world, the Mainland still has little tolerance for religious development. Buddhist temples have been reduced to aesthetic gardens and ancient relics, unaccompanied by any religious practice or belief. For more than a thousand years, Buddhism has been an undercurrent in Chinese culture, but to blossom again, it will have to wait longer for causes and conditions to ripen. Before that happens, Hsing Yun must spread as many bodhi seeds as he possibly can.

In the current context of tangible exchange, free issues of *Universal Gate* and *Awakening the World* are distributed regularly to the Mainland even though they might never reach their intended readers. The dozen or so letters each month from China requesting financial assistance for the sangha and monasteries are all answered. A joint effort between Hsing Yun and Pan Hsiao-jui provides annual scholarships for twenty students from the Mainland to study in the United States. Scholarships are also given to two hundred local Buddhist college students. Hsing Yun's publications continue to be widely reprinted, and *Universal Gate* is considered a gem in many monasteries.

Hsing Yun's latest project is publishing the *Anthology of Buddhist Scholarly Essays,* edited by Fo Guang Shan's Culture Council consultant Chi Kuang-yu. The anthology's content centers around the problems and future of Chinese Buddhism. Academics on the Mainland have been invited to contribute. The publication, to be produced in Taiwan and distributed on the Mainland, is anticipated to be an instrument of scholarly exchange between both Buddhist circles.

Tending to a Future Cause

As long as the Mainland continues with its economic advancement and political moderation, Hsing Yun foresees opportunities for communication. "All conscientious Chinese people want a unified China," he asserts. "It is not as if one side is swallowing up the other but rather a peaceful, equal form of unification."

"Prior to unification, attainment of the following must be complete: first, mutual strengthening of the economy; second, cultural dialogue; third, respect for religion; and fourth, political democracy. China isn't the exclusive property of a few. The country is the convergence of the majority."

On being labeled a unionist, he says: "No partisan politics for me, only this affection for Taiwan and this heart for China."

As a monastic, Hsing Yun does not intend to budge from the principle that "politics are politics and religion is religion." He hopes that both governments will tend to the future of the Chinese people with graciousness.

Part Five

Buddha's Light Held High

Showing former California Secretary of State, now U.S. Ambassador, March Fong Eu the site of Hsi Lai Temple, Hacienda Heights, California.

With graduates and faculty members of Hsi Lai University.

At the office of Diosdado Macapagal, President of the Phillipines, 1963.

With the President of the Commonwealth of Dominica, Clarence
Seignoret at the inauguration of Hsi Lai Temple, 1988.

The first-ever meeting with the leader of a Muslim country, Malaysian Prime Minister, Dr. Mahathir Mohammad.

Visiting Taipei International Book Exhibition at Taipei World Trade Center, Taiwan, 2001.

Delegates at the Buddha's Light International Association's
Seventh General Conference in Toronto, Canada.

Escorting the Buddha's Tooth Relic with the vice-abbot of Thailand's
Dhammakaya Foundation.

Special Photo Edition

Newsweek

THE INTERNATIONAL NEWSMAGAZINE

BUDDHA'S LIGHT INTERNATIONAL ASSOCIATION

APRIL 6, 1995

COCONUT PALACE MANILA, PHILIPPINES

WITH MASTER HSING YUN

On the cover of *Newsweek* and accepting an interview by the magazine, 1995.

Conferring certificates to new chapters during the Sixth General Conference of the B.L.I.A. held at the Hong Kong International Trade and Exhibition Center, 1997.

Singing on stage with B.L.I.A. adults, young adults, and scouts, 2002.

Opening Ceremony of the Eighth General Conference held at
Taipei International Convention Center, Taiwan, 2000.

Flags are raised at the Closing Ceremony of the Ninth General
Conference of B.L.I.A. held at Motosu Temple, Japan, 2002.

Chapter 16

The Dharma Coming West

*F*our decades ago, Buddhists were expelled from Mainland China. Hsing Yun rode the crest of Taiwan's economic boom and in doing so took the Buddha's light around the world. He traveled to Southeast Asia in the 1950s, Japan and Korea in the 1960s, Europe and the Americas in the 1970s, and to Africa in the 1990s. The globalization of Chinese Buddhism has become a historical reality, and its maturation has been phenomenal.

The construction of Hsi Lai Temple is perhaps the most momentous example of this maturation.

The Largest in the Western Hemisphere

Hsi Lai Temple is approximately twenty miles east of Los Angeles and twenty minutes by car from Monterey Park, also known as "Little Taipei." Spring breezes are always kind and gentle and daybreak is spectacular. Less than an hour's drive from the Los Angeles International Airport, the road gently winds through the hills of Hacienda Heights. One is then pleasantly surprised. The temple's golden walls and glittering rooftop tiles light up the entire area. The colossal Mountain Gate welcomes all who pass through it. The inscription, designed by its founder, reads *Fo Guang Shan Hsi Lai Temple*.

Officially registered in the name of International Buddhist Progress Society [I.B.P.S.], Hsi Lai Temple is a milestone that marks the Dharma coming to the Western world. In addition, it is a major platform on which traditional Buddhism plays out its social role in modern society. The temple sits atop fifteen acres. The sprawling 102,432 sq. meter structure was designed by U.S.-based architect Yang Zuming. The temple's groundbreaking took place in 1986 and it was completed in November 1988. To symbolize the continuity of the Dharma teaching and lineage over the centuries, Hsing Yun made a request for the traditional five-grain bricks from India, the sacred sand from the River Ganges, and soil from Fo Guang Shan. These traditional symbols of the roots of the Dharma were then incorporated into the foundation of the Main Shrine.

The palatial temple was featured in *Life* magazine, singled out as "the largest Buddhist temple in the Western hemisphere" and dubbed "the Forbidden City in America," in reference to its classic architecture. The temple was also the subject of a feature in *Reader's Digest* the following April.

Hsi Lai Temple carries the torch of Fo Guang Shan as a spiritual and cultural center in America. It is a learning ground of Buddhism for Westerners, and the convergence of cultures, both East and West. Devotees and visitors of all nationalities stroll the grounds each day. Lamas from India and bhiksus from Spain are frequent guests in the guesthouse, and exchanges in various languages and dialects reverberate beneath the Buddha's feet.

Marvelous Showcase of Eastern Culture

Because of its direct descendancy from Fo Guang Shan, Hsi Lai Temple has inevitably become a West Coast stopover for political and social celebrities from Taiwan. Former Chairperson Hao Po-tsun of the Executive Council, Legislator Kang Ning-hsiang, General Chiang Wei-kuo, Presidential Political Advisor Li Huan, and former Mayor of Kaohsiung Yu-Chen Yueh-ying are among a few. Once Hsing Yun told Chang Ching-yen, former head of the

Los Angeles office of the Coordination Council for North American Affairs: "Please feel free to utilize the facility for hospitality and entertainment purposes!" More importantly, the temple transcends the tension between the isle and the Mainland by providing a buffer zone. The temple has hosted many officials including Zhu Qizhen, China's ambassador to the United States; Xu Jiatun, former head of the Hong Kong office of the New China News Agency; Wuer Kaixi, leader of the June 4th Tiananmen Student Movement; and Peng Ming-min, one of Taiwan's most vocal political dissidents. Local notables also frequent the temple. California's former Secretary of State, Dr. March Fong Eu, in particular, marvels at such a fine presence in her home state.

Today Hsi Lai Temple showcases Eastern culture and is recognized as one of the main headquarters for the spread of Buddhism in the West. However, its inception was an incredibly difficult and daunting struggle, which is typical of any pioneering effort.

The seed was sown when Hsing Yun first came to America as a guest during its Bicentennial Celebration approximately twenty years ago. The country's cultural diversity and openness made a lasting impression. Hsing Yun saw the need for a spiritual anchor serving the numerous Chinese immigrants in the United States. However, Hsing Yun also had to consider whether the West would come to accept Buddhism. He was still affected by the sometimes violent and intrusive manner in which Christianity was introduced to China during the last century. Could Buddhism be peacefully taught in the West?

Inspired by the urging of eager devotees, Hsing Yun sent Venerable Tzu Chuang, accompanied by the English-speaking Venerable Yi Hang, to the United States with $50,000. The two were to explore the possibility of building a temple in America. Venerable Tzu Chuang, as it turned out, was utterly taken aback as she learned, firsthand, the price of real estate in California. A single house could easily sell for $70,000 to $80,000 at the time. Considering the entire endeavor too costly, she was ready to return to Taiwan when instead, Hsing Yun joined them on their quest in California. They eventually located a church building for sale. While disciples ruminated over the notion of having to convert a church into a Buddhist temple, the Master immediately finalized the purchase with $20,000 down payment. To him, a building designed for religious purposes would only make things easier, not harder. With the down payment, the loan application was soon approved, and the beginning of a new venture for Chinese Buddhism in America was established.

The monastics repaired the walls and painted images of the Buddha. The first chanting session drew devotees from a great distance, and the ensuing gatherings filled the temple each time. Due to its success, the Baita Temple was established in Maywood, California. This laid the causes and conditions for a grander facility.

The Resistance of Hacienda Heights

Hsing Yun's longtime follower, Chang-Yao Hung-ying, was the major driving force behind the vision. Her $300,000 donation, combined with that of others, helped purchase a hilly property in Hacienda Heights. However, the application for the state of California's approval to begin construction met with tremendous resistance from the affluent, conservative, and predominantly white suburb. The resistance of the community of Hacienda Heights was bitter. Residents were concerned about everything from the annihilation of the natural landscape, disturbances from the chanting and festivities, the potentially negative impact of monastic attire on the young, to the safety of their own household pets caused by the mistaken belief that Chinese Buddhists dine on dog meat.

Subsequent legal proceedings took the form of six public hearings and over a hundred explanatory sessions. Discussion centered on concerns that the temple would be too big, or too tall, or the colors would clash with the surrounding neighborhood. Actually, the legal issues masked the true motivation behind many of the proceedings, which was a fear and distrust of a different culture. This was occasionally expressed with rock throwing, name-calling, and a general lack of understanding or respect for the intentions of the temple community. However, Hsing Yun, long skilled in insight, tolerance, and perseverance, waited patiently for things to improve. Community representatives were invited to informal chats and tours of the site. The Master, too, demonstrated his sense of community by leading disciples and devotees in many community service programs, and showing that the temple was committed to sharing funds with local charities. Slowly, the local residents put aside their suspicions, touched by all the temple was doing. During one of the public hearings, a Protestant minister literally pleaded on behalf of Hsi Lai Temple, proclaiming, "My wife is Vietnamese. She hasn't passed a day without crying about missing home since coming to America. I hope this can be a place where she will find solace."

Home for the Buddhist Body and Mind

Hsi Lai Temple was established after a decade of struggle. Well-wishers both within and without Buddhist circles offered their genuine congratulations. A message from U.S. congressman Matthew G. Martinez read: "The majestic Hsi Lai Temple will not only benefit its devotees and the local community with endless activities but also bridge the gap between the cultures and thoughts of East and West." Venerable H. Ratanasara, the executive president of the American Buddhist Congress added, "Hsi Lai Temple is destined to be the lighthouse for the spread of Buddhism. A supreme glory for the Dharma in the Western Hemisphere."

The temple set the stage for worldwide Buddhism when it hosted the Sixteenth General Conference of the World Fellowship of Buddhists. This would be the first time the conference was held outside of Asia.

During the past ten years, Hsi Lai Temple has evolved into an international and multifaceted center of cultural exchange. There the Buddhist population in America finds sanctuary for its spirit and stability for its body and mind. Temple activities include Dharma functions such as the Great Compassion Repentance Ceremony (which takes place monthly), the Eight Precepts Retreat, the Seven-day Amitabha Retreat, and many Buddhist lectures. Counseling provided by the monastics assists immigrants in finding solutions to their daily problems and helps them with the emotional and psychological frustrations that arise with the adjustment to a new culture. Sociologically speaking, the temple is where social interaction and social identification occur for many among the American Buddhist population.

Each Lunar New Year, devotees of Chinese, (with roots in the Mainland, Taiwan, and Hong Kong), Vietnamese, and Cambodian heritage join others of various backgrounds to pay homage to the Buddha. Many individuals drive two or three hours for the occasion. When the temple's 200 parking spaces are filled, many must park quite a distance from the temple and walk uphill to the main gate. An incredulous bystander jokingly described the spectacle, "One closely behind another, they're like a line of focused, homecoming ants!"

Visitors are welcome to lodge at the guesthouse and are treated with genuine hospitality. One immigrant was allowed to stay there until he found a job and settled into his own residence.

To enrich the life of the entire community, the Hsi Lai Cultural Training Center offers classes in floral arrangement, vegetarian cooking, tai chi, Chinese zither, calligraphy, and the Dharma. To assist working couples that attend services, a daycare center for children is being considered. An ideal weekend pastime for neighboring families is learning a craft or two, making new friends, and enjoying the vegetarian cuisine served at Hsi Lai Temple.

Coming from Near and Far

To serve Westerners who have traveled from near and far seeking the joys of the Dharma, Hsi Lai Temple sponsors Buddhist camps and English Dharma classes and hosts dinners for community residents. The temple also provides simultaneous English interpretation for all regular Dharma functions. Western devotees account for approximately twenty percent of the three hundred people who annually participate in the traditional refuge ceremony that marks the official recognition of oneself as a Buddhist. Temple participation continues to increase with the most recent record showing 20,000 temple members. The distrust and hostility expressed over a decade ago have been replaced by congeniality and enthusiasm. On average, 18,000 visitors from educational, religious, and professional groups visit the temple each year. Seventy-five percent of the visitors are from the United States and the remaining are from Europe and other continents. Comprehensive guided tours in English are provided for groups, or the individual visitor may use a handy headset complete with an instructive CD to guide himself around the beautiful temple grounds.

Last year, five large and thirty-three small conferences, were held at the temple. Composed of Buddhist, civic, and educational groups, all were happy to take advantage of the temple's spacious location and up-to-date facilities. However, not only have others come to the temple to conduct their business, but the temple's role has been extended beyond its walls as well. A California State Council meeting was inaugurated with a Buddhist Purification

Ceremony presided over by Hsing Yun.

Mondays and Thursdays on Channel 53, telecasts of weekly features and updates revolve around the topic, "Buddha's Light Coming West." The benefits of increased efforts by individual devotees to translate Buddhist literature into English are having a positive effect within the non-Chinese speaking community as well. For instance, Vice Chancellor Wayne Huang of Los Angeles City College has just published an English translation of the *Diamond Sutra* and *Heart Sutra*.

The five-year-old Hsi Lai University, temporarily accommodated in the temple, is a small and specialized institution of higher learning with a distinguished faculty. Attending classes conducted entirely in English, students pursue bachelor's degrees in Buddhism and master's degrees in religious studies. In the words of Vice President Venerable Tzu Hui, "Many of the most respected schools are one hundred to two hundred years old. It takes at least fifty years for any institution of higher learning to even begin to establish itself. The growth of a respected university takes a long time, so Hsi Lai University has a long, long way to go. But I have every confidence it will succeed."

French cyclist Bénédict Storme, originally intending to spend ten years traveling around the world, stopped at the temple gate midway through her travels two years ago and still remains there today. Although raised Catholic, she has taken both the Five Precepts and Bodhisattva Precepts at Hsi Lai Temple and studies at Hsi Lai University. "I used to be so frightened of the unknown future," she says, recounting the impact of Buddhism on her life. "Twice, I saw my own life imperiled. But I'm a Buddhist now and am no longer fearful for I know that the Buddha resides in my heart, not just in the temple."

Karl Uth, a Buddhist of German descent, is preparing to publish German translations of the Master's writings in his home country. He has spent countless hours of work to complete them. Not satisfied to stop there, he has also begun planning an early retirement so he can devote all his energy to Buddhism. In addition, Uth is presently in the process of donating a scenic family property in Germany for the site of a new temple. With construction slated to be completed in three years, it will serve as a base for the spread of Buddhism in Germany.

A Global Network

Like the Master, Hsi Lai Temple has never failed to keep its word to the surrounding community over the last ten years. Aware that loud chanting may offend neighbors, the temple always does so in a quiet and serene manner. Temple grounds are kept immaculate and pleasing to the eye for those who pass through as visitors and friends. Donations of funds and books are made to local schools on an ongoing basis. An example of Hsi Lai Temple's sincere concern for the well-being of the community was demonstrated by the swift organization and allocation of funds to those in need after the recent disastrous earthquake in Los Angeles. Conference facilities and services are free to educational and cultural organizations. Real estate prices in Hacienda Heights remain stable despite the general economic slump. The Chinese community believes that "it is safe to be around Fo Guang Shan."

The small step that Hsi Lai Temple has taken is one gigantic advancement in the evolving history of Buddhism. Patterned after Hsi Lai Temple, other Fo Guang branches have spread throughout the world, including twelve in Asia and thirteen in the United States and Canada. Others have sprung up as well in London, Berlin, Paris, and Switzerland. The International Buddhist Progress Society (I.B.P.S.) has also been established in Queensland, Australia and North Island and South Island in New Zealand. Brazil and Paraguay are the newest branch organizations in South America.

Venerable Hui Li, the first Buddhist monastic in the history of Buddhism to spread the Dharma in South Africa, is currently planning construction of Nan Hua Temple in South Africa. Last September, Hsing Yun conducted the historic ordination of ten African Buddhist monastics in South Africa, many of whom hold doctorates and other academic credentials. For Chinese Buddhism, this was the epochal spreading of the light to the vast African continent.

Hsing Yun, with much humility, attributes the rapid spread of Buddhism to several facilitating causes. First, government policies in Taiwan since the mid-1970s have relaxed, resulting in the emigration of very well-educated and affluent individuals abroad. Second, there has been increased immigration to the British Commonwealth countries from Hong Kong, where concerns over post-1997 uncertainties have intensified. Third, the influx of refugees from Indochina countries has continued. All of these immigrants of Chinese ancestry who are Buddhists, have needed a haven for the mind. It has been with their support that Buddhism has been able to survive and grow.

Fulfilling Dreams

Facing the future, Hsing Yun acknowledges the long and winding road ahead of him. Historically, Buddhism in America did not reach beyond the devotees of Asian descent until 1893, when the Parliament of the World's Religions met in Chicago. The first Buddhist organization in Europe, the Buddhist Preaching Society of Germany, was not formed until 1903 in Leipzig, Germany.

Buddhism, which was first introduced to China from India, required more than 400 years of adaptation and harmonization within Chinese thought and culture before evolving into the "Chinese" version of Buddhism. Likewise, it might take hundreds of years before Buddhism will take root and be able to exert influence in other countries. Therefore, the training of teachers to introduce the Buddhist faith throughout the world will be essential.

In light of this, there are already many monastics pursuing higher education abroad. Venerable Yi Fa is expected to be the first bhiksuni with a doctorate from Yale University, and Venerable Hui Kai is a Ph.D. candidate in religion from Temple University. Six years of teaching the Dharma in America has convinced Venerable Hui Kai that in order to open others' minds to Buddhist teachings, one must first take into account their background, culture, customs, habits, and circumstances. Therefore, he has actively explored all aspects of Western culture—including religion, philosophy, sociology, and their interrelation—and studied other religions such as Christianity and Hinduism.

Knowing his master's goals for him, Venerable Hui Kai resides in a predominantly non-Chinese suburban neighborhood, befriends Christian ministers, and speaks often at neighboring institutions. He closely follows the daily news in order to gain a picture of the American mentality pertaining to the economy, education, family values, gun control, drugs, and the like. In the process, he reflects on what the Dharma can do to help alleviate problems in America.

Sharon Silver, an ardent admirer of Chinese culture and an elementary school teacher, first visited Fo Guang Shan more than ten years ago. Each year she invites her good friend, Venerable Hui Kai, to speak to her class about the teachings of Buddhism. At the conclusion of the class, students are invited to participate in a simple meditation exercise. Mrs. Silver is always astounded to see her restless students, who rarely settle down for more than a minute, sitting still during the entire exercise. From the Dharma, these children learn the proper Buddhist etiquette for the classroom: they rise before each class and join their palms together to greet their teacher. They have even learned how to greet and thank their monastic mentor in Chinese. Last year, their welcoming song for Venerable Hui Kai touched him deeply; it was "Fo Guang Buddhists in the Four Seas"—sung in Chinese, of course!

Integration of Buddhism and Western Culture

Chan meditation is therapy for both the body and the mind. Meditation is becoming increasingly popular in the West. However, when compared to Tibetan and Thai Buddhism and Japanese Zen (introduced to the West by Dr. D.T. Suzuki, whose scholarly works were extensively translated into English), Chinese Buddhism in the West has been a late development. One can only wonder what Buddhism will be like 500 years from now and which school will be the major source of influence at that time.

The Dalai Lama also addressed the same question following the completion of Hsi Lai Temple: "Interest in Buddhism in recent years has led to the construction of Buddhist places of worship in the West. We must be aware that, like the integration of Tibetan Buddhism and Tibetan culture or that of Chinese Buddhism and Chinese culture, Western Buddhism must integrate with Western culture. Integration of Buddhism with the existing culture facilitates societal acceptance and practice. So long as the fundamental doctrine remains intact, integration is only beneficial to and supportive of the normal development of Buddhism. While we practice, we should learn to respect other religions. This is especially vital for those of us who are new in our faith. Let us remember that personal inner cultivation and progress are far more important than superficial appearances."

Three Decades of International Efforts

Hsing Yun began dissolving international boundaries much earlier than one would have expected. He was only thirty at the time. In an article for *Awakening the World*, he wrote of his plans to lecture internationally and proposed training English-speaking teachers of the Dharma. During the next two decades, he would travel to India, Thailand, Malaysia, Singapore, the Philippines, Hong Kong, and Japan, laying the groundwork for the worldwide dissemination of Buddhism. On one occasion, in a refuge ceremony in Malaysia, offerings by devotees took three hours to complete. Another time, 3,000 people packed themselves into Dewan Tunku Abdul Rahman, which only has a capacity of 2,000 seats, to hear Hsing Yun speak. "What happened this evening," stated Penang's Chief Minister Tan Sri Dr. Koh Tsu Koon in the opening speech, "reaffirms my resolution to put up an indoor stadium with a 10,000 seat capacity, so that when Master Hsing Yun teaches in this city again, everyone who wishes to attend will be able to."

Buddhist devotees in Islamic Indonesia, vowing to remain vegetarian for three months, ultimately convinced the government to lift the ban on the public teaching of Buddhism. Consequently, Hsing Yun was able to speak to a historic gathering of over a thousand Buddhist devotees.

Last year in San Francisco, the Master's lecture on the *Heart Sutra*, with simultaneous translation by Venerable Hui Qun, amazed his American audience. Journalist Lu Keng observed, "In developing Humanistic Buddhism, founding the Buddha's Light International Association, and organizing international events, you're the master of social movement. What we have failed to notice is that you are also a profound Buddhist scholar."

The globalization of Buddhism has united Buddhists worldwide. It is also a form of religious diplomacy with disciples and devotees of various branch temples acting as informal diplomats. Fo Guang Shan's branch temples even surpass the number of Taiwan's foreign consulates worldwide. The language experts of Fo Guang Shan include over a hundred of those conversant in English, over sixty in Japanese, over forty in Cantonese, and others in German, French, Spanish, Portuguese, Tibetan, Thai, and Malaysian. "I'm afraid that Fo Guang Shan's pool of foreign language experts," Chiang Hsiao-wu, former consul to Japan, once lamented, "is more diversified than ours."

Fo Guang Shan also influences overseas Chinese communities. In Paris, most residents of Chinese descent are concentrated in the 13th district. Because they are incredibly busy running their businesses, it is difficult to congregate even 200 people for a Dharma function. Yet when Master Hsing Yun conducted a refuge ceremony there, over 2,000 members of the Chinese community were present.

Bodhi Seeds from the East

Two thousand years ago, the Buddha spent four decades propagating Buddhism across the five regions of India. Today, Hsing Yun, with the selfsame spirit, has continued to spread Bodhi seeds from the East to the rest of the world. He is truly able to "let the Buddha's light shine through the great chiliocosm, and to let the Dharma water flow across all five continents."

Chapter 17

Buddha's Light International Association

What differentiates a human from a Buddha?

Buddha is a sanskrit word for the Enlightened One.

It was well over 2,500 years ago that Sakyamuni Buddha attained enlightenment while meditating seated on the diamond throne beneath the Bodhi tree and gazing into the starlit skies. He awoke to the innate goodness of all living beings, which is simply hidden or obscured by the five desires and three poisons. During the next forty-five years, the Buddha taught the Dharma in an effort to bring the deluded back to their true nature. Buddhism was then introduced to China, Japan, and Korea in the north, and Sri Lanka, Thailand, among others in the south.

Presently, Hsing Yun, expending a lifetime to uphold the Buddha's teachings and to transform Humanistic Buddhism into a reality, has come to realize that the sangha alone cannot revitalize Buddhism. Buddhism's growth can only be enhanced through the combined efforts of the sangha and lay community. Empowering the lay community became his goal after he had stepped down from the abbotship of Fo Guang Shan.

Correct Knowledge and Correct View

A Buddha's Light member can be a member of the sangha, a student, a teacher, an attendant, a devotee, or anyone sharing a good affinity with Fo Guang Shan. Hsing Yun had the vision in the early 1970s that Fo Guang Shan would not simply be the creation of another school of Buddhism. He hoped to establish a consensus and a set of principles so that Buddhists would have correct knowledge and correct view, thereby raising standards.

The next decade witnessed Taiwan's unprecedented economic growth, societal diversification, and universal education. At the same time, Buddhism, after decades of cultivation and effort, was finally coming into its own. For the first time, the Buddhist lay community was composed of business, political, and academic leaders.

Buddhist scholar Cheng Chen-huang points out that Buddhism in Taiwan appears to be developing extremely well, when in actuality, it is like loose sand–scattered because it lacks a strong group of leaders to organize the lay devotees. Hsing Yun agrees with this assessment and believes that the number of monasteries and monastics are limited. To let more people enjoy the benefits of Buddhism, the participation of the vast number of devotees must be recruited.

As the community of Buddha's Light members has expanded for nearly three decades, the branch temples have continued to be at the center of Buddhist practice and refinement. The temples provide social education in conjunction with public institutions, emphasizing that religion and life are interwoven at all times. After martial law had ended, democratic policy was introduced in Taiwan by President Chiang Ching-kuo,[88] which allowed people to form public organizations. The causes and conditions were perfect for the continuation of the spirit and principle of Fo Guang Shan.

Alliance of Sangha and Devotees

The Buddha's Light International Association (B.L.I.A.), R.O.C. was formed on February 3, 1991 in Taipei. It was another pioneering feat in the history of Buddhism.

How would the organization be assimilated into Buddhism and society at large? In essence, the B.L.I.A. is a manifestation of Hsing Yun's long-standing concern for the continuation of social involvement and a society lacking in order, values, and faith. He is optimistic that with the sangha and the laity joining forces, people will be assisted in their study of the Buddhist Tripitaka and in upholding the Five Precepts. As a result, society will be able to achieve a state of purity and serenity.

Hsing Yun was specific about his direction for B.L.I.A., R.O.C.:

> People used to think that Buddhism was mainly for monastics, not for laypeople. The creation of B.L.I.A., R.O.C. marked the transition of a Buddhism for the sangha-only to a Buddhism for everyone. Buddhism will no longer be isolated from the world. B.L.I.A., R.O.C. will re-energize Buddhism and benefit the people.
>
> In the past, people believed that there were Buddhists only in Taiwan. However, due to the establishment of B.L.I.A., R.O.C., it is now possible to spread Buddhist teachings to every corner of the world. In the past, even if a layperson had developed a very deep understanding and practice of Buddhism, they were still viewed as spiritually inferior to any monastic. Only by becoming a monastic could they assume the status of a teacher. The coming of B.L.I.A., R.O.C. enables qualified devotees to assist others in their spiritual growth and contribute to the happiness and prosperity of society and nation by teaching the Dharma.

That is, B.L.I.A., R.O.C. has encouraged the direction of the development of Buddhism to proceed from:

- monastics to lay devotees
- temple to society
- self-cultivation to altruism
- a tranquil state to an active state
- disciple to teacher
- Taiwan to the rest of the world

Those who understand Buddhism know how much vision and courage are required to promote such ideals. In traditional Buddhist circles, monastics are thought of as superior and laypeople as inferior. B.L.I.A., R.O.C. emphasizes the inclusion of laypeople in "shouldering the responsibility of the Tathagata." This could easily be misinterpreted as the decline of monastic sovereignty. However, Hsing Yun is not inclined to submit to the pressure of convention or to promote class distinctions. Hsing Yun believes that monastics and laypeople should share equal importance and join hands in bringing Buddhism into a new era.

The Mushroom Effect

Built on the solidity of Fo Guang Shan, B.L.I.A., R.O.C. began with a membership of over 3,000. Across Taiwan, there are four district chapters located in the north, central, south, and east. Based on location, these chapters are further divided into subchapters. In addition, there are lateral branches such as Tainan's Buddha's Light Subchapter for teachers, the Tathagata Subchapter established within the Immigration Department, and the Precious Light Subchapter organized by finance and business professionals.

The mushroom effect has been phenomenal. Hsing Yun once sanctioned the establishment of fifteen subchapters in one single day. Membership is categorized into individual, group, and preliminary. There are also family and associate memberships. The list of benefits is extensive: Buddhist studies, career and general counseling, social activities, consultation for weddings, funerals, etc. No matter where you go, as soon as you see the golden vest embroidered with the nine-petal lotus trademark and introduce yourself as another B.L.I.A. member, you will immediately perceive such kindred warmth.

The inauguration of the Buddha's Light International Association World Headquarters a year later on May 16, 1992 at Hsi Lai Temple in Los Angeles, was in response to the rapid growth of Fo Guang Shan overseas. It also illustrated the strength of the B.L.I.A. as an international organization.

Manifesting the Impact of Buddhism

Four thousand members representing fifty-one districts from thirty countries on five continents were present for the opening ceremony of Buddha's Light International Association. Many international dignitaries also attended. This was a milestone for the further development of Buddhism into the next century. During the inauguration ceremony of the B.L.I.A., Sir Clarence Seignoret, President of the Commonwealth of Dominica; Dr. March Fong Eu, Secretary of the State of California; Mr. Jung-chi Chung, Chairperson of the Social Workers' Association; and Venerable Sharma Rinpoche of Tibet came to celebrate this auspicious event. To commemorate the occasion, Monterey Park Mayor Samuel Kiang expressly proclaimed May 16, 1992, the city's Buddha's Light Day.

The festive gala was a historic union for the Buddhist sangha and devotees. Participants came from countries and regions such as China, Japan, Korea, India, and Tibet. The various schools within Buddhism were also represented, such as the Northern and Southern schools and the Sutric and Tantric. Nishihara Yuichi, the President of B.L.I.A., Tokyo, elatedly said, "In a single day, I've become friends with 4,000 fellow Buddhists."

Prior to the opening, Los Angeles had erupted with riots in the inner-city due to severe racial unrest. The turmoil shocked the world and intimidated visitors. It was against such a backdrop, at such a time, that Hsing Yun founded the B.L.I.A. Headquarters. He rallied Buddhists from all countries and races in "joy and harmony," in true openness and mutual acceptance. In stark contrast to the violence, Hsing Yun's attitude exemplifies the peace and tolerance of the Buddhist doctrine.

At the end of 1994, the international organization of B.L.I.A., founded by the Chinese Buddhists, consisted of one head association,[89] seventy-nine chapters,[90] and seventeen preparatory committees.

The Omnipresent Buddha's Light Member

B.L.I.A.'s golden vest worn by people of all races is living proof of the prevalence of the Buddha's Light members everywhere. The B.L.I.A.'s five-color, striped flag symbolizes the ultimate transcendence "across ten directions and throughout the three time periods." It now flies in fifty-one countries and regions on all five continents: these include Canada and the United States; Central and South America; the Commonwealth of Dominica, Brazil, Paraguay, Argentina, and Costa Rica; France (Paris), England (London), Switzerland (Zurich), Germany (Berlin), Russia (St. Petersburg), and Holland; South Africa; Australia and New Zealand; Taiwan, Japan, Hong Kong, Macao, Malaysia, the Philippines, Indonesia, Thailand, Singapore, Sri Lanka, Sikkim, and India.

Why has the B.L.I.A. spread so rapidly? Legislator Pan Wei-kang, a member of the Board of Directors of B.L.I.A., R.O.C. and a veteran of board meetings, marvels at the open-mindedness and delightful harmony that typify the association's meetings. Vice President Chang Nai-pin of the Los Angeles Chapter, founder of a social service hotline in Taiwan, speaks for the Chinese community in America. She says, "The presence of B.L.I.A. calms the anxiety of living overseas, uncovers the infinite treasure of our minds, and links together the hearts of every Chinese person around the globe."

Hsing Yun, known for his organizational capabilities, has devised for B.L.I.A. an ingenious developmental strategy that serves a dual function. First, influential public figures are invited to chair the local chapters and help recruit local members. Second, both regularly scheduled and special activities are designed to encourage individual participation. For example, to assist the members of the Chinese community in Germany, most of whom are in the restaurant business and do not have the time to socialize, Venerable Man Che of I.B.P.S., Berlin, has established a nonalcoholic happy hour. It is held from midnight to two in the morning each Tuesday. Participants are able to forget the discomforts of kitchen grease and the noise of the workplace with a friendly chat, a Dharma class, or a philosophical exchange. President Ting Cheng-kuo of the Berlin Chapter was among the many thankful attendees of these gatherings. After completing the refuge ceremony with Master Hsing Yun in Paris, the 2,000 plus participants immediately became B.L.I.A. members as well.

Awash in the Dharma Rain Together

Membership is approaching one million, and more and more Buddhists of other races and origins are joining the B.L.I.A.

For example, Fred Webb, one of three vice presidents of the Los Angeles Chapter, has been diligent in his service and devout in his faith for the past two years.

Approximately thirty English-speaking members who make up the Hsi Lai Subchapter hold group discussions on Fridays at the home of B.L.I.A. President, Al Duffy. They also attend the English Dharma Class each Sunday. Duffy, who is of Scottish descent, has taken the Five Precepts and is proud to be Buddhist. He volunteers at Hsi Lai Temple, and greets all he meets by lowering his head, joining his palms, and saying with his American accent: "Ni hao, Omito Fo!"[91] His visit to Fo Guang Shan made such a strong impression on him that he is planning to become a Hsi Lai Temple resident in two years. The thirty-year veteran in marketing is preparing himself for more active participation in spreading the Dharma among the English-speaking community.

Not just another religious body, the Buddha's Light International Association is also a cultural bridge leading from Taiwan to the rest of the world. For example, when the Second B.L.I.A. General Conference was held in Taipei's Linkou Stadium, 30,000 representatives from around the world assembled. President of the Republic of China, Li Teng-hui addressed the audience. The international visitors were invited on an excursion to see present-day Taiwan. This was another outstanding public relations event.

Hsing Yun hopes that eventually there will be a hundred more national headquarters; and the entire world shall bask in the Buddha's light and all humankind will be awash in the Dharma rain.

Integration and Coexistence

The theme of the Second B.L.I.A. General Conference emphasized the richness of B.L.I.A.'s universal message of integration and coexistence. Its theme originated from the important Buddhist principle of cultivating universal kindness and compassion.

Hsing Yun elaborates: "When I came to Taiwan four decades ago, I was called a monk from the Mainland; after four decades, I'm still called a monk from the Mainland. Then, when I returned to the Mainland after an absence of four decades, I was called Master Hsing Yun from Taiwan! After years of traveling in America, Europe, and Australia, however, I don't see the bridge of my nose rising or my eyes turning blue; nor has anybody called me American or Australian. I can't help but wonder where I belong.

"It is all self-interest and intolerance, I've come to realize, that brews conflict among nations and biases between races. So long as the planet Earth doesn't desert me, I'm willing to just be an earthling. After all, we are all members of the same human family. So let us treat male and female, old and young as one; let us treat rich and poor, noble and common as one; let us treat all cultures and races as one. Buddhists should not limit their philanthropic activities to other Buddhists alone; the Chinese should not limit their aid and assistance to other Chinese alone. Let us all share the same existence on Earth.

"The concept of integration and coexistence gives hope and security to those who live in this turbulent age. At the opening of the Paris Chapter, President Jiang Jiming of the Third Subchapter tried to articulate the inner struggle he experienced as a multicultural Chinese person. "I'm Chinese-Cambodian, but I fled to France when the Communists took over my country. However, China wouldn't acknowledge me as Chinese. Back home, Cambodia would not acknowledge me as Cambodian. Now that I live in France, the French will not acknowledge me as French either. For the longest time I was pained and disheartened. That is, until what the Master said struck me. I finally got it! I need to grieve no more. From this day on, I'm simply going to be an open-minded, compassionate, joyful, and generous earthling."

The Beauty of Affinities

The tolerance and selflessness exhibited by the B.L.I.A. under Hsing Yun's leadership, has enabled the organization to extend its influence as far as Moscow in the upper north to the mountain city of Ladakh, India, 15,000 feet above sea level. Venerable Sanghasena, President of Ladakh's Buddhist Association, recounts what it feels like to be part of the B.L.I.A.: "I've served for eight long years in Ladakh, but my reputation, my influence, and my efforts had no way of reaching beyond it. Now, as Vice President of the B.L.I.A. Ladakh Chapter, I am able to make contact with Buddhists the world over."

In addition to providing devotees with everything ranging from a spiritual haven to study and discussion groups, lectures and cultural trips, meditation classes and visits, the association opens windows in their lives. Feng Derong, who works in the Department of Economy and has just taken over the presidency of the Precious Light Subchapter from his wife Guo Lifen, is equally animated when discussing the B.L.I.A. He says, "Although I am in Taipei, I can communicate with the whole world. How global networking maximizes the space and scope of life for me!"

Behind B.L.I.A.'s charitable undertakings is an all-embracing theme: All living beings belong together. The various branches in the United States responded immediately in providing emergency relief for recent disasters, such as the flood in the Midwest and the fire in Los Angeles. During the winter before last, the Los Angeles Chapter donated 300 relief packages of everyday necessities to the homeless, who were then given shelter by the First African Methodist Episcopal Church in South Central Los Angeles. The sight of these tired, unkempt people, some curled up in fetal position, receiving help from the Buddhists so moved Reverend Murray that he said gratefully, "This is a flight across the gigantic racial and religious gap, and the transformation of love into a beautiful affinity."

Such Potency of Resolve

As Hsing Yun handed over the abbotship of Fo Guang Shan to ride the crest of yet another set of causes and conditions, he was swept to an even broader and wider platform. Indeed, those who give to others reap the rewards.

Watching him travel from place to place as he establishes one B.L.I.A. branch after another, one has to wonder how he has survived. Hsing Yun has had to adapt, maximize his use of time, and bear the unbearable. A flight from New York to Sao Paulo, Brazil took twenty-six hours instead of the scheduled eleven due to engine problems. Another time, almost everyone in his party became ill with acute mountain sickness due to Ladakh's high altitude. In Ladakh, the temperature ranges from thirty-seven degrees Celsius in summer to subzero degrees in winter. The annual rainfall averages ninety-two millimeters (3.6 inches). While others rested, Hsing Yun continued to conduct ceremonies and visit with guests in spite of having a splitting headache, swollen cheeks, and shortness of breath.

Hsing Yun's fortitude propelled the three-year-old B.L.I.A., R.O.C. to gain recognition as one of the most outstanding organizations in Taiwan for two consecutive years. In 1994, the B.L.I.A. placed first out of almost 2,000 candidates. Additionally, it is the world's fourth largest private organization. Notably, the B.L.I.A. is in the process of applying for nonpolitical group membership in the United Nations, even though Taiwan is not currently a member of the United Nations. The B.L.I.A. may break the diplomatic deadlock.

Of Wheels, of Wings

The big brother of Buddhist circles, the Chinese Buddhist Association, is slowly being replaced by the B.L.I.A. It has been speculated that the B.L.I.A. is Hsing Yun's declaration of independence after years under the oppression of the Chinese Buddhist Association, and possibly even a challenge. He has never formally responded to this idea except to say that, "the founding of the B.L.I.A. does not conflict with the Chinese Buddhist Association.

It is like the implementation of a courier service on the freeway system, both of which are good."

In reality, the two *are* different. The Chinese Buddhist Association consists primarily of monastics, while the B.L.I.A. consists of lay devotees. Many are members of social and intellectual circles with a more cultivated and progressive attitude toward their faith than traditional Buddhists. Hsing Yun ensures that devotees play the lead role with monastics lending support and guidance to the devotees.

Under the guidelines of Hsing Yun's perspective of Humanistic Buddhism, monastic-run temples collaborate with the devotee-run B.L.I.A. For a strong foundation, the sangha is the cement and the devotees are the sand and stones. In order to make any progress, the two must work together like the wheels on a cart and the wings on a bird.

A century ago, British colonists sailed the four seas, and through military conquest, built an empire where "the sun would never set—its flag rising wherever the sun rises." A century later, a Chinese monk emulating the compassion, wisdom, vows, and practice of the four great bodhisattvas,[92] sowed seeds of the Dharma throughout the world. With peace and tolerance, he founded the Buddha's Light International Association, thereby letting the Buddha's light shine and Dharma water flow wherever the sun rises.

Chapter 18

Holding Space
in an Embrace

Religion is one aspect of human civilization that is constantly evolving into new forms along with ever-changing cultural and social structures in different times. For example, Christianity evolved into both Catholic and Protestant schools. The Western church has many branches, sometimes formed out of bloody conflict. History records innumerable battles between warring religious factions, leaving deep scars that affect people even to this very day. It seems that, religion has not yet developed a cure for the prejudice and selfishness of humankind. Living beings have yet to learn compassion and tolerance on a grand scale.

Many Doors to Cultivation

Buddhism is an ancient religion. How did it develop?

Over 2,500 years ago, Sakyamuni Buddha taught various methods of cultivation in accordance with the diverse natural capacities of all living beings. After he entered nirvana, disciples interpreted his teachings based upon their own understanding, and ultimately, compiled a written record of his teachings. Later generations of eminent masters have studied these works and formulated their own interpretations, resulting in various Buddhist schools.

In the footsteps of masters who traveled to teach the Dharma, Buddhism was introduced in the south to Cambodia, Burma,

Thailand, and Sri Lanka, developing in Theravada Buddhism. In the north, in the countries of China, Japan, Korea, and Vietnam, it developed into Mahayana Buddhism. In the process, the Buddhist faith interacted with the cultural and social conditions present at the time. Additional subdivisions were established, as evidenced in Japan, which has over fifty schools.

Buddhism in China was introduced during the reign of Emperor Ming of the Eastern Han Dynasty [58–75 C.E.]. It intermingled and harmonized with the existing philosophies, Confucianism and Daoism, and ultimately blossomed into eight primary schools, each with its own practice, and emphasis–as illustrated by the following verse:

> *Tantric for the rich,*
> *Chan for the poor,*
> *Pure Land for the convenience of all,*
> *Yogacara for the patient,*
> *Sanlun stressing emptiness,*
> *Huayan for orthodoxy,*
> *Vinaya for cultivation,*
> *And Tiantai stressing structure of doctrine.*

The Tiantai School emphasizes teaching and its organization. The Huayan, Yogacara, and Sanlun Schools emphasize textual study. The Vinaya, Chan, Tantric, and Pure Land Schools emphasize practice. The Tantric School is also known as Tibetan Buddhism due to its prevalence there. Tantric cultivation requires the guidance of masters, as well as generous offerings by devotees, which only the more affluent can sustain. The Chan practitioners, with their straw sandals and chipped alms-bowls, aspire to enlightenment by way of simplicity, frugality, and freedom from desires. Regardless of intellect, gender, or location, those who chant the

Buddha's name with utmost dedication shall attain rebirth in the Pure Land, which is why it is known as convenient.

Unlike other religions, each of the Buddhist schools was established through independent, spontaneous growth rather than through struggle and conflict. In China, all eight Buddhist schools took center stage to further enhance the cultural pageantry of the Sui and Tang Dynasties. More than once, fickle imperial favoritism ignited persecution of the sangha,[93] yet the harmony and respect between Buddhism and other religions, or among the Buddhist schools themselves, has never been tarnished.

One Master, One Way

Throughout history, some of the eight schools of Mahayana Buddhism faded while others emerged more vibrantly than ever. The evolution of Buddhism as an integral force in world history was undermined when the Southern, Northern, and Tibetan divisions drifted apart due to geographical and cultural factors, and barriers were established. Visionaries across the years requested the unification of teaching of all eight schools to establish harmony between the Sutric and Tantric,[94] and the dual practice of Chan and Pure Land. Hsing Yun made these dreams a reality.

Hsing Yun believes that there is only one founder, Sakyamuni Buddha, and only one direction for us to go. All beings should be mutually caring and supportive, nondiscriminating and collaborative. Modern Buddhism must be able to rely on the stability of this kind of outlook in order to foster its own growth and development.

Efforts during the past ten years have led to healing within Buddhist circles. A feat worthy of celebration was the friendship between Hsing Yun and the Dalai Lama.

In the past, due to political and cultural differences, Tibet was cautious regarding relations with Taiwan. As a result, the exiled Dalai Lama has never visited Taiwan. However, the construction of Hsi Lai Temple changed everything. This temple in the West played a key role in the developing relationship between the Tibetan sangha and devotees, and the emerging Buddhist populace in Taiwan. In July of 1989, the Dalai Lama and his entourage visited Hsing Yun at Hsi Lai Temple, where they chatted for over three hours. Their discussion was followed with a speech given by the Dalai Lama.

The following day, on the Dalai Lama's fifty-fifth birthday, Hsing Yun and approximately a thousand guests attended festivities. The Dalai Lama requested that Hsing Yun be seated next to him during dinner so they could continue their discussion. Those who attended noted the historic nature of the encounter and were encouraged by the atmosphere of the entire event.

In five days, the two eminent masters met four times and established a specific agenda: first, scholarships at Hsi Lai University for the Tibetan sangha and secondly, student exchange between Buddhist colleges in India, Tibet, and Taiwan. As a result, Venerable Yi Hua is currently studying at International University in India.

The Tantric and Sutric Join Forces

The meeting was no coincidence. It was the product of years of painstaking cultivation and the sowing of good seeds for the alliance of both Sutric and Tantric traditions.

Early in 1985, Hsing Yun initiated the Chinese-Tibetan Cultural Association of the Republic of China. Subsequently, a joint Dharma function of the two traditions for the preservation of the nation was held in Taipei. This was the cornerstone of the collaboration. Approximately ten thousand Chinese and Tibetan devotees were present.

The next year, Fo Guang Shan hosted the World Sutric and

Tantric Buddhist Conference to discuss harmony in relationship to the evolution of global cultures. Three hundred participants from nineteen countries and regions attended, including lamas and scholars from Nepal and India.

"Modern Buddhism is no longer regional or divisional," Hsing Yun stated. He presented his purpose for calling the meeting and said: "Buddhist development should be a harmonization between Mahayana and Theravada, between the lineage of both North and South, between the sangha and the lay community, of all four orders,[95] and between orthodoxy and modernity. However, the most crucial of all is the harmony between the Sutric and Tantric traditions."

The sad state of affairs in Tibetan Buddhism was clearly communicated when the head of the Tibetan Sakya School spoke: "Buddhism, which has been vital to the life of Tibet, has been devastated by the Communists. So I am especially elated to see it back on its feet in Taiwan."

This was the series of events that laid the proper conditions for the historic meeting between Hsing Yun and the Dalai Lama. During the following years, Tantric monastics were ordained at Hsi Lai Temple and many furthered their studies at Fo Guang Shan. Lamas and rinpoches also began to spread the Dharma in Taiwan. Hsing Yun's vision of harmony between the Sutric and Tantric traditions was finally beginning to take form.

Mahayana and Theravada Under One Roof

Sutric or Tantric, Mahayana or Theravada, Hsing Yun wants to see all schools united. The various schools of teachings resemble flowers with different hues and shades, which, when gathered together, form a delightful bouquet. "After all," he asserts, "there is but one Sakyamuni Buddha!" Hsing Yun's book of travels, *Traces of Wandering in the Seas and Skies*, indicates that he also visited the Thai monarch and the head monastic of Thailand in 1961. His visit has been reciprocated many times by visiting Buddhist dignitaries from that country. Due to his interaction with Theravada Buddhism, Hsing Yun became aware that not only has the status of female monastics depreciated in Theravada Buddhism, there is also no full ordination for bhiksunis. Consequently, he daringly proposed that the sangha of bhiksunis be restored.

In 1988, a remarkable number of Theravada participants attended the month-long Triple Platform Full Ordination Ceremony at Hsi Lai Temple. In the process, the wall of regionalism that has separated the South and North for more than a thousand years began to crumble. Those invited to pass on the precepts included eminent masters from the Southern and Northern Schools. Among the 200 or so preceptors were monastics of the Theravada tradition as well as disciples of the Tibetan Tantric Schools. Many of them were monastics of high seniority seeking to repeat their vows. Others possessed advanced academic degrees and were devoting themselves to Buddhism.

Mandarin, the Taiwanese dialect, and English were spoken for the precept ceremony, and those who took the precepts came irrespective of gender or school. So overwhelming was the number of participants, nations, and schools that the success of the event was unprecedented in the history of Buddhism.

At the end of the month-long ceremony, preceptors learned a great deal from a stimulating exchange among themselves in regard to traditions, concepts, ceremonies, discipline, and doctrine. Many regarded this event as the most inclusive and global experience thus far in the history of Buddhism.

Last spring, Hsing Yun visited a sister temple Thailand's Dhammakaya Foundation, for the casting ceremony of its golden Buddha. He was driven through streets strewn with flowers and lined with 100,000 people there to greet him. This was an unprecedented honor for a Mahayana monastic in a Theravada country. Consequently, Baita Temple in Los Angeles, which was the predecessor of Hsi Lai Temple, has been turned over to the Dhammakaya International Society of California to serve as the base of Thai Buddhism in America.

Others closely associated with Fo Guang Shan include Todai Temple in Nara, Japan; the Japanese Buddhist pilgrimage group; the Nichiren School; and the Soto School. Venerable Jung Woo of Tong-do Sa, Korea, heads the Asian Liaison Committee of B.L.I.A.

Dual Practice of Chan and Pure Land

Having achieved the harmony of both the Sutric and Tantric Schools, and the inclusion of the Mahayana and Theravada, Hsing Yun resolves to foster collaboration among all eight schools of Buddhism. He even chooses to view in a positive light the criticism of sectarianism from Taiwan's Buddhist circle. He states that it is an indication of prosperity and a sign of versatility. "Like the four legendary mountains in China coexisting over time," he says, "it is from the school of Sakyamuni Buddha that all Buddhists invariably descend."

Despite the similar dominance of Chan and Pure Land in Taiwan, Hsing Yun, being the forty-eighth Patriarch of the Linji School of Chan, will not be confined to a certain school. By creating the first chanting services in Ilan, he also boosted the Pure Land method of aspiring for rebirth in the Pure Land of Ultimate Bliss by calling on Amitabha Buddha's name. Hsing Yun is also given credit for the resurgence in popularity of the practice of meditation. Meditation instruction is now a regular feature in all branch temples of Fo Guang Shan. Fo Guang Shan's new meditation hall is the largest and best equipped in Taiwan and is already most renowned for its vigorous discipline. The Taipei Vihara, close to the Sung Shan Train Station, provides busy city dwellers with a convenient location for meditation practice.

Revering the Masters, Motivating the Newcomers

Hsing Yun is cordial and courteous to all the venerables and masters in Taiwan. Master Ching Kung was invited to the Tsung-lin University to speak on the concept of Yogacara and Master Liaozong spoke on the *Sandhi-nirmocana Sutra*. Master Dong-chu lectured on the monastic system. Master Yin-shun and Mr. Nanhuai Jin were both invited to teach the Dharma and conduct seven-day meditation retreats respectively.

Universal Gate magazine, headquartered at Fo Guang Shan, reports monthly on temples all over Taiwan and serves as a clearinghouse for communication throughout the Buddhist community.

Hsing Yun is very supportive of the new generation of monastics, and has encouraged the formation of the Chinese Buddhist Youth Association and the founding of Venerable Cheng Yen's Jingsi Vihara. Each time he lectures in Hualien where Jingsi Vihara is located, he opens by saying, "What a wonderful place Hualien is! The landscape is so lovely, and the air so fresh. Above all, Hualien is where the Buddhist Compassion Relief Tzu Chi Foundation[96] is!"

His advice for young monastics is to break the stubborn habit adopted by previous generations of not fostering communication amongst themselves. He urges dialogue and teamwork regardless of differing schools or opinions. The common goal is to bring Buddhism to new heights. Over time, many of the younger generation come to rally around these sentiments, showing their support by joining Hsing Yun on his lecture tours.

The Beauty of Religious Harmony

What does it mean to hold space in one embrace and measure worlds as numerous as the sands of the Ganges?

Hsing Yun upholds harmony both within and without Buddhism. He once described the human quest for the true, the good, and the beautiful as a journey to a common destination. The yearning being the same, it is only the means that differ. Whether we choose to bike, drive, ride, fly, or sail to get there, different religions are actually heading towards the same end.

Once, in the early years of Fo Guang Shan, approximately eighty Dominican priests and nuns traveled to Fo Guang Shan with the purpose of learning the Dharma. Two years ago, a bishop from the Vatican also visited. Hsing Yun and Archbishop Luo Guang once held a stimulating exchange on religion, philosophy, life, and faith. The two masters, both compassionate and wise, agreed that religions must be tolerant of one another. There will always be differences amidst similarities and similarities to be found amidst differences. In their mutual concern for the welfare of all and the purification of human minds, the respect and affirmation they had for each other was beautiful to behold.

Later, at the request of the Archbishop, Hsing Yun spoke about "The Wondrous Use of Chan" at Fu Jen Catholic University.

As a religionist faced with the recent chaos of society, Hsing Yun was certainly concerned, but wished to dedicate his efforts to improve it. On one occasion, at a gathering arranged by *Global View Monthly*, Hsing Yun was invited to join Archbishop Luo Guang, Protestant Minister Reverend Zhou Lianhua, and Vice Secretary-General of the Daoist Association Zhang Shengqi for an in-depth discussion on the reconstruction of social values as prevention against social disintegration.

Following the completion of the Taipei Vihara in February 1994, a forty-nine day lecture series was provided to the public. The series, entitled "The Running Water of Life," featured such animated speakers from various religions as Father Ding Songyun of the Catholic Institute of Guangqi She and Shi Yonggui, a Muslim. The event and the lectures offered were a wonderful display of the beauty of religious harmony.

On another occasion, Zhong Jongji invited many religious leaders including Muslims, Protestants, and Catholics to an event hosted by Hsing Yun for a discussion on Chan over a vegetarian meal.

Last year, Hsing Yun donated the royalties from his writings to six needy organizations. They were the Taipei Relief Foundation for Women, Sunshine Foundation, Xinlu Cultural Foundation, Christian Chenxi Society, Yiguang Society for Volunteers, and Shanmu Society for Catholic Nuns. With utmost sincerity, he later expressed, "To give is not just about asking society to give alms to Buddhism. We as Buddhists must give alms, too!"

Tolerance for Folk Religions

What about the numerous folk religions in the world?

Hsing Yun could not have phrased it better when he commented, "Correct belief surpasses superstitious belief; superstitious belief surpasses non-belief; and non-belief surpasses deviant belief."

Beliefs, like learning, vary widely in depth and sophistication. So long as a "religion" encourages people to do good, Hsing Yun believes that it is one to be valued.

Hsing Yun recounts:

I remember back home in Yangzhou, there wasn't a police station within ten miles or a courthouse within a hundred. So what could be done when people got into a dispute?

What happened was that the parties involved would pray at the temples of the earth gods and all would eventually be solved. The townsfolk were unwavering believers in the law of causality and harbored a perfect willingness to try their cases before the deities.

Although Hsing Yun has been viewed as an orthodox Buddhist, he has never perceived of himself as superior to others. Quite to the contrary, he affirms that deities such as Mazu and the earth god have given the common folk the correct mind. He takes a stance of tolerance and respect toward folk religions. However, he does not tolerate the charlatans whose practice does nothing but jeopardize the social well-being of others under the guise of possessing supernatural powers. They belong to what Hsing Yun describes as deviant belief because of the way they dupe well-meaning but naïve people into parting with hard-earned money for the supposed benefits of association with supernatural powers.

Buddhism is not superstition, nor is Hsing Yun superstitious. Many, speculating on the sophistication of his personal practice, bombard him with questions about divination, physiognomy,[97] and geomancy.[98] They are also curious about the supernatural powers he may or may not possess. These are his least favorite topics. Instructions in the *Sutra of the Teachings Bequeathed by the Buddha* direct the Buddhist practitioner not to engage in divination and not to practice astrology. These are not in accord with the Buddhist principles of causes and conditions, and correct livelihood. Therefore, one of Hsing Yun's favorite sayings is, "When there is joy in the heart, every day is a good day and every place a good place."

Ahead of His Time

History has been riddled with human strife and conflict, and all the world's wars have yet to awaken the innate goodness in mankind. As the end of another century looms, scenes of carnage and destruction have not ceased. This is most certainly a time when Hsing Yun's example can serve as a light leading us out of the darkness. The visionary and gallant Hsing Yun has expended half a lifetime patching and repairing Buddhism, bonding with other religions, tapping social resources, and creating a diversified and all-encompassing paragon. Ahead of his time, Hsing Yun sheds a light on peaceful coexistence among human beings.

Part Six

RETURNING ON THE WINGS OF HIS VOWS

Awarded the Top Honor Medal by the Ministry of Interior Affairs, R.O.C.

At the groundbreaking ceremony for Fo Guang University, 1993.

Master encourages members of B.L.I.A.—Y.A.D. Malaysia who visit
Fo Guang Shan for a "Searching For Our Roots Trip," 2003.

Celebrating his sixtieth birthday at Fo Guang Shan, 1987.

Always with a smile and tender loving heart for the young.

Greeted by B.L.I.A. members from all over the globe at the
General Conference.

With Australian dignitaries at the inauguration of Nan Tien Temple,
Australia.

The Master with devotees of Fo Guang Shan.

Conferring the Dharma Scroll during the Conferment of Mantle Ceremony for the Third Abbot of Fo Guang Shan, Venerable Hsin Ting, 1997.

Leading his disciples in an alms procession during the Ullambana Festival at Fo Guang Shan, 1992.

Dharma Lecture and Refuge Taking Ceremony at
Massachusetts Institute of Technology (M.I.T.) in 1998.

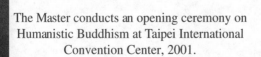

The Master conducts an opening ceremony on
Humanistic Buddhism at Taipei International
Convention Center, 2001.

At Fo Guang Shan.

Chapter 19

Heart of a Child

*O*nce somebody asked the Master, "What is the reality of life?"

"Life," he replied, "is half in the Buddha's world and half in the samsaric world; it is half advancing and half retreating."

Because he has mastered this *half-and-half* principle, at the end of nearly seventy years, he is able to:

> *Follow the heart and be carefree,*
> *Follow circumstances and be at peace,*
> *Follow joy and do everything willingly,*
> *Follow conditions and live life accordingly.*

Living in the Spiritual and Material Worlds

Considered by many to be enlightened above and beyond the three realms, Master Hsing Yun has chosen to remain engaged in everyday activities. To those who do not know him personally, he is as enigmatic as he is approachable. Understandably, many are eager to catch a glimpse of his personal life and private feelings. Those who know him concur that he has always been the master of his own heart; in his own independent way, he has managed to balance spiritual and material concerns.

In the early days of his monkhood, the teenaged Hsing Yun could not help but miss his mother, siblings, and home. However, since he had already renounced, the austere discipline and his master's high expectations did not allow him to go home whenever he pleased. Through this difficult experience, Hsing Yun learned to cope with his personal emotions with the help of religious practice. Later, on the eve of his flight from the Mainland, he chose to bid farewell and reveal his plans of spreading the Dharma in Taiwan to his master rather than to his mother. His family had not the slightest inkling of where he had gone to for over forty years.

In Taiwan, the pursuit of establishing schools and housing for the sangha, and sacrificing for the Dharma in myriad ways left little time for his individual needs. However, thoughts of his loved ones would often invade the stillness of the night. Ever since he reconnected with them a few years ago, he has taken upon himself the responsibility to care for them—a hundred or more relatives in all—as though he were repaying some mountainous debt of forty years. He was willing to bend in any way possible to bring pleasure to his mother, who was stunned when she eventually met the thousand or so monastics inhabiting Fo Guang Shan.

"Do they all answer to you?" she asked him.

"Yes," he replied, "but I answer to you alone!"

He made every effort to be with her on her birthday over the past two years. Back in Yuhua Vihara, Nanjing, the Master was but the son of a local family once again. He would devotedly cool his mother's porridge, or sit by her bedside and reminisce with her. A master of international repute then became the humblest of listeners.

Caught up as people sometimes are in the stress and strife of everyday life, we often find out too late that we have failed to appreciate the people and opportunities in our lives. A tree, about to fall down, finds the wind unceasing as ever; a child, prepared to repay his parents, discovers they are no longer around. While he treasures every chance to fulfill his duty to his mother, Hsing Yun regrets that he never had the opportunity to repay his teacher, Master Zhikai. It took him years to fully comprehend the profound caring and concern beneath the stern facade of his master, who was killed during the Cultural Revolution. On his homecoming five years ago, a stricken Hsing Yun broke down completely at the graveside of Master Zhikai; on subsequent visits, he has made it a point to go and chant a sutra there.

Repay a Drop of Water with an Overflowing Spring

To the mother who gave birth to him and the master who taught him the Dharma, Hsing Yun's grateful repayment to them is a matter of course. Hsing Yun bears in mind everyone who has ever helped or supported him, and he is sure to repay every single drop received with an overflowing spring.

It was a time of extreme turmoil when he graduated from Jiaoshan Buddhist College and became the principal of Baita Primary School in 1947. To evade the bandits, guerrillas, and soldiers, he was compelled to go into hiding with his teaching staff for days. A loyal worker at the school would bring them food daily at great risk to himself. Never has Hsing Yun forgotten him. On his first homecoming in 1989, he made a point of reestablishing contact with this worker. Eventually, Hsing Yun located the man's family, and braving a heavy downpour, visited them, bearing gifts and goodwill. "Even though the man who helped us is no longer with us," he told his disciples later, "his son is, and I'm no less grateful. That's why I have every reason to go on taking care of his offspring."

Another person to whom he shall forever be appreciative is Sun-Chang Ching-yang. From the time he came alone to Taiwan, to the founding of Fo Guang Shan, Mrs. Sun treated Hsing Yun as one of her own, and supported and protected the Dharma with all her might. During her last days, Hsing Yun took time out to be with her whenever he could. When he could not, he would ensure that his disciples would take his place. Upon her death, he conducted her funeral and undertook efforts to execute her will with utter meticulousness. Zhang Foqian, a writer, described the memorial service presided over by Hsing Yun for Mrs. Sun as the most impressive and solemn he had ever seen.

This tender care is extended to his teachers as well. As an expression of his gratitude, he had Masters Yuanzhan, Xuefan, Hechen, and Huizhuang flown to America. When Master Shengpu fell ill last year, Hsing Yun made sure that his Chinese language teacher was amply provided for and properly treated.

Although tradition has it that monastics are to see everything as empty and act apathetically, this is not quite Hsing Yun's way. When it is time to be warm and tender, his warmth and tenderness surpass that of most people.

More Than a Few Embarrassing Moments

Many wonder about the private world of his inner feelings. Those who have known Hsing Yun since the early days, and those who have chanced upon photographs taken in his youth, usually comment on the young monk's handsome and distinguished looks. His tall stature and piercing eyes, his stately bearing and eloquence, are all qualities that deeply ingrain themselves in the minds of others. The question arises then, as to whether a monk of his quality has ever been attracted to others in a way unbecoming a monk. Or, have others sought his presence as more than simply a Dharma lecturer?

A seasoned master today, Hsing Yun has no qualms about telling how, when he was a twenty-something monasterial director at Dajue Temple, overly doting parents were seized by the wishful thought of adopting him with the happiness of their daughters in mind. Often, they would try to dissuade him from pursuing the monastic life. More than a few young female devotees were seen to frequent the two temples, Leiyin and Shoushan, out of a special regard for the attractive young monk rather than for the Buddha.

Su Xiuqin, a longtime follower in Kaohsiung, recalls how she and others used to share the purest admiration for the Master's attractive Dharma appearance. Unlike some others, they were able to appreciate the Master for his spiritual contributions, drawing the line between their feelings for the Dharma and feelings of love. However, since female devotees are proportionately higher in Taiwan, the media would often publish rumors about Hsing Yun's secret life: his wife or his children. Although he has not confronted these rumors, they have unfortunately bought him some trouble. Over the past few years, he has dismissed these reports as sheer unfounded gossip, no longer allowing them to bother him.

One of the more extreme cases of unsolicited attention was that of a woman in her seventies who was obsessed with what she considered to be an ongoing relationship with the Master through seven lifetimes. One day, she dropped by Fo Guang Shan, and as usual, demanded to see the Master. This time, however, her two handsome young sons accompanied her. While on the grounds of the temple, the trio ran into the Master, who was giving visitors a tour of the premises. The next instant, the woman ordered the young men to get down on their knees, claiming, "This is your father! Quickly, call him 'Father.'" The young men, visibly embarrassed, had to comply. They later returned to apologize for their mother's mental instability. While Hsing Yun remained totally unfazed by the episode, it is anyone's guess what the members of his tour group thought.

An equally obsessive high school teacher used to approach the podium with copies of books midway through Hsing Yun's lectures. When asked about her intent, her reply was a cryptic: "I want to pluck that cloud from the sky."[99] Once she caught Hsing

Yun totally by surprise as he was waiting for an elevator. Emerging out of nowhere, she deftly reached over and adjusted the Master's collar for him, leaving everyone else present utterly flabbergasted. Unable to do anything about the bizarre incident, Hsing Yun simply proceeded into the elevator.

Yet another time, one of Fo Guang Shan's most ardent supporters suddenly announced her dissociation for the most ludicrous of reasons: the Master had supposedly taken a fifth concubine, or so she had heard. It turned out that the instigator of the vicious rumor was a former teacher at the nursery school who had been dismissed for misconduct. The Master did not have the slightest inkling of who she was.

Faithful for Half a Century

Throughout the half century since his tonsure, Hsing Yun has abided by the monastic precepts, and his conscience is clear in the face of temptation and misunderstanding. He has been faithful to Buddhism, never allowing any personal affection to distract him from the task at hand. He has been true to his commitment of sharing his love with all sentient beings. Deep within is a boundless world of sentiment, and his love is not for one, but for all. Hsing Yun says, "The monastic is committed to a more boundless and sublime expression of love. This love is for the benefit of all beings, not simply a partner or family member. All elders under heaven are my parents, all children are my own, and all people are my family." He wisely resists individual attachment while rendering his devotion to everyone, saying, "Unconditional love becomes compassion, while asking nothing in return is true wisdom."

Many seek to repay his kindness with demonstrations of love and respect. Unsatisfied with just a birthday party, devotees from every corner of Taiwan came to Fo Guang Shan on the Master's

sixty-eighth birthday in 1993 and gave him a three-night gala sa-
lute.

Love for All Creatures

He loves all creatures large and small. Pigeons have been
his favorite companions since he was young, and for years they
would stop by and feed on his windowsill at Fo Guang Shan.
Whenever he had to go away, he would prepare more feed or hand
over his tending chores to another so that the birds were constantly cared for.

Xiaojun, a stray puppy who took shelter at the Buddhist
College, displayed Buddha Nature by attending every lecture with
amazing concentration. As a young puppy, Xiaojun would always
rise at the approach of Hsing Yun but started to slow down visibly
as he advanced in years. One day, Hsing Yun was speaking with
students in the corridor when he spotted Xiaojun struggling to get
up. Out of consideration for the aging dog, the Master simply
slipped into an office, allowing Xiaojun to save his energy without
disturbing him any further.

Laifa, another puppy, was barely a month old when he was
taken to Fo Guang Shan. His home for the next six or seven years
would be at Hsing Yun's door. He stood guard there whether the
Master was entertaining or out lecturing. Then, one day, Laifa
was missing. Hsing Yun could not help but feel sadness. A few
months later, someone brought along another puppy, which strange-
ly enough, resembled Laifa in color, disposition, and even behavior. Everyone called him Laifa, Jr. Hsing Yun cared for Junior the
same way he did for Senior until the second Laifa died of old age.
A chanting service was held in his memory.

Keeping It Simple

Visitors at Fo Guang Shan marvel at how a temple can be so

magnificent, modern, and traditional, all at the same time. The aesthetic appeal of the temple is for the enjoyment and convenience of all. It is an extension of goodwill and, most of all, a reflection of the *progressive* movement of Hsing Yun's life. Yet if we examine how he conducts his daily life, we will see the traditional aspect of his life.

In contrast to the splendor of the temple grounds, the Master has different views regarding clothing. He lives by the maxim: "Simplicity is fundamental for a monastic." The Master alternates between a couple of robes all year round, adding thermal wear or a knit sweater underneath when temperatures plunge. A curious, small, centipede-like pattern on his left shoe was a tear, which he had neatly sewn back together himself. In fact, both shoes are quite battered in the sole, their linen padding showing through. When asked why he does not simply replace them, he quips, "They've been like this for a while. I guess they can't get any worse, can they?"

The manner in which he eats is sometimes astonishing. He will run into a room holding a bowl of steaming plain noodles, cool it before the air-conditioner, devour it, and then dash off to his next commitment. Hsing Yun has rushed through decades in this fashion, and it can be said that he has mastered the art of eating on the run. Dining with him is both a pleasure and a burden. While acting as host, he keeps helping his guests to copious amounts of food, yet he merely touches a couple of the dishes closest to him. He never replenishes his bowl by taking from more than one dish, and he completes his meal quickly.

A little-known fact is that Hsing Yun takes after his father, who was skilled in vegetarian cooking. On the long list of Hsing Yun's culinary creations—peanut tofu, tomato noodles, imperial bean noodles, and arhat soup–are among Fo Guang Shan's most popular dishes; all the cooking staff are required to know how to prepare them. Whenever the temple was swamped with visitors in the early days, Hsing Yun could be seen in his apron helping out with the fried noodles. He has not done much of that lately, but last year in Hong Kong, I was thrilled to feast on a heavenly dish he made for everyone: twisted fritters and tender pea shoots. Our plates were emptied in no time.

His favorite food is a simple dish of plain noodles sprinkled with soy sauce and sesame oil, or rice soaked in water and served with fermented bean curd from Ilan. As he travels from place to place, his tastes have become quite eclectic; he is perfectly at home with anything from Japanese pickles or Korean Kimchee to American bread. The only things that he excludes from his diet are fruit, nutritional supplements, and vitamins.

Home Is Nowhere and Everywhere

"Even heaven and earth feel small when the heart is bound, but a small bed feels spacious when the heart is free," Hsing Yun says. As monumental as Fo Guang Shan is, for years his quarters consisted of only a cubicle in the corridor of Chuan Deng Lou, until he moved into the Founder's Quarters, which Venerable Hsin Ping built in his honor two years ago.

Without a permanent home, the roving monk is equally comfortable and at ease aboard a transpacific jet as he is in a car on the freeway. However, what really bothers him is extravagance. Once, on a lecture tour, the Korean master who was the host reserved the presidential suite in a five star hotel for the Master. Hsing Yun did no more than sit in one of the chairs and, pulling up a corner of the bedding, he curled up for the night. Totally unaccustomed to luxury, he could not bear to spoil the impeccable setting. Like many who have seen the worst of times, Hsing Yun learned to be frugal the hard way, and fame has not changed that. There is an anecdote that his disciples love to tell that illustrates his thriftiness. Each time the Master is abroad preaching, he has at hand a sizeable amount of ready cash to help those he meets along the way who may be in need of financial help. At the same time, whenever the Master uses paper napkins on a plane, in restaurants, or in washrooms, he folds each piece neatly and keeps it in his pocket after one use, conscious of the fact that it can be used again. Once, upon his return, an attendant helping him unpack his bags found seventy or more paper napkins stashed in his pocket. "The Master left home with U.S. dollars, and returned with napkins!" the attendant declared in amusement.

Vimalakirti once said, "With Dharma joy, I no longer relish worldly joys." Hsing Yun, too, rarely buys for himself, and the last time he did so, he had to borrow money from Venerable Tzu Hui. While in transit in Japan, he borrowed the money to purchase a wristwatch with large numerals because his eyesight is failing.

A disciple was moved beyond words one day when she saw the Master cautiously pull out neatly folded bills worth NT $1000 and hand it to another disciple, saying, "If you respect it, there will be more!" Because he is willing to relinquish all things, he views the five desires and six defilements as illusions; because he is willing to receive all things, he views all living beings within the chiliocosms as his wealth. His enlightened perception of the ebb and flow of the universe makes him magnanimous and open, able to give and receive.

Hard on Himself, Easy on Others

Hsing Yun has always demanded much of himself but not of others. Conscientiously, he sees to it that offerings from devotees are channeled directly to the temple to facilitate a multitude of projects. "I don't know whether it's a positive or negative aspect of my character," he remarks, "but I am unable to keep any money. I tend to look for every chance to part with it." With his stipend, for instance, he loves bringing everyone a little something each time he comes home from a trip. These small souvenirs, though inexpensive, coupled with his care and appreciation, are his way of expressing his gratitude and connection with all who work alongside him.

His heaviest investment, as such, is in the young monastics. Fo Guang Shan finances all the disciples currently studying abroad. Moreover, Hsing Yun visits them whenever he can and leaves them extra funds from his own pocket.

The summer before last, he met Venerable Jiqun and Xiuyong from Xiamen Buddhist College in Hong Kong, and they had a cordial exchange. Hsing Yun gave them a handsome collection of texts, including the *Fo Guang Encyclopedia* and *Hsing Yun's Lecture Series*, and urged them to return home to work hard for Buddhism on the Mainland. On parting, they prostrated to thank him. Hsing Yun hastened to help them up and handed them a red envelope, which he had received from a devotee just ten minutes before. The pair left with tears in their eyes. Monetary matters may be mundane, but when given with a sincere heart, money can become a resource that benefits all beings.

Indeed, as a monastic, Hsing Yun lives a simple and frugal life. He notes, "I've never held the key to my room, nor are any of my letters ever hidden, or my whereabouts unknown."

The World Is as Large as the Heart that Can Hold It

Truly, the world is as large as the heart that can hold it. In the same way, how much we can achieve depends on how much we can tolerate. Hsing Yun's ability to create the most expansive Buddhist establishment worldwide hinges on his broad-mindedness, which has enabled him to break through the customs of conventional monasticism.

Author Lin Ching-hsuan and director Liu Weibin were filming a documentary on location at Fo Guang Shan years ago when Liu was suddenly taken with the idea of shooting from the top of the offering table before the Buddha, which is normally off-limits. Pleased with Liu's innovative spirit, Hsing Yun's approval was prompt. Liu also recalls his wonder and glee in watching the sangha engaged in a game of basketball at Fo Guang Shan—led by the Master himself!

Hsing Yun once said that what holds the most indelible place in his heart is not the majestic structures of Fo Guang Shan but the basketball court at Dongshan. Sports enthusiast that he is, he almost faced expulsion when he resorted to building his own basketball goal because the Buddhist College curriculum then did not include physical education. Therefore, he yearned for a basketball court, especially when he came to have his own temple. He used to have the time of his life playing in the evenings with the disciples, the only distraction being the occasional interruption which would force him to quit halfway and hurry off to greet visitors—still sweating from the game.

An advocate for basketball among the sangha, he hopes that more exercise will foster better health for all of the monastics. Aside from this, Hsing Yun outlines the benefits of playing basketball as a means of personal development that fosters fairness, justice, openness, personal progress, valiance, and agility. It encourages group spirit, collaboration, and glory for all. The sport engenders honesty, humility, obedience, and kindness. Furthermore, it develops love for one's opponents, without whom there could not be a game in the first place.

On the basketball court, the Dharma—not just the ball—is passed on between master and disciples; and bonding—not just competition—occurs. Although his doctor banned him from the sport after he fractured his leg, he still shoots three-pointers from a wheelchair. For twenty-seven years, those at Fo Guang Shan have all turned out to play in the annual basketball tournament celebrating the Master's birthday.

Heart of a Child

Those close to Hsing Yun often describe him as a personable and fun-loving character. Author Yao Zhuoqi spent a month with Hsing Yun on his homecoming to the Mainland in 1989. Yao remembers how the Master bought a panda hand puppet at the entrance to the Ming Tombs in Beijing and became very dexterous with it, handling it with three fingers. He would hide it in his sleeve and pull it out to greet passersby, winning laughs and hearts.

A good number of those traveling with him at the time were lay devotees for whom the abrupt switch to a totally vegetarian diet was somewhat taxing, especially in light of the delicious meat dishes included in the cuisine. Finally in Xian, seven of them could no longer refrain and, at the direction of the local guide, were about to sneak out for a feast of mutton when they bumped into the Master.

"Why, going somewhere for a bite?" he laughed.

Sheepishly, the group confided their plan to the Master.

"Be careful," he cautioned. "It's probably safer to have the chef at the hotel prepare it for you."

The next day, a full-course non-vegetarian meal was laid out before them—including mutton. Everyone had a pretty good idea where it all came from. Another time, at the close of the B.L.I.A. Executive Meeting in Japan, he amused others by wearing his cane across his chest as though it were a rifle and saluting everyone at the hotel entrance.

Do Not Disturb the Heart of the Practitioner

To be a monastic of exceptional caliber in an age of professionalism, one must be more diligent than others. Hsing Yun's meticulousness makes him an infallible host; one who makes sure that all the lights are on and the roads are clear before a tour commences, that seats are in order, air-conditioning functioning, and tea ample before a meeting begins, all so that guests will feel at home.

After three years of working alongside Hsing Yun on the television program *Hsing Yun's Dharma Words*, producer Chen Tai has only this to say: "He is top-notch!" Chen recalls the Master having no misgivings whatsoever about going to great lengths for a perfect shot. Once, after three or four hours of sitting under seven 5,000-volt spotlights, his disciples were ready to leap out of their chairs and cry, "The Master is going to roast!" The Master, however, remained composed and smiling.

Although nearing the age of seventy, Hsing Yun is nonetheless young at heart and receptive, an impeccable role model to disciples and followers. In the way he walks, opens the door, or pulls out a drawer, he causes no disturbance. He takes care of his own chores: shaving his own head, laundering his clothes, and cleaning up after himself at each bath—even in hotels. As the saying goes, "One would rather stir up a thousand rivers than disturb the mind of the practitioner."

Demonstrating mindfulness and humility, the Master teaches by example. He is most attentive to thoughts of the young and the needs of disciples and followers, and rarely vetoes them. Never chastising, his words for anyone acting out of line are, "If I were in your place, I might try another approach–it may bring better results." Hsing Yun's manner of dealing with people embodies the maxim, "Criticism should not be too harsh, for it must be acceptable; instructions should not be too demanding—they must be viable."

Unlike the stereotypical graying monk deep in meditation, Hsing Yun heartily supports having fun. "Joy," he often tells those who are downcast, "is the inner sunshine." He refuses to be persuaded that anything is unsolvable. Coming up with the perfect analogy, the Master adds, "Joy is like perfume. When we spray it on others generously, we're sure to catch a few drops ourselves."

A wise person said, "When one rule is understood, all else shall be clear." Striving to build good rapport with all beings, Hsing Yun has developed a certain fluidity and sophistication in his interactions with others over time. He often says, "To fail in work is acceptable, but we should not fail in getting along with others." Only when time, space, and human relationships are pursued to perfection can all be happy.

A Self-Made Bibliophile

Hsing Yun's credentials, though informal, stem from a lifetime of self-directed study. After he reads them, text after text has gone to the various collections of Fo Guang Shan's many cultural departments and libraries. He relishes the few pages he reads before bedtime no matter how long the day has been. His reading selections include the biographies of the eminent Buddhist masters, the classics, martial arts fiction, science fiction, journals, and newspapers.

He frequently gives books as gifts to disciples and friends, and he often speaks of reading as a source of happiness. He says it must not result in defilement but joy, and must accord with one's nature and inclinations. The ability to learn, not qualifications on paper, should underlie true professionalism, he believes. Most of all, the truly learned person should be a thorough reader of the texts of life and humanity.

Many are curious as to how a monk reared in such seclusion has such a good understanding of everyday problems and affairs. His listening skills are the reason for this. He greets visitors, friends, devotees, and disciples with patience and humility, and he learns a great deal from them. He once compared himself to a sponge soaking up information and retaining it, or a good computer storing good views and ideas and turning them into his own.

Make It Acceptable, Make It Viable

Tang poet Du Fu once said, "One who reads thousands of texts composes with utmost spontaneity and eloquence." Hsing Yun is one of the most prolific authors among the monastics in Taiwan. He took years to train himself. He will never forget the lean years during which, lacking pen and paper to jot down his thoughts, he could only keep them close to his heart. He used to compose mental drafts while at meals or in line for the shrine and still does the same while on the road. Perhaps that is one reason for the spontaneity and compactness of his writing.

Understandably, Hsing Yun's style is easy and popular. He does not hesitate to pick up colloquial phrases and incorporate them into his writing. Lauded as "seasoned and essential, simple and lasting," his format is lively and his language unpretentious, but his intent is profound. His own favorite author is Kumarajiva, a brilliant translator of some of the most popular sutras. Hsing Yun's principle in writing is that it should be simple understandable, readily accepted, and easily incorporated into life.

A Living Treasure-Trove

Followers have long realized that the Master is a living treasure-trove. A recent discovery is his calligraphy. In his spare time, he renders Dharma sayings in brush and ink. He gives these to devotees in appreciation of their dedication. He is humble about his own ancestral background, which was nowhere near an academic one, and about his lack of practice, which he says has consisted of no more than writing up posters and couplets for lecture halls. That he is able to make gifts of his calligraphy is, first and foremost, of surprise to him.

Hsing Yun has dedication of character, forgetting both the world and the self, and treating oneself and others as one. This quality permeates his calligraphy, which has become increasingly sought after among collectors. Some of these works now fetch hundreds and thousands of dollars, as in the recent fundraising art auctions for Fo Guang University. At the same time he does not think twice about rendering a piece expressly for a twelve-year-old who only pledged NT $100 (US $3.30).

Living Is Joy; Dying, Not Necessarily Sorrow

Despite basking in the Dharma for half a century, Hsing Yun, like all others, is merely sojourning in a physical body, which is subject to the vicissitudes of birth, aging, infirmity, and death. Long principled in creating joy for others, he rarely mentions his health concerns. However, the fact remains that diabetes is affecting his vision and memory, and even his skin is showing the effects of the disease. Disciples and followers often ask him to slow down, and some have offered herbal medications and other remedies. Li Wuyen, a follower of thirty years and a radiologist, has pleaded on his knees many times for the Master to go in for his medical check-up. "There is only one human, one life, and one heart," he answers with characteristic lightness.

Others have not been as casual about the Master's increasing age and the condition of Hsing Yun's health. "The position can be replaced, but not the person or the prestige," they say. Understandably, many speculate about the future of Fo Guang Shan after the Master passes away. To that, his answer is ready: "I have no fear of death," he says, "for death is a matter of course. This is not to say that we as Buddhists won't die. No, it's just that, in the face of death, we know that it is not the end but the beginning of another existence."

"I often use the analogy of death as moving to a new residence or changing into a new garment. Life and death, death and life, are really two in one, one in two. Living is certainly joy; dying is not necessarily sorrow."

"Do not worry about Fo Guang Shan when I'm gone. Hasn't it fared well since I left the abbotship? It has been established to be in accordance with the Dharma and it is systematized under healthy leadership. This is the pure, harmonious, and joyful sangha. There is no need to draw any connection between the destiny of Fo Guang Shan and mine," he assures his followers.

Free to Follow Conditions

Irrespective of others' admiration, concerns, or doubts, Hsing Yun's self-evaluation is this: lift the weighty as though it were light; follow conditions to be carefree through one's life. Chan Master Xiangyen Zhixian gave verse to the same sentiment: "Devoid of marks and traces anywhere, splendor rules beyond sights and sounds." Thus, Hsing Yun wrote in his diary:

> *Embrace the vow of compassion to deliver all beings,*
> *Float like an untethered boat in the Dharma sea.*
> *Ask me what merits have I over a lifetime,*
> *They are the Buddha's Light across five continents.*

Indeed, that is how he views his whole existence. Simply put, everyone is the architect of his or her own destiny. A Buddhist who has undertaken to revive his own faith and live out his life marches on, never turning back. While leading a sincere and pious life, Master Hsing Yun is an ordinary monk who is an extraordinary leader.

Chapter 20

Devoted to the Buddhist Path

Hsing Yun is a vigorous monastic who weaves his way in and out between the Buddha gate and the secular world. He possesses a marvelous gift of discernment and clearly comprehends the connections of the past, present, and future. The Master is an erudite man of letters who writes and speaks with the utmost eloquence, and also a peaceful character of countless affinities who befriends all levels of beings. He is a dynamic manager of international repute who devises and handles enormous corporate planning and financial tasks. Such versatility makes one consider whether he might be one of a kind. Critics have even suggested that he has strayed far from the traditional monastic concerns.

An examination of his past—his thoughts, sayings, and deeds—reveals a life that has been principled in Buddhahood and little else. Bearing the surname of Shih,[100] the same as the Buddha himself, Hsing Yun is committed to revitalizing Buddhism and, moreover, to aiding the world by means of the Dharma.

As a study of life, the teachings of the Buddha are about the truth of all matters and things within the universe. Methods of interpretation and dissemination may vary in accordance with changing times and circumstances, but the doctrine and spirit are essential and inextricable from their Buddhist ancestry. Hence, in advocating Humanistic Buddhism, Hsing Yun aspires to transform traditional Buddhism into a new tool for the resolution of contemporary issues.

The Dharma, Environmentally Friendly for the Mind

The world of the twentieth century seems to be spiraling, both visibly and audibly, into a maelstrom of natural disasters, human hostilities, deceit, and corruption. All living beings find themselves struggling to catch their breaths or trying to survive amid constant fear, uncertainty, and restlessness. Environmental preservation of the physical world is crucial on a planet stricken with problems of waste management, air pollution, sewage, and unrelenting land exploitation. Social concern must address a society afflicted with problems of politics, crime, and family dysfunction; human relationships are distant, hollow, and contentious, so people need spiritual preservation even more.

In the particularly engaging style of the humanistic bodhisattva, Hsing Yun offers a rational and workable approach to solving the problems of living. The Master teaches people how to live with family and interact with relatives; how to love spouses and care for friends; how to relate to society; how to handle everyday life; and how to tackle matters of finance, religion, health, medicine, and politics.

Apart from its manifestations in education, culture, and charitable causes, Hsing Yun's Humanistic Buddhism also assumes many other forms, including classes taught by qualified speakers from both the sangha and lay community, consultation for those seeking guidance and advice in career and family, and emergency relief and shelter for the aged and disabled.

"Believers are many, but practitioners are few," comments Chen Luan, head of the Control Yuan in Taiwan. He is aware that there is a greater enthusiasm for material donations to gather personal merits than in spiritual cultivation for the elevation of the mind and betterment of society. Hsing Yun agrees, and he looks forward to a more deeply rooted understanding of the Dharma, not merely blind adherence. He hopes to see a much broader adaptation of its values.

Laying the Groundwork

Many today proclaim the coming of a new epoch in Buddhism, one of unprecedented influence, esteem, and promise. On hearing this, Hsing Yun is both elated and wary. He is astutely aware that beneath the apparent prosperity of the Buddhist faith, a range of internal structural issues remains unresolved.

For years, Hsing Yun, who has pledged his life to the Triple Gem, has called for a progressively solidified groundwork: the establishment of a modern system; the betterment of the quality of the sangha; the expansion of Buddhist efforts; and the promotion of Humanistic Buddhism.

In fact, the absence of a unified system in Buddhism worries him greatly. The state of affairs in Taiwan resembles loose sand. In particular, the increasingly affluent society has no problem supporting a proportionately growing sangha. Furthermore, even monastics relatively superficial in spiritual cultivation and knowledge are now able to attract a cadre of devotees, establish their own temples, conduct Dharma functions, receive their own disciples, confer precepts, and enjoy their share of financial contributions. Ungoverned by any administrative body, many are susceptible to fraudulent or lawless practices.

These circumstances, however, are directly addressed by Fo Guang Shan's comprehensive systemization covering all possible areas: personnel, finance, monasterial administration, preaching, Dharma functions, tonsure, precepts, and many more. A far cry from the traditional feudal monastic hierarchy, the systematic rules and disciplines in Hsing Yun's mind are modern and convenient. They are instrumental in the unification and progress of Buddhism as a whole.

A Lame-Duck Law

The existence of a lame-duck law has kept a unified system from prevailing in the Buddhist circles of Taiwan. The supervisory regulations for monasteries implemented by the Nationalist government as far back as 1929 are mandatory only for Buddhism and Daoism. No other religions, even the occult, are subjected to any kind of supervisory agency. Alive and well to this day, the consequences of this law are grave. With the abbot playing second fiddle to the monasterial supervisor, the sangha is all too often overpowered by the laypeople, or the two groups become locked in constant battle. The ambiguity of the existing laws creates confusion over such matters as the legitimate boundaries between purely monastic affairs and those of the laity. No legal stipulations exist regarding the selection of a qualified abbot or monastics. Consequently, the monastics often use the absence of a defined term of abbotship as an excuse to develop an individual monopoly.

Hsing Yun has, on many occasions, made public pleas for fairer, healthier circumstances under which all religions may be enabled to grow. He insists that both the devotees and monastery be integral parts of Buddhism at large, and therefore not dependent on individual followings or private ownership. He also advocates that administrative supervision by laypeople be abolished, making way for professional management by the sangha and ending the strife between the two parties once and for all. He insists that abbots be required to train in orthodox Buddhist colleges, thus ensuring that they hold legitimate and professional credentials. He also believes that terms for abbotships should be clearly defined to facilitate proper succession.

Pleas for Buddhist Education

To elevate the quality of the sangha, Buddhist education is key. In Taiwan, Fu Jen Catholic University has a full-scale Religious Studies Department and curriculum, and the Protestant Tung Hai University has its own legitimate school chapel. The courses offered by Buddhist colleges, however, are not officially recognized by law; therefore Buddhist college graduates do not enjoy the same status as the graduates of other religious universities simply because their opportunity to study certain subjects is curtailed by existing laws. Worse yet, within the very same governing body that gives other religious institutions full endorsement, there are still threats to abolish Buddhist colleges altogether. Even the Communist Regime of the Mainland runs a centralized educational operation that includes religious studies, despite its intrinsic atheism. All Buddhist colleges are funded and directed by the Chinese government, and their faculties are salaried like their counterparts in teacher training colleges. By contrast, in America, all types of theological institutions are allowed to thrive. Likewise, both national and private universities in Japan are known to foster well-developed religious studies programs.

Somehow, in Taiwan alone, the Buddhist college seems orphaned within the educational system. After promoting Buddhist education for three decades, Hsing Yun is still fighting for the legitimate status of Buddhist education. He is calling for official registration of all Buddhist colleges, the general acceptance of official guidelines from Taiwan's Ministry of Education, official recognition of student credentials, and official permission to recruit students publicly.

Hsing Yun's proposals for the promotion of Buddhist education include:

- clearly defined levels of elementary, middle, and advanced

Buddhist education

- eligible teachers certified by examination and standard qualification procedures
- the standardization of curriculum and facilities
- training and official recognition for educational administrators
- centralized leadership
- encouragement of the pursuit of higher learning for outstanding graduates
- intercollegiate activities such as lectures and contests
- the recognition of student credentials
- positions such as Dharma teachers, abbots, and directors be assumed by Buddhist college graduates only
- joint examinations devised for Buddhist student bodies in college-level institutions that enable eligible examinees to serve in Buddhist circles in the future, and
- the offering of scholarships, grants, and loans by Buddhist circles.

History reveals that a nation's power is directly linked to its advancement in education. By the same token, as much as religion is accountable for educating society, how can it purify minds and affect moral trends if the qualifications of its proponents are questionable?

Self-Sufficiency Benefits All Sentient Beings

Traditionally, as long as monastics carry on their efforts in chanting sutras and conducting Dharma functions, they can make a decent living, thereby allowing their temple to thrive. An old saying describes the monastic mindset as thus: "As clouds of incense gather above me, I can be assured that a vegetarian feast awaits me." This adage proves true even today, and it is evident that these attitudes about monastic livelihood have not changed much. Monastics still compete for devotees and solicit donations for the purpose of maintaining the monastery itself—a sign of material dependence and one of the reasons that Buddhism has yet to command the respect of society.

The agrarian Chan livelihood, which Chan Master Huaihai of the Tang Dynasty led and advocated, was committed to self-sufficiency by way of day-to-day labor and productivity. In 1911, Master Taixu went as far as to urge that factories be set up and run by monastics, not only for self-sufficiency but also for the benefit of society. Hsing Yun, sharing the same orthodox training as the two Chan masters, believes firmly that Buddhist circles should be as productive and service-oriented as the Catholic and Protestant circles so acclaimed for their medical and educational undertakings. The Buddhist circles in Japan, too, have ventured into the retail and hotel businesses, and society appears to have no objection. The Master insists that Taiwan's Buddhist circles cease regarding business enterprises as taboo, and become economically self-sufficient to better serve society and benefit all living beings.

As for Hsing Yun, his business ventures span decades, starting some thirty years ago with his founding of Zhiguang, a school of commerce, with fellow monastics Wu I and Nanting. From Pumen High School at Fo Guang Shan founded eighteen years ago to Hsi Lai University, the newly launched and feverishly pursued project established in 1990 by Fo Guang University, Hsing Yun has occupied himself with a wide range of ongoing enterprises. In addition to these educational endeavors, the Fo Guang television and radio stations, the Buddhist daily newspaper, and the mass-communications center, clearly reveal the Master's vision of the development of Buddhist enterprises.

Fo Guang University represents Hsing Yun's ultimate dream, a dream that is about to be fulfilled. On a sprawling fifty-six sq.

hectare property overlooking the sea in Linmei, Chiaohsi, in the county of Ilan, the groundbreaking ceremony was held in October 1993. Initially scheduled to open with seven departments—Chinese, philosophy, mass communications, business management, foreign languages and literature, fine art, and drama—it began accepting applications for its graduate school in 1995.

Hsing Yun's vision for Fo Guang University is one of breadth and depth, and one that balances academics with applications to daily life. Its first chancellor is Dr. Kung Peng-cheng, a young scholar of Chinese literature.

In the meantime, effective fundraising done through public donations and auctions has amassed a remarkable financial foundation for the institution, and demonstrates a mutually supportive connection between Buddhism and society at large. No one puts it better than Hsing Yun himself when he says, "Who owns Fo Guang University? Certainly not myself nor Fo Guang Shan. This is an institution that belongs to society. Indeed, Fo Guang University belongs to everyone!"

Riding the Crest of a Universal Wave

More often than not, the Master's concerns for the state of affairs around him, when articulated, either annoy the privileged few or simply fall on deaf ears. But Hsing Yun knows all too well that the home base, one's own grass roots, is where everything begins.

So this branded liberal in Buddhist circles has vowed to create a monasterial institution of modern character named Fo Guang Shan, whose system is healthy and viable, and whose operation is organized and efficient. To this day, its Buddhist colleges have this day generated over a thousand graduates, all vibrant new blood in the monastic lineage. Moreover, other Buddhist establishments in recent years have been seen to pattern themselves on Fo Guang

Shan in the network establishment of educational, medical, charitable, and cultural enterprises.

Hsing Yun is never overly excited or afraid of anything; instead, he is devoted to the Buddhist path, and the Buddhist path only, and rides the universal crest of undertaking. Nevertheless, problems abound, and perfection has yet to be attained. Indeed, the fruit of Buddhahood takes much more than a mere lifetime to mature. Hsing Yun has great faith that the undertaking of Fo Guang Shan shall continue through succeeding generations, and someday soon, Chinese Buddhism will enjoy a bright new lineage.

Chapter 21

No Regrets Whatsoever

*O*ut of the clear, cool nocturnal blue above southern Taiwan rains gold and silver and loose diamonds—fireworks! Among the shadows of trees and groves, ornate lanterns sway back and forth. Applause and cheering rise and fall and rise again.

This is the Dharma function known as the Festival of Light and Peace, featured each Lunar New Year at Fo Guang Shan from the first to the fifteenth day of the first moon. Then, on the first day of the second moon—also the anniversary of Hsing Yun's entrance into the monkhood–devotees converge again for the annual general meeting, which happens year after year without fail. In that month alone, hundreds of thousands of devotees from all over head toward the Great Welcoming Buddha and the Main Shrine feeling like they have come home.

From the rubble of postwar poverty, Taiwan rose like a phoenix out of the tumult of world events. Hsing Yun was wrought from a similar foundation. But then again, Hsing Yun's story is much more than a fabulous tale, for he inherited no lineal prominence and earned no formal credentials, nor was he ever anywhere close to being a child prodigy. Still, as a child, he lost a parent; becoming a novice monk, he faced infinite chaos; he was alone, yet he survived.

His odyssey is an inspiration to those of us who seek the extraordinary despite our own ordinariness. He is the light that reflects our inner nature and illuminates our future.

Focus Your Effort, Then Strive Onward

"Focus your effort, then strive on to the end" is the motto that summarizes his career and characterizes his life. This determined focus brings him success. Choosing monkhood over home at the tender age of twelve, this child implored his mother to let him leave the family and enter the sangha. Thereafter, he was able to brave a decade of tribulations in monastic training because, even from a young age, he fully realized the importance of the initial inspiration of his vows.

Picking a winding path to Taiwan in 1949, the young monk found himself a total stranger in a strange land with limited means and no knowledge of the language. He was hungry, cold, sick, jailed, wronged; battered; he saw many around him succumb to similar trials. What kept him going was the pact he made with Master Zhiyong, for one to defend their faith on the Mainland while the other carried the Buddha's light across the strait, forever dedicating their lives to Buddhism. This involved four years of learning how to live under someone else's roof, twelve years in Ilan learning how to lay the groundwork for the future, and many years learning how to build Fo Guang Shan step by step. Throughout this time, when things and people around him changed, the choice of living his faith did not.

Like the economic progress of Taiwan and the maturation of its social conditions, Hsing Yun's diligence, has also borne bountiful fruit. His first-generation disciples, torch in hand, have taken their positions in an astounding global network, and the second generation is ready and waiting. The body of Buddhist enterprises known collectively as Fo Guang Shan embraces close to one hundred branch temples worldwide. The branch temples are joined by 180 outlying establishments such as the Buddhist colleges, high schools, kindergartens, nurseries, publishing houses, hospitals, and homes for the elderly.

Continuously Handing Down the Light

Hsing Yun has been very successful in raising the young in the Buddhist faith. Whether viewed from the standpoint of modern education or that of orthodoxy, the fact that Fo Guang Shan has produced a total of over 1,100 monastics is a phenomenal record in the history of Buddhism. He has made such achievements because he believes that Buddhism needs to hand down the light continuously.

To make sure the development of Buddhism is strong and enduring, Hsing Yun harmonizes the orthodox monastery with the modern institution. He has come up with a versatile system that is capable of keeping up with the times in terms of administration, economy, finance, personnel, education, and welfare. According to Hsing Yun's design, all those who head the hundred or so branches abide by the system; it is a network built upon monastic fellowship. A mighty mechanism, it is fair and open, yet finely tuned and efficiently run.

Fo Guang Shan embodies the spirit of Mahayana Buddhism, which Hsing Yun seeks to manifest in the forms of Humanistic Buddhism and Living Buddhism. Employing modern preaching methods, he seeks to spread such concepts as life preceding death—emphasizing the importance of living mindfully in the here and now—and Buddhism as a religion of blessedness. In the meantime, Taiwan's economic boom, social diversity, and educational progress together create fertile ground for the growth of Humanistic Buddhism. Presently, Fo Guang Shan's devotees number over one million in Taiwan, along with hundreds of thousands worldwide. Overall, Buddhism has become a popular faith among the rich, the famous, and the intellectual, as well as the common folk.

While it is true that Fo Guang Shan began with Hsing Yun's creative vision, "the Dharma, not the preacher, is to be relied on," he says, and the system must be adhered to. A decade ago, to ensure that Fo Guang Shan's growth would never cease, the Master decided to pass the baton of abbotship on to Venerable Hsin Ping.

Put It Down So You Can Pick It Up Again

You have to "put it down so you can pick it up again." As if liberated from some cocoon, Hsing Yun went on to teach across the continents and eventually founded the Buddha's Light International Association. Destined to be a major player in the future of Buddhism, B.L.I.A.'s hundred or so chapters are already injecting new strength into the propagation of the Dharma all over the world.

Hsing Yun is frank about his inward journey: "All my life I have deplored broken promises above all. To me, honor is of the essence. The reality is, regardless of how many trials and tribulations you have endured, people only seem to care about the result and not your efforts. I just set my goal and thereafter refuse to be shaken or to change my mind no matter how bitterly trying it is along the way. The knottiest problems can be solved, just like that. Indeed, one who is determined always has hundreds of thousands of solutions, while one who is not determined, hundreds of thousands of obstacles." Hsing Yun's philosophy is that, irrespective of our role upon the stage called life, we should always play our part as though we were the protagonists.

A Thoroughfare to Modernity

The *Diamond Sutra* states: "All conditioned dharmas are like dreams and illusions, bubbles and shadows, dew and lightning. They should all be contemplated in this way." This means that whatever is seen and heard is empty, lacking any substantial, independent reality. On the other hand, for the public to fully appreciate Master Hsing Yun from an everyday point of view, it makes sense to analyze his career and contributions in the context of history and as a projection into the future.

A lifetime of engagement has aged him markedly. His greatest achievement is that, in bringing orthodox Chinese Buddhism to Taiwan, he has transformed a desert deprived of the Dharma rain into a pure land blossoming with bodhi. Furthermore, he has opened up for Buddhism a thoroughfare to modernity. Under Hsing Yun, the doctrine remains orthodox while the format is contemporary; thinking remains transcendent while endeavors are very practical; lifestyle remains conservative while preaching is progressive. As more and more people are drawn to Buddhism, some even attribute Buddhism's comeback to Hsing Yun—in Taiwan, if nowhere else.

Second, he has nurtured generation after generation of talented individuals to perpetuate the Dharma lineage. Especially noteworthy is that he has been far ahead of his time and his peers in acknowledging the aptitude and competence of the bhiksunis, and in promoting them to positions historically beyond their reach. This is especially significant since Buddhist convention dictates that the bhiksus always come before bhiksunis. The latter are subjugated to the extent that in Thai, Sri Lankan, and Tibetan Buddhism, no bhiksuni precepts are conferred.

Not so in Taiwan, which has produced a constellation of brilliant bhiksunis, like Venerables Xiaoyun, Cheng Yen, and many others, together with Hsing Yun's first-generation disciples, Venerables Tzu Chuang, Tzu Hui, Tzu Jung, Tzu Chia, and Tzu I. In fact, Fo Guang Shan's bhiksu and bhiksuni population is a record 3:7 proportion. In addition to this, is Venerable Tzu Hui's vice presidency in the World Fellowship of Buddhists under the auspices of Hsing Yun. Traditionally the domain of representatives from the Theravada tradition was closed to women, the tight-knit executive circle has been broken with the addition of Tzu Hui. In the hearty words of Venerable Zhaohui, "Hsing Yun has genuinely attained equality among all living beings as taught by the Buddha."

Third, Hsing Yun has established an order for the coexistence and mutual respect between the sangha and devotees. Contrary to the traditional view of monastic superiority regardless of personal dedication or practice (which has historically been a factor in the alienation of the two groups), Hsing Yun stresses a Fo Guang Shan free from distinctions of class or status.

"Just as a nation cannot be without people," he says, "a temple cannot be without devotees." In his eyes, nothing invigorates Buddhism more than the joining of forces between the sangha and the lay community. An outstanding group of lay preachers and teachers of the Dharma has been elected in Buddha's Light International Association, which is the consummate affirmation of the role of the lay community in Buddhism.

The Master's Vision of Buddha's Light

Even beyond the realm of religion, Hsing Yun has never stopped giving, directly or indirectly. Taiwan's four million Buddhists are appropriately a major source of stability, and their practice of Buddhism helps to regulate individual behavior amidst the nation's political, economic, and social strife. His own sensitivity to his status as a monastic originally from the Mainland helped him to demolish the barrier of regionalism by leading a majority of indigenous devotees in Taiwan. In truth, the breakdown of regionalism is giving Buddhism in Taiwan a fresh outlook.

Overseas, the intricate web of organizations under Fo Guang Shan and the Buddha's Light International Association smoothly executes its function in diplomacy. From the chateau in France, to the grasslands of Australia, to the deserts of South Africa, Hsing Yun and his followers have replaced the centuries-old impression of an isolated nation with a glittering new image of a vibrant people—the Chinese of today.

"Look to the future, and do whatever is closest at hand. Willingly consider the doubtful as well as the probable, and use your energy where it is needed most"—these are the principles of Hsing Yun's undertakings. Some consider his religious leadership a product of Taiwan's social evolvement and see the Master himself as a heroic figure made by circumstance. However, even if that proves to be so, Hsing Yun, in dispatching the message of Buddhism across the world, can still be considered a master who has carved out a unique and remarkable vision.

Hsing Yun: His Name and Its Meaning

If slander is a twin to acclaim, now and again Master Hsing Yun finds himself in some whirlpool of controversy. These encounters are helpful in reflecting the kaleidoscope of views that are held concerning Hsing Yun. While some wait in awe on the temple grounds, hoping to catch a glimpse of his elegant figure, others snort at how completely uninspiring the cement Buddha images are. For those whose hearts have been touched in some way, there are tears shed while they sit listening to the Dharma teachings. Others consider his presence in the national political arena to be totally unsuitable for a monastic. While most devotees donate in earnest to gather merits for themselves and loved ones, others attempt to profit under the shingles of Fo Guang Shan. Even while many pay homage and offer incense, there are others who scrutinize each record book of donations and speculate on how much he must have pocketed.

The ultimate irony is how harsh people tend to be on the

subject of their hero-worship, which they happen to have created themselves. But, is that truly the intent of the hero himself?

"Who am I?" Hsing Yun asks. "Only a regular monk! Only a peasant!"

Criticism and praise are to him as swans across the sky and snow on the ground, for he has always formed his own definition of life.

Once, while he was on the road traveling with a group of monastics, the weather forecast on the radio stated: "Satellite pictures of the clouds indicate...." At that, Venerable Tzu Jung was struck with a question. She asked, "Master, first the grand master named you Chin Chueh. Then you named yourself Hsing Yun. What is the story behind your name?"

"I remember while learning to use the dictionary in the monastery, I stumbled upon the term *Hsingyun Tuan*, (masses of stars and clouds)," Hsing Yun replied. "I read on and its definition described it as: 'Huge, ancient, and without bounds.' There was a union of countless cloud-like stars before the universe took form. How I admired that state! While I vowed to bring light to those in the dark, I ventured to be always above and beyond care and bondage. So I took the Dharma name *Hsing Yun*."

On his portrait rendered by Li Zijian, Hsing Yun wrote a verse, which is in essence a summary of his life:

> *Who was he?*
> *Living atop Buddha's Light Mountain,*
> *Founding it twenty-seven years before.*
> *Speaking the Dharma through forty seasons of fall,*
> *Teaching disciples, one thousand and more.*
> *Spreading the light over five continents,*
> *Donning the mantle of countless roles,*
> *Always befriending and purifying the world.*

Paving the Way for the Next Five Hundred Years

Against the backdrop of turbulent times, Hsing Yun has emerged from ordinariness to attain extraordinariness through broad-mindedness, insight, flair, and resolve. In an article titled "The Next 500 Years in Buddhism," U.S.-based historian and author Tang Degang summarizes Hsing Yun's role in religious history as follows:

"In teaching the major religions of the world, I make sure that students bear in mind the old Chinese proverb, 'Every 500 years a benevolent king shall rise.' This is an easy way for them to keep track of historical events.

"In regards to the dates of various religious founders, that of Jesus is the easiest to remember. Five hundred years before him came Sakyamuni Buddha (563–483 B.C.E.), Laozi, and Confucius. Still another 500 years earlier is the time of Moses, founder of Judaism.

"Moving forward in time, it was Mohammed (570–630?), founder of Islam, who came 500 years after Jesus. Five hundred years after that came Martin Luther (1483–1546), founder of Protestantism. Now, as the clock ticks toward the end of another 500 years since the religious reformation [in Christianity] of 1520, the next epochal leadership in religion is again anticipated.

"A circumspect look at the world's cultural, philosophical, political, and economic developments today reveals that Buddhism is the source of a new life force… for Buddhism today is not only sweeping across Southeast Asia but also penetrating the five continents. So potent is its impact and so excellent are its conditions that it has long surpassed the Christian Reformation [of the sixteenth century].

"With the emerging four young dragons of the Pacific Rim and China racing feverishly to catch up, the enormous middle class that results is asking for a religion of their own—a Buddhism which is adaptable to modern circumstances, and one which is home-oriented instead of monastery-oriented as in orthodoxy. Hence, a Buddhist reform is in the works, and a reformer is here.

"The new state of Buddhism is such that, at long last, the Mahayana and Theravada, along with the ten schools, are at last joining forces, and together they shall take China and the rest of the world by storm. The question arises as to who is capable of leading Buddhism into what appears to be a new era of prosperity and growth. Apart from Venerable Master Hsing Yun, founder of Fo Guang Shan, I honestly cannot think of anyone else."

Once a Monk, Always a Monk

Like his mother giving her son away to the world, Hsing Yun, too, has long given himself to all living beings. Over his lifetime, has he ever regretted that decision or contemplated another way of spending his life?

"The greatest blessing in this life of mine has been attaining monkhood," he remarks. "I pledge to be a monk in my next life, and in the many, many lives to come." Emperor Shunzhi of the Qing Dynasty once penned a poem to honor monkhood. It stated:

> *"As rare as gold and white jade are;*
> *Rarer still is the donning of the robe."*

For Hsing Yun, monkhood has been a task for a man of fortitude and courage, something beyond even what great generals and ministers must tackle. Should he return as a monastic in the next life, he would still have no regrets.

ENDNOTES, GLOSSARY, AND APPENDIX

Endnotes

[1] Jiangnan: The region south of the Yangtze River.

[2] Mrs. Li: She is fondly known as "Grandma Li" to many Chinese people who regard her as a caring and compassionate woman. She passed away in May 1996.

[3] *Dao*: Refers to rice, and is a pun for *dao*, the way. This is also an intimation on the mother's part that her child's life shall be fruitful due to his many accomplishments.

[4] Li Chengbao: Master Hsing Yun's father.

[5] Plum of the Li Family: Li, Master Hsing Yun 's secular surname, is a pun for *li*, plum or a choice object; it is the same character in the Chinese language.

[6] *Qizi Duan*: Folkloric literature primarily of mythological, historical, and chivalrous themes, written in a prose made up of structured seven-character sentences (approximately equal to seven-word sentences in English).

[7] *The Water Margin* [*Shuihu Zhuan*]: A masterful work of fiction set in thirteenth-century China about 108 characters compelled to flee social chaos under the decaying Song Dynasty. It is authored by Shi Naian. Many English translations exist.

[8] Mrs. Li, at ninety-four: She was ninety-four years old in 1994.

[9] Xinhai Revolution: The revolution led by Dr. Sun Yat-sen, which overthrew the Manchurian Qing regime in 1911, and resulted in that the Republic of China which was founded in 1912.

[10] the Sino-Japanese War: Or Chino-Japanese War. The Japanese Empire began the invasion of China at Marco Polo Bridge in 1937. This war lasted for eight years and the Japanese finally surrendered in 1945.

[11] the civil war between the Nationalists and Communists: It began in 1946, and Mao Tse-tung led the Communists to overrun China and to proclaim the People's Republic of China. And the Nationalist government, led by Chiang Kai-shek, retreated to Taiwan in 1949.

[12] the Cultural Revolution: In most sources, it has been assigned the dates 1966 to 1969. However, the Chinese government considers the period of the movement from 1966 to 1976, during which Mao died and the "Gang of Four" was arrested.

[13] The Rape of Nanjing [1937 C.E.]: When the Japanese Empire invaded China in 1937, Nanjing was completely destroyed. In this invasion, Japanese troops massacred many innocent citizen, and raped many Chinese women.

[14] Vairocana: It literally means, "the sun."

[15] Relic: What is left after the cremation of a Buddha, bodhisattvas, or highly cultivated people.

[16] Kalavinka: It literally means, "wondrous sounds."

[17] a banking system offering interest-free and contract-free loans: This system was established by the Sanjie Sect during the period of the Sui and Tang Dynasties.

[18] *field of compassion*: Regular collections of financial contributions to aid the needy.

[19] *lixue:* Also known as "Neo-Confucianism," popular during the Song Dynasty, it employed a rational approach to the study of Confucianism.

[20] all-embracing faith: Refers to Buddhism as a religion that compassionately embraces all sentient beings regardless of their social status or positions. In ancient India where a hereditary caste system existed, social distinctions were made according to four castes—brahmans, rulers and warriors, farmers and traders, and serfs. In contrast, Sakyamuni Buddha taught compassion for and equality among all sentient beings, who all possess Buddha Nature and will all attain Buddhahood. Such an advocacy invariably gave hope to the despairing lower classes at the time, which rallied around in zealous support.

[21] Venerable Master Lianchi [1532-1612 C.E.]: Also know as "Zhuhong," he was one of four great masters during the Ming Dynasty. He emphasized the teachings of the Pure Land School.

[22] Hu Shizhi [1891-1962 C.E.]: Also known as "Hu Shi." He was a famous Chinese philosopher in the 20th Century. He also published many articles related to the study of Chan Buddhism.

[23] Zheng Chenggong [1624–1662 C.E.]: A leader of resistance against the Manchu invaders at the fall of the Ming Dynasty, who later regained Taiwan from the Dutch.

[24] Tangshan: Refers to Mainland China. After the Tang Dynasty, China was often known as "*Tangshan*" (mountain of Tang), and the Chinese people were commonly known as "*Tangren*" (people of Tang). In the title, "Tangshan monk" refers to a monk who sailed from Mainland China; here it refers to Master Hsing Yun.

[25] Mazu: Goddess of the sea.

[26] Lu Dongbin: An immortal Daoist during the Tang Dynasty.

[27] Chiang Kai-shek and his wife: Chiang [1887-1975 C.E.] was the head of the Republic of China during World War II, who led the Chinese army against the invasion of the Japanese Empire. After World War II, he was elected the President of the Republic of China in 1943 and re-elected again in 1948. In 1949, he led the Nationalist government retreat to Taiwan. His wife, Soong Mei-ling [1898-2003 C.E.], also known as Madame Chiang, was Chiang's close adviser and sometimes his spokesperson during international meetings due to her superbly fluent English. Brought up in a Methodist family, she had a strong influence on Chiang's conversion to Christianity.

[28] Dr. Sun Yat-sen: [1866-1925 C.E.] He is recognized as the Father of the Republic of China. He led the Xinhai Revolution, and overthrew the Qing Dynasty in 1911 and founded the Republic of China in 1912.

[29] Mi'le Neiyuan: "Mi'le" refers to Maitreya Bodhisattva; "Neiyuan" means "inner palace." This refers to the inner palace of the Tusita Heaven, over which Maitreya Bodhisattva presides and expounds the Dharma to celestial beings.

[30] the period of "white terror": It started from the 228 Incident, which took place on Feb. 28, 1947, and lasted until 1987, when martial law was annulled. During these four decades, many people were arrested, mysteriously disappeared, or were massacred by the military police.

[31] Chinese Buddhist Association: Established in Shanghai in 1912.

[32] *Shigu*: Female lay-disciples of the sangha, who also maintain a celibate life.

[33] Master Lcan-Skya: Referring to the 19th Lcan-Skya; his Dharma name was Yeses Rdorje [1891-1957].

[34] srivatsalaksana: Literally means "auspicious."

[35] over one hundred branch temples around the globe: As of 2004, there are now over 200 branch temples around the globe.

[36] Vairocana Buddha: Also known as "the Great Sun Buddha."

[37] Master Yulin: Also known as Yulin Tongxiu; a Chan master [1614–1675 C.E.] in Qing Dynasty, belonging to the Dharma lineage of the Linji School. He was appointed the National Master during the reign of Emperor Shizu.

[38] Prajna: Literally means "wisdom."

[39] Mahabrahma: Referring to the third heaven of the first dhyana state in the realm of form. Dhyana literally means "meditative concentration."

[40] the *pipa*, the *zheng*, the *qin*: *Pipa* is the Chinese lute, *zheng* is the Chinese zither with 12, 16, 21, or 23 strings, and *qin* is the Chinese zither with 5 or 7 strings.

[41] KTV: Similar to Karaoke, except in KTV, customers have their own private rooms.

[42] Master Zhiyi: The founder of the Tiantai School in Chinese Buddhism [538-597 C.E.]; also known as the Great Master of Zhizhe (the Wise) or Tiantai.

[43] the *Sutra of the Wondrous Truth of the Lotus*: This sutra is more commonly known as the *Lotus Sutra*.

[44] *Prajnaparamita*: *Prajna* literally means "wisdom," and *paramita* means "perfection." This term indicates the perfection of wisdom.

45 Pattra: Palm leaves used as writing material.

46 Ermei, Wutai, Putuo, and Jiuhua: Four famous mountains in Chinese Buddhism. Ermei is located in Sichuan Province, well known as the sacred mountain of Samantabhadra Bodhisattva; Wutai is in Shanxi Province and is considered to be the mountain where Manjusri Bodhisattva manifests to give discourses on the Dharma. Putuo is located in Zhijiang Province, well known as the sacred mountain of Avalokitesvara Bodhisattva; Jiuhua is in Anhui Province and considered as the Dharma site where Ksitigarbha Bodhisattva manifests to help sentient beings.

47 Religious Affairs Committee: The highest policy-making body of Fo Guang Shan.

48 the Guanyin Release Pool: A pool where devotees and visitors set free the live fish, turtles, or other aquatic animals rescued from the market.

49 Taishan: Also known as "Mount Tai," a famous mountain in Shandong Province, China.

50 One flower, one world; one leaf, one Buddha: This statement emphasizes that Dharma can be manifested and experienced through one flower, one leaf, or other ordinary things in our daily life.

51 the offering of bright lanterns: It is an annual ceremony at the beginning of Chinese New Year, in which devotees offer a candle to the Buddha, and pray that the light of the mind (i.e., wisdom) can become bright.

52 Dharma transmission ceremonies: It refers to the ceremony of passing on the torch. For example, Master Hsing Yun passed the torch to Master Hsin Ping.

53 International Buddhist examinations: An annual examination for

devotees; its purpose was to encourage devotees to study Buddhism.

[54] Return to the Epoch of the Buddha: The aim of this activity is to allow participants to experience the Dharma assembly in the time of the Buddha.

[55] formation, abiding, destruction, and emptiness: In Buddhism, all phenomena will experience these four phases in the process from arising to extinguishing.

[56] greed, anger, and ignorance: Also known as "three poisons." In Buddhism they are the fundamental elements that produce afflictions, sufferings, and the cycle of birth and death.

[57] Chan Master Baizhang Huaihai [720-814 C.E.]: He studied with Chan Master Mazu Daoyi and established the system in which the Sangha provides for its own daily necessities by cultivating vegetables. This kind of system is called "the monastic regulations of Baizhang" (*Ch. Baizhang Qing Gui*). His work is known as *Sayings of Chan Master Baizhang*.

[58] Dunhuang: A famous Buddhist site, located on the Silk Road in Gansu Province. There are over four hundred thirty caves, in which thousands of Buddhist paintings are carved on the wall.

[59] solitary retreats: Intense individual practices. During this period, the practitioners cannot have any contact with the outside world, and must focus on the practices of meditation, chanting, or other cultivation.

[60] the Eight Precepts Retreat: Also known as the Retreat of Eight Purification Precepts. Precepts are the rules of conduct and discipline established by the Buddha. Sakyamuni Buddha established the eight purification precepts for the purpose of offering the laity an opportunity to live in the monastery for one day-and-night to

learn and experience the monastic life. They are the basic five precepts plus three additional disciplines: 1. no killing; 2. no stealing; 3. no sexual conduct; 4. no lying; 5. no intoxicants; 6. no use of perfumes and no singing or dancing; 7. no sleeping on a high or luxurious bed; 8. no eating food during non-regulated hours.

[61] the Seven-day Amitabha Retreat: An intense practice in reciting Amitabha Buddha's name over seven days.

[62] pilgrimages to the founding temple: A pilgrimage event in which the monastics and devotees walk from the main gate to the Buddha Hall while chanting a Buddha's name and making a full prostration on every third step.

[63] Nalanda: Also known as Nalanda University, founded in the 5th century by the Gupta Emperor Baragaon. It was a famous Buddhist university, and thousands of students and teachers studied and taught there. One of the most famous scholar monastics in Chinese Buddhism, Xuanzang, traveled to India and studied Buddhism at Nalanda.

[64] *Wooden fish*: A type of musical instrument commonly used in Buddhist ceremonies. It is made of wood, and shaped like a fish.

[65] Sariputra: One of the ten chief disciples of the Buddha, known as the foremost in wisdom.

[66] the traditional monastery of Tang Dynasty: In the original text, it is called "conglin," which literally means "forest," and refers to the number of monastics as many as the trees in the forest. This system was first established by Chan Master Mazu Daoyi in the Tang Dynasty, and later made complete by Chan Master Baizhang Huihai.

[67] Venerable Hsin Ping: He passed away in April of 1995. The new abbot of Fo Guang Shan, Kaohsiung is Venerable Hsin Ting.

[68] the Office of Sangha Affairs: The committee in charge of looking after all monastics of Fo Guang Shan, including issues pertaining to their education, welfare, reward and punishment, medication, and even the welfare of the monastics' parents.

[69] the six points of reverent harmony: These are: 1. physical unity by living together; 2. verbal unity by not criticizing others; 3. mental unity through sharing joy; 4. moral unity through upholding the same precepts; 5. doctrinal unity in views; and 6. economic unity through sharing.

[70] the five contemplations: Also known as "five contemplations at meal time" and these are: 1. by considering the work required in producing the food, I shall be grateful for its source; 2. reflecting on my own conduct, I shall deserve this offering only if it accords with morality; 3. I shall guard my mind cautiously from greed; 4. to cure the ailment of hunger, I shall consume this food as medicine; and 5. to tread on the spiritual path, I shall accept this offering.

[71] mantra: "Mantra" is same as "dharani," which literally means "spell."

[72] The diamond throne: Referring to the seat upon which Sakyamuni Buddha attained his enlightenment.

[73] began to turn the wheel of the Dharma: It refers to the first time the Buddha discoursed on the Four Noble Truths and the Eightfold Noble Path to the first five bhiksus. This is also known as the Three Turnings of the Dharma Wheel.

[74] Sal trees: Teak trees.

[75] *To search for bodhi*: Searching for perfect wisdom and enlightenment.

[76] Burma: Currently known as "Myanmar."

[77] Ceylon: Currently known as Sri Lanka.

[78] Sangha Day Celebration: Once a year (usually takes place in Lunar July), on this day the laity gather to make offerings to monastics.

[79] *red dust*: Referring to the secular world.

[80] *Mojia*: Referring to Master Hsing Yun. Mojia is his pen name.

[81] Po Leung Kuk: An orphanage.

[82] Better to perish taking one step west than to survive taking one step east: To go "west" means to advance to an intended destination, referring to India. To go "east" is to retreat home to China.

[83] conflict over Chinese representation: The delegation from the Mainland withdrew in protest against the election of Taiwan representative T'ien-Liu Shih-lun as Vice Chair during the 14th meeting in Sri Lanka. The Taiwan delegation was ousted altogether from the 15th gathering in Nepal as a result of pressure from Beijing.

[84] *highly formalized*: This is a diplomatic terminology of the Chinese government, referring to a reception that is highly adorned.

[85] stone-sculptures of Dazu: Images of the Buddha sculpted from cliffs that are masterpieces dating from the Tang Dynasty.

[86] subversive elements: According to the Communist government, the subversive elements refer to Master Hsing Yun and journalist Lu Keng.

[87] protection: Involuntary "full-time accompaniment" in the protocol of the Communist government.

[88] Chiang Ching-kuo: [1910-1988 C.E.] The eldest son of Chiang

Kai-shek.

[89] head association: A country with more than four chapters is eligible for the establishment of a head association.

[90] chapters: A chapter has ten subchapters, and a subchapter has a hundred members or more.

[91] Ni hao, Omito Fo!: It means "How do you do? May Amitabha Buddha bless you!"

[92] the four great bodhisattvas: Indicating Avalokitesvara, Manjusri, Ksitigarbha, and Samantabhadra Bodhisattvas.

[93] More than once, fickle imperial favoritism ignited persecution of the sangha: Textual mention of the four most catastrophic cases in Chinese history during which enraged monarchs ordered the annihilation of texts, images, and the sangha, or monastics were forced to renounce their vows. The incidents took place, namely, in the 7th year [446 C.E.] of the reign of Emperor Taiwu of Northern Wei; the 2nd year [573 C.E.] of the reign of Emperor Wu of Northern Zhou; the 5th year [845 C.E.] of the reign of Emperor Wuzong of Tang; and the 2nd year [955 C.E.] of the reign of Emperor Shizong of Later Zhou.

[94] Sutric and Tantric: The twofold categorization of Buddhism according to practice. The Sutric division, also known as the exoteric, comprises seven of the eight schools except the Tantric school. The Tantric school is also known as the esoteric school and stands in its own division.

[95] four orders: Bhiksus, bhiksunis, upasakas (male devotees), and upasikas (female devotees).

[96] Tzu Chi Foundation: One of the most acclaimed Buddhist charitable organizations in Taiwan. Its founder is Reverend Cheng Yen.

[97] physiognomy: The art of determining personal character from the form or features of the body.

[98] geomancy: Divination by geographic features or by figures or lines.

[99] cloud from the sky: A pun on the Master's name, which translates into "stars and clouds" in English.

[100] Shih: As in *Shih Jia Moni*, the Chinese transliteration of Sakya-muni Buddha. Hence, the surname Shih is given to all Chinese monastics.

Glossary

Amitabha Sutra: It is one of the three sutras that form the doctrinal basis for the Pure Land School of Mahayana Buddhism. It is also known as "the *Smaller Sutra on Amitayus*."

Arhatship: Arhat literally means "being worthy of." Arhatship refers to the state of having eliminated all afflictions and passions, which will never arise again.

Avalokitesvara Bodhisattva: Literally, "He who hears the sounds of the world." In Mahayana Buddhism, Avalokitesvara is known as the Bodhisattva of Compassion and can manifest in any conceivable form to bring help to whoever is in need. In Chinese Buddhism, Avalokitesvara is one of the four great bodhisattvas and is usually portrayed in female form, known as "Kuan Yin" (Guanyin).

Bodhi: It means enlightenment. In the state of bodhi, one is awakened to the true nature of self; one is enlightened to one's own Buddha Nature. Such a person has already eliminated all afflictions and delusions and achieved prajna wisdom.

Buddha: Literally, "awakened one." When "the Buddha" is used, it usually refers to the historical Buddha, Sakyamuni Buddha.

Buddha Nature: The inherent nature that exists in all beings. It is the capability to achieve Buddhahood.

Buddha's Light International Association (B.L.I.A.): A worldwide Buddhist organization dedicated to the propagation of Humanistic Buddhism, which was founded by Master Hsing Yun in 1992. Today, the B.L.I.A. has over one million members.

Buddhism: One of the Eastern religions, founded by Sakyamuni Buddha around 2,500 years ago in India. There are three major schools–Mahayana, Theravada, and Vajrayana. Mahayana is also known as Northern Buddhism, prevailing throughout East Asia (China, Japan, Korea, etc.). Theravada is also known as Southern Buddhism, spreading over South and Southeast Asia (Burma, Kampuchea, Laos, Sri Lanka, Thailand, etc.). Vajrayana is also called the "Diamond Vehicle," popular in Central Asia, India, and Tibet, as well as in China and Japan.

Cause and condition: Referring to the primary causes (cause) and the secondary causes (conditions). The seed out of which a plant or a flower grows is a good illustration of a primary cause; the element of soil, humidity, sunlight, and so forth, can be considered secondary causes.

Cause and Effect: This is the most basic doctrine in Buddhism, which explains the formation of all relations and connections in the world. This law means that the arising of each and every phenomenon is due to its own causes and conditions, and the actual form, or appearance, of all phenomena is the effect.

Chan: The form of the Chinese transliteration of the Sanskrit term, dhyana. It refers to meditative concentration.

Chan School: One school of Chinese Buddhism. It was founded by Bodhidharma, emphasizes the cultivation of intrinsic wisdom, and teaches that enlightenment is clarifying the mind and seeing one's own true nature. Another major statement of the Chan School is that Dharma is wordlessly transmitted from mind to mind.

Diamond Sutra: Skt. "*Vajracchedika Prajnaparamita Sutra*"; Ch. "*Jingang Jing.*" There are several versions, translated into Chinese by Kumarajiva, Bodhiruci, and Zhendi (T: vol.8, no.235, 236 & 237). "*Vajracchedika*" means the diamond that cuts through afflictions, ignorance, delusions, or illusions; "*prajnaparamita*" is the perfection of wisdom, and it brings sentient beings across the sea of suffering to the other shore.

Dharma: With a capital "D": 1) the ultimate truth, and 2) the teachings of the Buddha. When the Dharma is applied or practiced in life, it is 3) righteousness or virtues. With a lowercase "d": 4) anything that can be thought of, experienced, or named; close to "phenomena."

Five desires: Wealth, beauty, fame, food and drink, and sleep.

Guanyin: Or Kuan Yin, also known as Avalokitesvara Bodhisattva.

Huayan School: One school of Chinese Buddhism, its founder was Chan Master Dushun in the Tang Dyansty; and its teachings rely on the *Flower Ornament Sutra* (*Avatamsaks Sutra*). Another one of its major characteristics is its emphasis on doctrinal classifications.

Humanistic Buddhism: The primary teaching of Venerable Master Hsing Yun, its philosophy emphasizes practicing Buddhism in daily life, and building a pure land in our living world.

Ksitigarbha: One of the great bodhisattvas of Mahayana Buddhism. Ksitigarbha Bodhisattva vowed to remain in hell until all sentient beings are released from it.

Kumarajiva: [344-413 C.E.] One of the four great translators in the history of Chinese Buddhism. His numerous works include the *Treatise on the Middle Way* (*Mulamadhyamaka Karika*), the *Sutras of Prajna-Wisdom*, the *Diamond Sutra*, the *Lotus Sutra*, the *Amitabha Sutra*, and many others. He also systematically explicated the philosophy of the Middle Way.

Lama: Translated from the Sanskrit term, "guru." It is a respectful title in Tibetan Buddhism, originally only used to denote the highly cultivated teachers or masters. Presently it is widely used as a title for any Tibetan monks.

Linji School: One of the Chan Schools in Chinese Buddhism, also known as Rinzai School in Japanese. It was founded by Chan Master Linji Yixuan [?-867 C.E.] of the Tang Dynasty.

Mahayana: Also known as "Great Vehicle." Literally, it means the vehicle that can carry many people. It is one of the Buddhist traditions, and its main characteristic upholds that aiding others to achieve liberation is as important as self-liberation. Mahayana prevails throughout East Asia.

Maitreya Bodhisattva: The future Buddha. It is said that he currently presides over Tusita Heaven, where he is expounding the Dharma to heavenly beings in the inner palace.

Nichiren School: One school of Japanese Buddhism, named after Nichiren, its founder [1222-1282 C.E.]. This school relies on the doctrines of the *Lotus Sutra*, and advocates that chanting the title of the *Lotus Sutra* is the expedient means to reach enlightenment.

Nirvana: Pali, "nibbana." The original meaning of this word is "extinguished, calmed, quieted, tamed, or dead." In Buddhism, it refers to the absolute extinction of individual existence, or of all afflictions and desires; it is the state of liberation, beyond birth and death. It is also the final goal in Buddhism.

Pure Land: Another term for a Buddha realm, which is established by the vows and cultivation of one who has achieved enlightenment.

Pure Land School: One school of Chinese Buddhism, its main aim is to be reborn into the Pure Land by the practice of reciting the Buddha's name. Its founder was Master Huiyuan in Eastern Jin Dynasty, who spent his lifetime promulgating the belief in Amitabha.

Sakya School: Or "Saskya Pa" in Tibetan, one of four major schools of Tibetan Buddhism. This tradition began with the establishment of the Sakya monastery, founded by Gonchok Gyelpo in the area called Sakya in 1073 C.E. Its major practice is known as "path and fruit" (lamdre).

Samantabhadra: He represents the transcendental practices and vows (ten great vows). He is usually depicted seated on an elephant with six tusks (symbolizing the six perfections).

Sanlun School: A school of Chinese Buddhism founded by Master Jiaxiang Jizang during the reign of Emperor An of the Eastern Jin Dynasty [397-419 C.E.]. This school emphasizes the doctrines of emptiness.

Soto School: One of two major Zen schools of Japanese Buddhism, originally transmitted from the Chinese Caodong School by Dogen in the 13th century.

Stupa: A religious monument built to commemorate the historical Buddha or other enlightened ones.

Tathagata: One of the ten titles of Buddha, literally translated as

"Thus-Come One," meaning the one who has attained full realization of suchness; i.e. the one with the absolute, so that he neither comes from anywhere nor goes anywhere.

Ten directions: In Buddhism, this term is used to refer to everywhere, indicating the eight points of the compass (north, west, east, south, southeast, southwest, northeast and northwest) plus the zenith and nadir.

Three poisons: Indicating greed, anger, and ignorance, which are the fundamental roots producing all afflictions, sufferings, and the cycle of rebirth.

Three realms: The realms where sentient beings reside and transmigrate: 1) the realm of sense-desires, 2) the realm of form, and the realm of formlessness.

Three time periods: Also known as "three periods of time," indicating the past, the present, and the future.

Tiantai School: One school of Chinese Buddhism, founded by Master Zhiyi in the Tang Dynasty. Its name was taken from the site of the head temple, Mount Tiantai in Zhejiang Province. Its major teachings are based on the works of Master Zhiyi, including the *Great Techniques of Stopping* [*Delusion*] *and Seeing* [*Truth*], *Profound Meanings of the Lotus Sutra* (*Fahua Jing Xuan Yi*), and *Explanations on the Passages and Sentences of the Lotus Sutra* (*Fahua Wen Ju*).

Triple Gem: The Buddha, the Dharma, and the Sangha.

Tripitaka: The *Buddhist Canon* known as the "Three Baskets." They are divided into three categories, the sutras (teachings of the Buddha), the vinayas (precepts and rules), and the abhidharma (commentary on the Buddha's teachings).

Venerable Master Taixu [1889-1947 C.E.]: Usually known as "Tai-hsu." He is the reformer of Chinese Buddhism in the late 19th and early 20th century. He is also the pioneer to who propagated Humanistic Buddhism. His works are included in the set of the *Complete Works of Taixu.*

Venerable Master Xuanzang: [602-664 C.E.] A great master of the Chinese Tang Dynasty. He is one of four great translators in Buddhist history. He studied in India for seventeen years and was responsible for bringing many collections of works, images, pictures, as well as 150 relics to China from India. One of his most famous works is the *Buddhist Records of the Western Regions.*

Vimalakirti: A famous lay disciple of Sakyamuni Buddha, and an elder of City Vaisali. Although he was a layperson, he was an expert on the Mahayana doctrines and already achieved high cultivation. An associated sutra is known as the *Vimalakirti Sutra,* discoursed by Vimalakirti, emphasizes the practices of the bodhisattva path.

Vinaya: Literally, it means precept, rule, or discipline. In Buddhism, it not only means precept, but also refers to one of the three groups of Buddhist Canon (*Tripitaka*).

Vinaya School: One school of Chinese Buddhism, founded by Master Daoxuan in the Tang Dynasty, specializes in the study of all aspects of the *Vinaya.*

Yogacara School: One school of Mahayana Buddhism; also known as the Mind-Only School (Vijnanavada). It was founded by Maitreyanatha between the 4th to 5th centuries, and emphasizes the teachings of the *Commentary on the Stages of Yogacara Practitioners* (*Yogacarabhumi*). After the founder, the famous masters included Asanga and Vasubandhu; both of whom accomplished great works on the Yogacara philosophy, for example the *Summary of Mahayana Doctrines* and the *Thirty Verses on Mind-Only*.

Appendix

Chronology of
Venerable Master
Hsing Yun

1927   Born on the twenty-second day of the seventh month of the lunar calendar in Jiangdu, Jiangsu Province, in China. Named Li Guoshen. Father is Li Huicheng; mother is Liu Yuying. Hsing Yun is third of four children, with an older brother and sister, and a younger brother.

1931   Becomes vegetarian along with maternal grandmother, a Buddhist.

1934   Enters rural school.

1937   Father disappears while on a business trip to Nanjing.

1938   Goes midway to Nanjing with mother in search of his father. Takes the tonsure under Venerable Master Zhikai at Qixia Temple; given the Dharma names Wuche and Jinjue. Becomes a disciple of the forty-eighth generation of the Linji Division in Chan School Buddhism.

1941   Is ordained at Qixia Temple.

1944   Studies at Tianning Temple, Changzhou.

1945   Transfers to Jiaoshan Buddhist College.

1947   Arrives in Dajue Temple, Baita Mountain. Becomes principal of Baita Elementary School. Founds monthly *Raging*

Billows with schoolmate Master Zhiyong. Is arrested by the Communists.

1948   Becomes director of Huazang Temple in Nanjing. Edits *Splendid Light*, supplement of newspaper *Xu Bao*.

1949   Arrives in Keelung, Taiwan, with a monastic relief group. Is arrested with Master Cihang and others on allegations of subversive activities, and is incarcerated for twenty-three days.

1950   Takes shelter at Yuanguang Temple in Chungli, under Master Miaoguo. Stands guard in the mountains around Fayun Temple in Miaoli, where he authors *Singing in Silence*, his first work.

1951   Takes charge of academic affairs in a Buddhist seminar conducted by Venerable Daxing. Edits *Life Monthly* and learns Japanese.

1952   Is elected to an executive post in the Chinese Buddhist Association. Raises emergency relief funds for victims of the flood in Hualien.

1953   Speaks on the Dharma at Leiyin Temple in Ilan at the invitation of Li Juehe. Publishes *Discourse on Avalokitesvara's Universal Gate Chapter*.

1954   Is stationed at Leiyin Temple and starts teaching in rural areas and prisons. Venerables Tzu Chuang, Tzu Hui, and Tzu Jung take refuge in the Triple Gem.

1955   Teaches throughout Taiwan while promoting the reprinting of the Buddhist Tripitaka. Suffers severe arthritis in his legs. Publishes *Biography of Sakyamuni Buddha*, the first hardbound Buddhist text ever published in Taiwan.

1956   Construction of the lecture hall for the Ilan chanting group is completed. Founds the first kindergarten, Ciai, and tutors arts and sciences at Guanghua. Teaches in prisons.

1957   Publishes *National Master Yulin*. Founds and becomes chief editor of *Awakening the World*, a magazine which is published three times a month.

1958   Conducts the Dharma function for the preservation of the nation held by the Chinese Buddhist Association in Taipei. Venerable Hsin Ping is tonsured.

1959   Supports the Tibetan Buddhist Movement against Communist suppression. Organizes the first float parade in celebration of the Buddha's birthday. Establishes a Buddhist cultural service in Sanchung, Taipei. Publishes *Biography of Sakyamuni Buddha's Ten Great Disciples*.

1960   Publishes the *Enlightenment Sutra*.

1961   Becomes publisher of *Buddhism Today*. Heads the Ilan youth choir and releases the first six Buddhist records in Taiwan.

1962   Takes over the publishing of *Awakening the World*.

1963   Organizes a Buddhist tour group with Venerable Baisheng, visiting India, Thailand, Malaysia, Singapore, the Philippines, Japan, and Hong Kong. Meets with King Bhumibol Adulyadej of Thailand, President Diosdado Macapagal of the Philippines, among others. Petitions for the release of seven hundred Chinese prisoners and rescues two fishing vessels in Kaohsiung.

1964   Shoushan Temple in Kaohsiung is completed, followed by the founding of Shoushan Buddhist College. Establishes a school of commerce named Zhihguang with Venerables

Wuyi and Nanting. Publishes a book of travels and a range of bilingual Buddhist texts in Chinese and English.

1965 Publishes a series of lectures titled *Awakening the World.*

1967 Construction begins on Fo Guang Shan. Shoushan Buddhist College renamed Dongfang Buddhist College. Takes over a Christian mission building, which is turned into a home for the elderly and poor.

1969 Holds the first Buddhist summer camp for college-level students. Founds the first Buddhist Sunday School for children. Builds Pilgrim's Lodge at Fo Guang Shan.

1970 Founds the Daci Nursery. Establishes a pilgrims' group.

1971 Great Compassion Shrine is completed, followed by the blessing of the Buddha's image. Founds Pumen Vihara in Taipei, which later becomes Pumen Temple. Is elected president of Sino-Japanese Buddhist Association.

1972 Introduces the constitution of Fo Guang Shan's Religious Affairs Committee.

1973 Chiang Ching-Kuo, head of Taiwan's Executive Council, visits Fo Guang Shan for the first time. Basketball court at Dongshan is officially opened. Fo Guang Shan Tsunglin College is founded, which is later renamed Chinese Buddhist Research Institute.

1974 Groundbreaking for Fushan Temple in Changhua.

1975 The foundation is laid for the Great Welcoming Buddha and the Main Shrine. Conducts a three-day lecture at the National Arts Hall, which is the first Buddhist lecture ever held within the halls of government.

1976   Attends the U.S. bicentennial festivities and teaches the Dharma for the first time in the country. Runs a Buddhist summer camp for senior citizens and starts an English Buddhist Center. Is founding publisher of *Fo Guang Scholarly Journal*. Launches Pumen Hospital as well as a clinic at Shoushan Temple in Kaohsiung.

1977   Lectures at Zhongshan Hall in Taipei. Founds Pumen High School. Establishes the editing and publishing center for the Fo Guang Buddhist Tripitaka. The Chinese Buddhist Research Institute and University of Oriental Studies in the United States become sister schools. Ten-thousand Buddhas Triple Platform Ordination is deemed a preceptoral model.

1978   After becoming president of Taiwan R.O.C., Chiang Ching-Kuo visits Fo Guang Shan again. Holds Dharma function for the preservation of the nation in Dr. Sun Yat-sen Memorial Hall. Raises funds for the establishment of a Chinese Buddhist Youth Association. Receives honorary Ph.D. from University of Oriental Studies. Becomes the first president of the International Buddhist Progress Society. Raises funds for the establishment of Hsi Lai Temple.

1979   Holds a Buddhist concert at Dr. Sun Yat-sen Memorial Hall in light of strained diplomatic ties between Taiwan and the United States to raise funds for a national foundation of self-sufficiency. Launches *Universal Gate* magazine. First Buddhist program, *Sweet Dew*, is televised. Leads pilgrimage to India. Holds first Buddhist summer camp for children. *National Master Yulin* is adapted for the stage at the National Arts Hall.

1980   Produces the first set of Buddhist bookmarks and a calendar. Becomes director of Chinese Culture University's Indian Research Institute. Telecast of the program *Gate of Faith.*

1981   Holds Buddhist summer camp for mothers. Teaches Buddhist philosophy at Tung Hai University.

1982   Becomes brother temples with Tongdo Sa, Korea. Conducts the fifth International Buddhist Scholars' Conference.

1983   Is honored by the Ministries of Legal Affairs and Education for outstanding educational achievements.

1984   Meets the Dalai Lama. Establishes a mobile clinic offering free medical care. Founds the first Buddhist City College at Puxian Temple in Kaohsiung.

1985   Holds the World Buddhist Youth Scholars' Conference. Passes the abbotship of Fo Guang Shan to Venerable Hsin Ping. Cultivates in isolation at Hsi Lai Temple in Los Angeles. Serves as Executive Officer of the Chinese-Tibetan Cultural Association of the Republic of China. The *Platform Sutra of the Sixth Patriarch* is televised, as well as *Venerable Master Hsing Yun's Lecture Series*, which is honored by the Department of Information of Taiwan.

1986   The World Sutric and Tantric Buddhist Conference is held at Fo Guang Shan. Takes office as Advisor of Nationalist Party Affairs. Launches a new annual lecture series at Kaohsiung Zhongzheng Cultural Center.

1987   Becomes founding president of the American Buddhist Youth Association. Visits Chinese Buddhist Temple in Sarnath, India. *Hsing Yun's Chan Talk* is televised.

1988   Inauguration of Hsi Lai Temple where the Sixteenth World

Fellowship of Buddhists Conference and the Seventh World Fellowship of Buddhist Youth Conference are held. Conducts Purifying Service for the openings of the California State and City of Los Angeles meetings. Teaches in Hong Kong for the first time at the City Hall. Holds the first alms-round fundraising event for the Fo Guang Foundation for Buddhist Culture and Education. Travels to Northern Thailand with a medical team and teaches there. *Fo Guang Encyclopedia* is honored by Taiwan's Department of Information.

1989   Holds International Chan Conference at Fo Guang Shan. On his first homecoming in four decades, pays homage to ancestral stupas in Qixia and visits his mother in Jiangdu. The Dalai Lama is a guest at Hsi Lai Temple. *Hsing Yun's Chan Talk* is honored by Taiwan's Department of Information. Speaks on the Dharma to the armed forces and their respective academies.

1990   Is invited to attend the inauguration of U.S. President George Bush. Receives his mother at Fo Guang. Begins an annual three-day lecture at Hunghom Coliseum in Hong Kong. Goes on lecturing tour through England, Holland, Belgium, France, Switzerland, Austria, Yugoslavia, and Italy. Plans for the construction of the International Buddhist Association of Australia underway on a thirty-six acre property donated by the city of Sydney, Australia.

1991   Hsi Lai University, temporarily housed at Hsi Lai Temple, opens. Founds the Buddha's Light International Association, R.O.C. and raises funds for floods on the Mainland. Is hospitalized for a broken right thigh. *Hsing Yun Dharma Words* is televised. Establishes a branch temple in a chateau outside of Paris and begins spreading the Dharma in Europe.

1992   Buddha's Light International Association is established and its first meeting is held at Hsi Lai Temple. Devotee Zhang Shengkai donates his own residence for the establishment of the first branch temple in South America, I.B.P.S. Do Brasil. Is requested by Dr. Hennie Senekal to start up a temple in Johannesburg, South Africa–the first step in spreading the Dharma in Africa. For the second year, is honored by Taiwan's Ministry of Education for outstanding educational achievements. Fo Guang Foundation of Buddhist Culture and Education is also honored.

1993   *National Master Yulin* is televised on CTS. The second B.L.I.A. World Conference is held in Taipei. Registration of Fo Guang University is officially approved by Taiwan's Ministry of Education, followed by a groundbreaking ceremony in Linmei, Jiaoxi, in Ilan county. Buddha's Light International Association is named the most outstanding social organization in Taiwan.

1994   Extensive fundraising for Fo Guang University is done through art auctions. Taipei Vihara is inaugurated. Receives key to the city and honorary citizenship from Austin, Texas. Third B.L.I.A. World Conference is held in Vancouver, Canada. Fo Guang Shan provides emergency relief for the massive floods in August at the request of President Li Tenghui. *Hsing Yun Says* opens on TTV. *Diary of Hsing Yun* is published in twenty volumes. Ten monastics of African descent are tonsured. Holds honorary presidency of World Fellowship of Buddhists and presidency of B.L.I.A.

1995   *Handing Down the Light: The Biography of Venerable Mas-*

ter Hsing Yun is authored by Fu Chi-ying and is published by Commonwealth Publishing. Receives a special award, the Buddhist equivalent of the Nobel Prize, at the "National Indian Buddhist Ceremony." Venerable Hsin Ping passes away. Presents copies of *The Buddhist Volumes* to devotees, Dharma lecturers, and benefactors of Fo Guang Shan.

1996   Is invited to preside over the Candlelight and Triple Gem Refuge Ceremony, held at Shah Alam Stadium in Kuala Lumpur and attended by at least 80,000 people. Hosts U.S. Vice President Al Gore when the latter visits Hsi Lai Temple. Taiwan's President Li Teng-hui presents congratulatory gift to commemorate Fo Guang Shan's thirtieth anniversary. Mother, Madame Li, passes away at Hsi Lai Temple at ninety-five years of age. Founds Nan Hua Management College.

1997   Has the "Religious Dialogue of the Century" with Pope John Paul II in Vatican City, Italy. Presides over the official installation ceremony of Venerable Hsin Ting as the third abbot of Fo Guang Shan. Is honored by both the Taiwan's Internal Affairs, and Foreign Relation Ministries with special awards of recognition. Official release of *You Qing You Yi*. Selected as one of the ten most influential people by the Canadian 1470AM Chinese radio station's Sunshine Project. *National Master Yulin* and *Handing Down the Light* selected as ten best publications. Receives the "Hua Xia" first class scroll.

1998   Retires as B.L.I.A., R.O.C. President. Wu Pohsiung is formally appointed as new president of B.L.I.A., R.O.C. Presides over the first combined Theravada, Mahayana, and Tibetan Triple Platform Ordination Ceremony in Bodhgaya,

India. Visits Thailand to officially receive the Buddha's Tooth Relic. Officiates at Hsi Lai University's first Commencement Ceremony. First official meeting with Malaysian Prime Minister Dr. Mahathir Mohammad in Kuala Lumpur, Malaysia. Groundbreaking ceremony in Houston, Texas. Mayor of Houston declares June 20, as Venerable Master Hsing Yun Day. On his seventy-second birthday, is presented with a special birthday gift by Taiwan's Vice President, Lian Zhan.

1999   President Li Teng-hui visits Fo Guang Shan to officially mark the start of the Fo Guang Shan Buddhist Music Concert tour in Taiwan. During his visit, President Li also announces that the Buddha's Birthday on April 8 will be a national holiday in Taiwan. Leads the Buddhist Music Concert tour in Europe for a month. Conducts prayer and memorial services for victims of the Taiwan 921 earthquake, which occurs during the European tour. Initiates the establishment of Emergency Relief Centers around the world. Publishes *Hsing Yun's Hundred Sayings Series*, and *The Buddhism Textbook*.

2000   Debut of *Merit Times Daily News* in Taiwan; its American edition is also published in the same year. Commencement of Fo Guang University with permission to recruit students for six research institutes; the university receives government subsidy in its first year of operation. An eighty-acre property is donated by the Wollongong City Council for Nan Tien Temple to construct Nan Tien University and Fo Guang Yuan Art Gallery. Is awarded the Buddhist Great Contribution Award by the Prime Minister of Thailand, Chuan Leekpai.

2001   Leads the Fo Guang Shan Hymn Choir on tour around the United States and Canada. Arrives at Ground Zero of the September 11 terrorist attacks for a Purification Ceremony, and reads a prayer for victims inside the New York Lincoln Center. Hosts an Inter-Religious Dialogue at University of Toronto on the topic of "How Would Religion Face Globalization?" Establishes the Humanistic Buddhist Reading Association. International Buddhist Youth Conference is held in Malaysia by B.L.I.A.-Y.A.D. World Headquarters to promote exchange between Buddhist youths worldwide; over a thousand delegates from twenty-six countries attend. Completion of Fo Guang Shan Nan Tien Vihara and Melbourne Fo Guang Yuan Art Gallery in Australia.

2002   Is authorized by the Chinese government to escort the Buddha's finger relic from Famen Temple to Xian, China to Taiwan. Arrives in Malaysia to propagate the Dharma in Penang, Kuantan, and Ipoh. Presides over the ninth General Conference of B.L.I.A. in Tokyo, Japan and gives keynote speech "To Resolve and To Develop." Establishes Motosu Temple near the foot of Mt. Fuji in Japan as a center for cultural and educational activities as well as training center for monastic and lay Buddhists. Hsi Lai University is granted candidacy to the Western Association of Schools and Colleges (WASC). Goes on a South East Asia Charity Tour (Laos, Myanmar, Cambodia, and Thailand). Conducts wheelchair donation ceremonies and enhances exchange between Northern and Southern Schools of Buddhism. Presides over the Buddha's Light International Young Executive Conference. Establishes the Fo Guang Shan Devotee's University at Jin Guang Ming Temple in Sanshia, Taipei.

2003   Presides over a Northern and Southern Schools Buddhist

Exchange Symposium. Conducts a Refuge Taking Ceremony for 700 Buddhist youths from Malaysia visiting Taiwan for the "Searching for Our Root in the Monastery" Trip. *Merit Times Daily News* celebrates its third anniversary, and is extended from twelve to sixteen pages. Attends the groundbreaking ceremony of Catholic Zhen Fu Shan Community Monastery by the invitation of His Eminence Paul Cardinal Shan, SJ. Announces "A Prayer to Stop SARS" and accepts interviews by the media to speak on his thoughts about the SARS epidemic. Is awarded an Honorary Ph.D. by Maha Chulalongkorn Buddhist University of Thailand. *Cloud and Water: A 50 Year Anniversary Photobiography of Master Hsing Yun*—the first photobiography of a master in Buddhism—is published.

Venerable Master Hsing Yun

Venerable Master Hsing Yun was born in Jiangdu, Jiangsu Province, China, in 1927. Tonsured under Venerable Master Zhikai at age twelve, he became a novice monk at Qixia Vinaya School and Jiaoshan Buddhist College. He was fully ordained in 1941, and is the 48th Patriarch of the Linji (Rinzai) Chan School.

He went to Taiwan in 1949 where he undertook the revitalization of Chinese Mahayana Buddhism on the island with a range of activities novel for its time. In 1967, he founded the Fo Guang Shan (Buddha's Light Mountain) Buddhist Order, and has since established more than a hundred temples in Taiwan and on every continent worldwide. Hsi Lai Temple, the United States Headquarters of Fo Guang Shan, was built outside Los Angeles in 1988.

At present, there are nearly two thousand monks and nuns in the Fo Guang Shan Buddhist Order. The organization also oversees sixteen Buddhist colleges; five publishing houses, including Buddha's Light Publishing and Hsi Lai University Press; four universities, one of which is Hsi Lai University in Los Angeles; two nursing homes for the elderly; a secondary school; a satellite television station; and an orphanage.

A prolific writer and an inspiring speaker, Master Hsing Yun has written many books on Buddhist sutras and a wide spectrum of topics over the past five decades. Most of his speeches and lectures have been compiled into essays defining Humanistic Buddhism and outlining its practice. Some of his writings and lectures have been translated into various languages, such as English, Spanish, German, Russian, Japanese, Korean, etc.

The Venerable Master is also the founder of the Buddha's Light International Association, a worldwide organization of lay Buddhists dedicated to the propagation of Buddhism, with over 130 chapters and a membership of more than a million.

Buddha's Light Publishing
Fo Guang Shan Int'l Translation Center

As long as Venerable Master Hsing Yun has been a Buddhist monk, he has had a strong belief that books and other documentation of the Buddha's teachings unite us emotionally, help us practice Buddhism at a higher altitude, and continuously challenge our views on how we define and live our lives.

In 1996, the Fo Guang Shan International Translation Center was established with this goal in mind. This marked the beginning of a string of publications translated into various languages from the Master's original writings in Chinese. Presently, several translation centers have been set up worldwide. Centers that coordinate translation or publication projects are located in Los Angeles and San Diego, USA; Sydney, Australia; Berlin, Germany; Argentina; South Africa; and Japan.

In 2001, Buddha's Light Publishing was established to publish Buddhist books translated by Fo Guang Shan International Translation Center as well as other valuable Buddhist works. Buddha's Light Publishing is committed to building bridges between East and West, Buddhist communities, and cultures. All proceeds from our book sales support Buddhist propagation efforts.